SURFING IN SOUTH CAROLINA

Front Cover: Jimmy Nolan and Merle Keels Witt pose for the camera on Myrtle Beach in 1964. (Courtesy of Henry Culbertson.)

Upper Back Cover: Kyle Busey lays into a strong bottom turn at The Washout on Folly Beach. (Courtesy of Paul Mulkey Sr.)

Lower Back Cover: At left, Erik Kirby cross steps to the nose at the Folly Beach Pier (courtesy of Justin Morris); at center, from left to right, Mike Garrett, Dean Monk, Glenn Tanner, Tommy Rhodes, and Lute Rhodes are looking dapper with their boards on Center Street at Folly Beach (courtesy of Dean Monk); Kate Barantini is spotted at the Folly Beach Pier in a stylish soul arch five (courtesy of Justin Morris).

Images of Modern America

SURFING IN SOUTH CAROLINA

Lilla O'Brien Folsom
and Foster Folsom

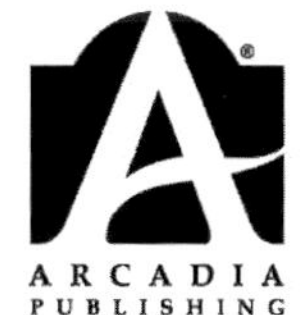

ISBN 978-1-4671-1513-1

Published by Arcadia Publishing
Charleston, South Carolina

Printed in the United States of America

Library of Congress Control Number: 2015944121

For all general information, please contact Arcadia Publishing:
Telephone 843-853-2070
Fax 843-853-0044
E-mail sales@arcadiapublishing.com
For customer service and orders:
Toll-Free 1-888-313-2665

Visit us on the Internet at www.arcadiapublishing.com

This book is dedicated to watermen and women everywhere. May your next wave be your best.

Contents

Acknowledgments

For their support and help with this book, we would like to thank the following: Ted Watts, Tim Holt, and Kelly Richards in Murrells Inlet; Nanci Polk-Weckhorst, Jerre Weckhorst, and John Tolly in Hilton Head; and Tim McKevlin, Bates Hagood, Folly Beach mayor Tim Goodwin, and Lucy Jacobs in Charleston. We would also like to thank all the surfers who shared their memories. Our sincere appreciation goes to Kent Ficklin, Paul Mulkey Sr., and Jesse Cadman, who so kindly helped by sharing their work and time. Any omissions are totally unintentional.

INTRODUCTION

In 1779, after Capt. James Cook's demise at the hands of angry Hawaiians, the new commander of the *Discovery* devoted two pages of Captain Cook's journal to the natives' skill and passion for wave riding. At the beginning of the 1800s, Calvinist missionaries were scandalized not only by the free-form fashion of the natives while surfing, but also the amount of time they spent having fun. They called for a ban on the past time for decency's sake. It took a South Carolinian, a Duke, and an Irishman to bring the royal sport back to its rightful place on the world stage.

Born in South Carolina in 1868, Alexander Hume Ford wanted to find adventure and write about it for a world audience. Ford was working for the *Charleston News and Courier* during the Great Earthquake of 1886. It terrified him.

Moving to New York, he was hired to write about the Trans-Siberian Railroad being built across Russia. Ford stopped in Hawaii on the return trip, fell in love with the Islands, and remained. He was a fearless promoter of the local culture, and when he first saw Hawaiians riding the waves, he was hooked. Realizing even then that access to prime Honolulu beachfront was getting scarce, he negotiated with Queen Emma's estate for an acre and a half of the shoreline in the shadows of Diamond Head. Promising that the land would only be used to revive and preserve the ancient Hawaiian sport of surfing on boards and in outrigger canoes, Ford founded the Outrigger Canoe Club. Established in 1908, the club guaranteed that men and boys would always have ocean access to "ride upright on the crest of waves." He became surfing's tireless promoter and champion of Duke Kahanamoku and legendary waterman George Freeth, who had taught Ford to surf.

One of Ford's first disciples was adventure writer Jack London. Charmaine London wrote about relaxing with her husband one evening in Honolulu after their famous cruise of the Snark. A very animated man sat down, introduced himself, and began to tell Jack London about wave riding. He vowed to make this island past time one of the most popular on earth. Caught up in Ford's enthusiasm, they never doubted that he would.

The Londons spent a full day trying wave after wave to learn the technique from Ford. The next day Jack was so sore and sunburned he could not move. Despite the horrible memory, the exhilaration he felt riding the waves shone through in his books and many magazine articles. The world was intrigued.

Agatha Christie was one of the first British to do it. Mark Twain never could do it. Duke Kahanamoku demonstrated the skill in California, on the East Coast, and in Australia. Famous in his own right after winning five Olympic medals, he brought out the crowds whenever he hit the beach. Word of the sport was spreading globally.

These people made the sport of surfing accessible to the masses, opening the world's eyes to the beauty of capturing a wave, if only for a few moments.

Across the globe from Hawaii, well before Europeans established their colonies, the waterways threading the Lowcountry sustained the indigenous population. In the 18th and 19th centuries, the ocean became crucial to the success of coastal communities, as ocean trade routes took rice and cotton to markets abroad, returning with the goods, fashions, and culture of cosmopolitan European capitals.

In the last century, South Carolina's strategic location, ports, and mild climate secured military base contracts along the coast with the Marines centering at Parris Island. Charleston hosted the Navy, Air Force, and Coast Guard, while another Air Force base located in Myrtle Beach. The buildup to the Vietnam War in the 1960s brought families and soldiers from the West Coast and Hawaii to tours in South Carolina.

Military families brought their hobbies, and surfboards began to appear on local beaches. Having practiced their moves on floats, local teens now had access to boards. Not too many pictures are around now from those early days. As one Myrtle Beach surfer summed it up, "We had enough money for a surfboard or a camera—you can guess which won."

Each geographic group thought they were unique and doing something no one else was attempting. Travel was not easy, and teens tended to surf where they lived. One older surfer said that one day he spotted someone way down the beach carrying a surfboard. It was like Robinson Crusoe discovering another human being on his deserted island.

Now that they compare stories, it seems the sport developed along the same timeline in each area. One thing everyone agrees on is that when a statewide contest was called and the groups got together, the rivalry was intense but good-natured. It was a chance to see what others were doing and watch the progress of the competition.

Surf clubs began to spring up around the state: representing the area from the mid-coast to the south were the Hunting Island Surfing Association in Beaufort, the West Coast East Surf Club at Folly Beach, and the Carolina Coast Surf Club east of the Cooper River; the stretch of coast above Georgetown included the 42nd Street Surf Club, and the Pawleys Island Surf Club, established in 1966. Club contests began to be held more frequently, and the pros started dropping in on their way from Florida to Virginia and New Jersey. Surfers were able to meet and watch their idols work the local breaks.

As boards got shorter and lighter, surfers grew into cars and driver's licenses and travel became easier. Super highways were rare, so a trip to Florida on two-lane Highway 17 could take teenage surfers a day or two. Parents were not happy about these trips and certainly did not finance them. Today, surfing has morphed into a family adventure. Parents are footing the bill for surf camps and vacations that were unimaginable in the 1960s.

Technology has also changed the face of the sport. Why go on dawn patrol when a click on the surf cam will give a wave report? If it is good, a text will go out and social media will announce the news. Cold weather? The new, lighter-than-air, fully flexible wet suits will take care of that; heck, there are heated vests if the temperature has really plummeted.

Yet no matter how fancy the gadgets, or how technically accurate the satellite reports get, the ancient challenge remains: it still comes down to one person and one wave.

One

Pawleys Island through the Grand Strand

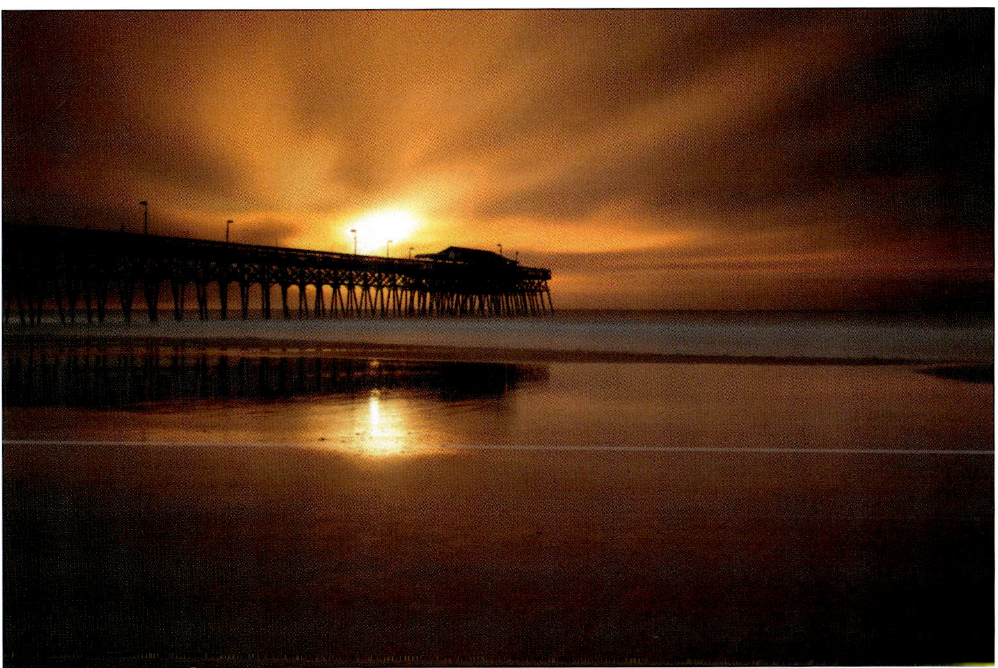

Pawleys Island is a hidden gem, a place where families have gathered for generations to enjoy casual summer days and escape the heat of the inland areas. The island seems removed from the hustle and bustle of summer visitors, more personal and moving at a slower pace. North of Pawleys Island, looking at a map, it is understandable why the change from one surf spot to the next happens seamlessly. The long, sweeping crescent shape of the Grand Strand affords a surfer many choices of beach breaks. Surfers tend to congregate at their favorite locations or simply sneak off to a secret spot. This stretch of the coast has produced a surprising number of champions. The surfing community is tightly knit and strong. The support and camaraderie is evident in the turnout for special events or a big swell. (Courtesy of Kent Ficklin.)

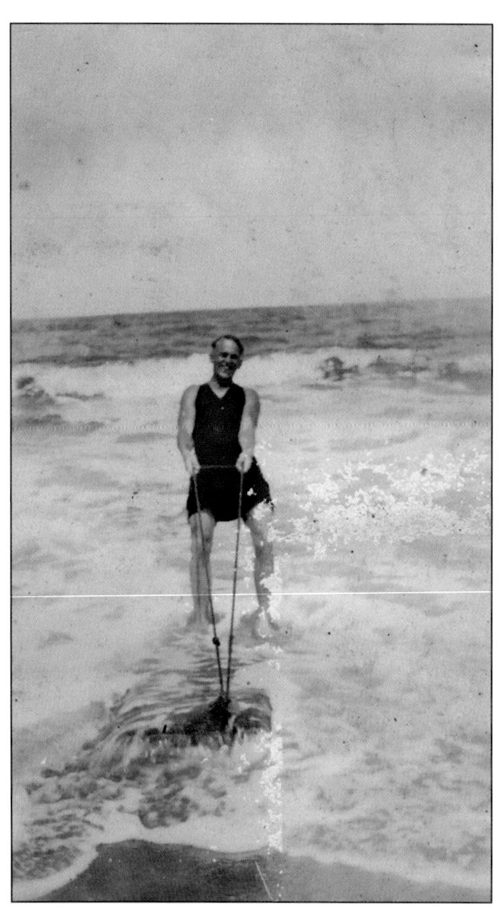

These two photographs were taken of Mr. Jones (at left) and Mr. Swanson (below) surfing at Pawleys Island Beach. There is a 1919 date penned on one of the photographs. Some claim they are much older, but the Pawleys Island Civic Association dates them to around 1905. These are the earliest South Carolina surfing photographs that could be found. (Both photos from the family archives of Virginia B. Skinner.)

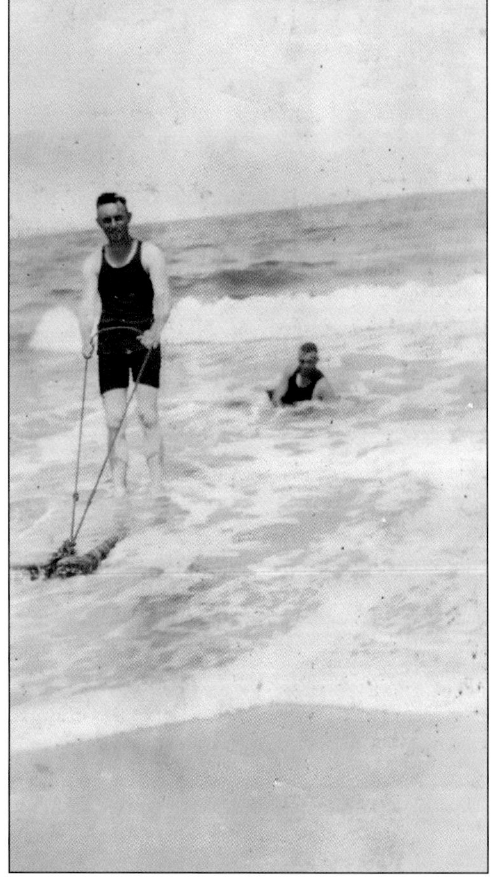

Pawleys Island Surf Club was established with 13 members on May 27, 1966, and in two short months the group had grown to 33 members. Craig Thomas shows off his original club jacket. (Authors' collection.)

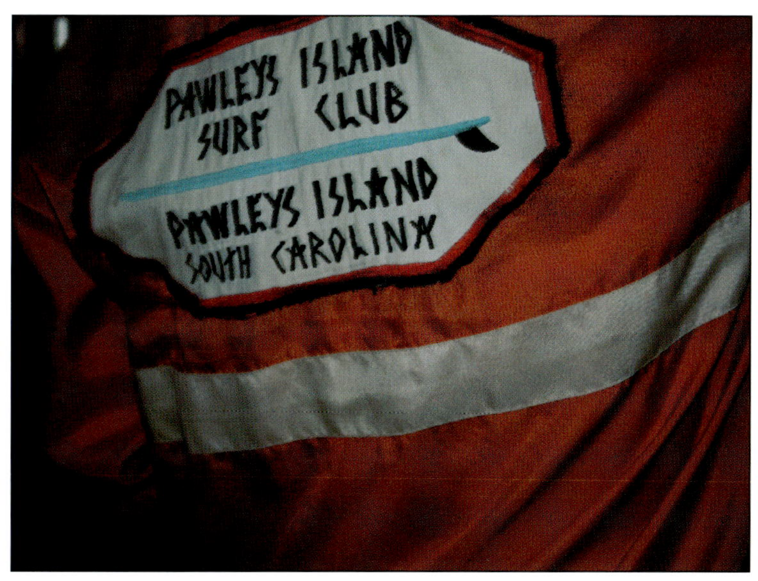

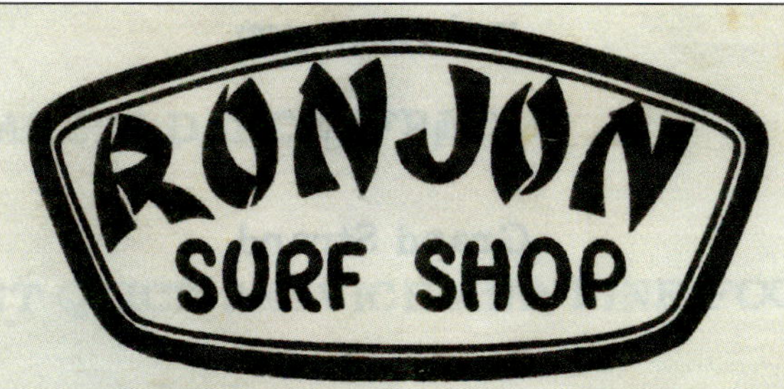

The club began showing surfing movies, and in August 1966 Dewey Weber introduced his new surf tour members during the intermission of *The Living Curl*. Club member Esther Johnson owned the Ron Jon Surf Shop on Pawleys Island Pier, where the club met. Her nephew Bill Perry, along with his wife, Betty Sue Cowsert, would later open Ocean Surf Shop on Center Street at Folly Beach, where he coined the popular phrase "Edge of America." (Courtesy of McKevlin's Surf Shop.)

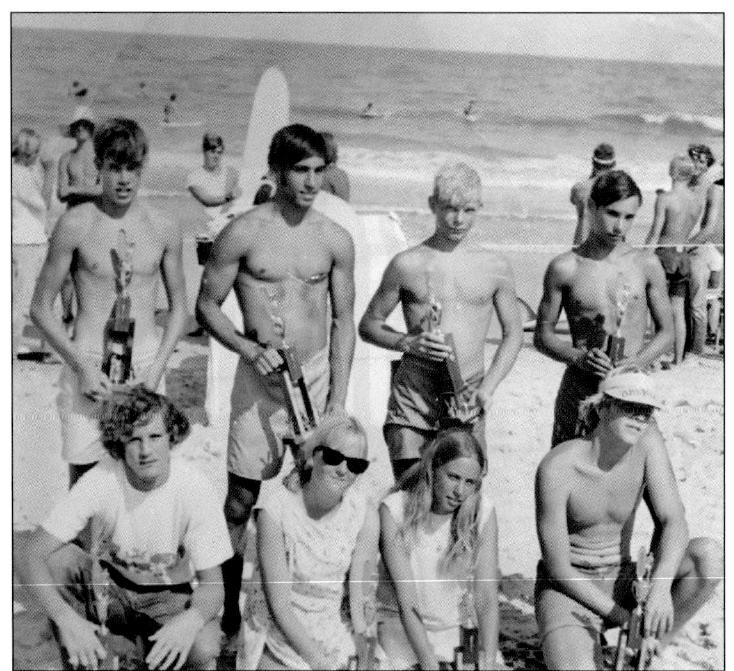

Winners of the 1969 Sun Fun Festival surf contest pose at the south side of Pawleys Island Pier with their trophies. Pictured are, from left to right, (first row) Ed Andrews, unidentified, Anna Anglin, and Keith Thompson; (second row) John Wilder, Ramon Basha, Mickey Marsh (from Emerald Isle, North Carolina), and Scott Beason. (Courtesy of Keith Thompson.)

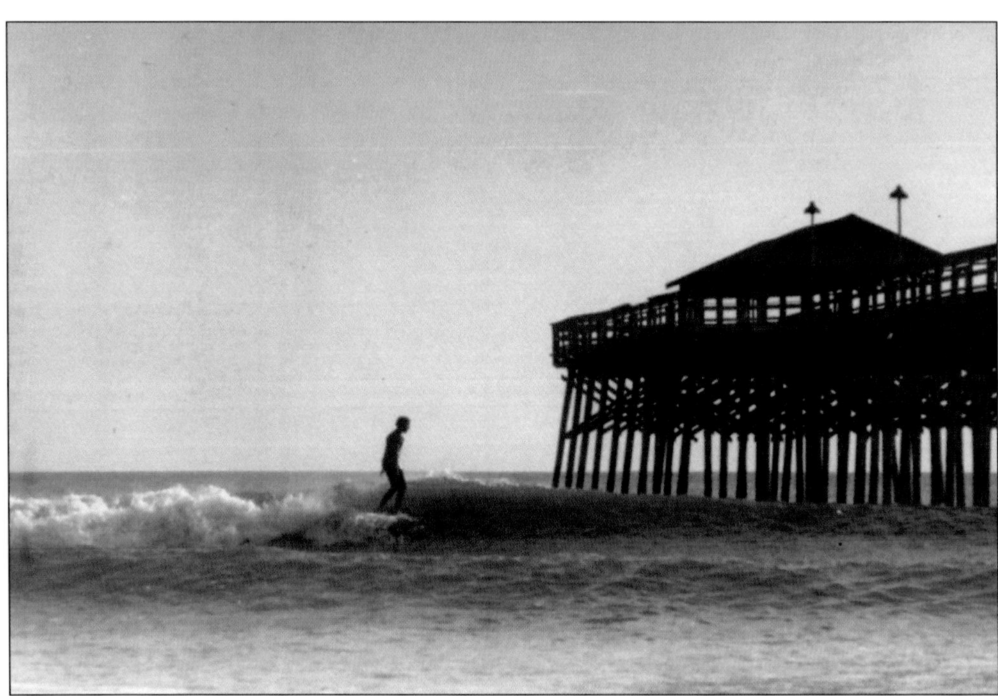

Keith Thompson, age 15, finds the nose (front tip of the board) on Christmas Day 1967 at Tilghman's Pier in Ocean Drive. Thompson's first board was a Delta pop-out that he bought in 1963 from Chapin Company, a one-stop hardware shop at the only shopping center in Myrtle Beach. Larry and Danny West had just gotten him started surfing at Forty-Second Avenue North, where all the north end surfers hung out. (Courtesy of Keith Thompson.)

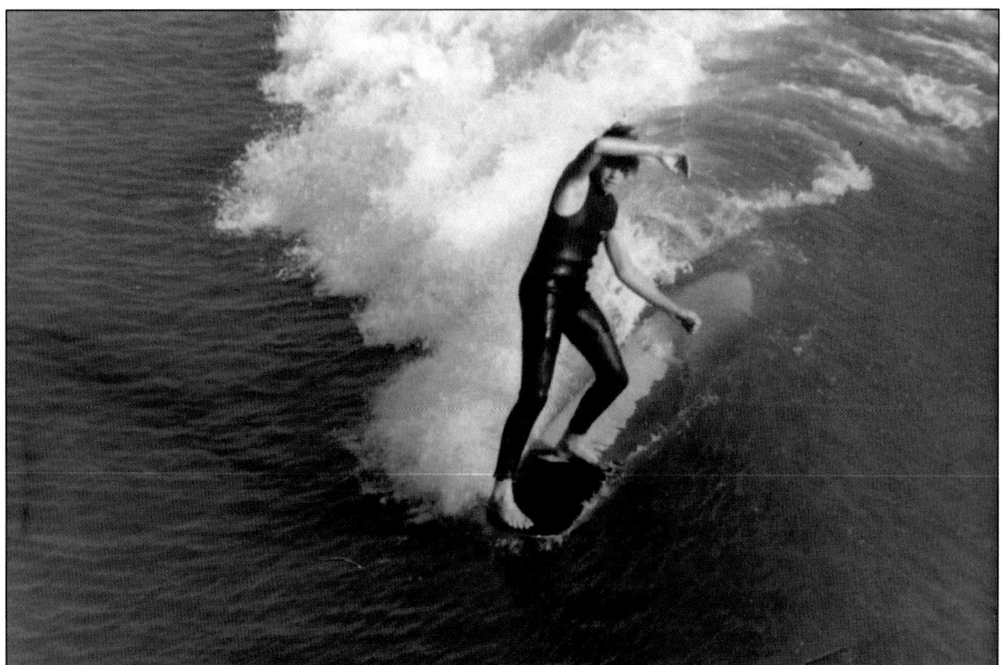

Keith Thompson, above, hangs five on his Gary Propper model in 1967 at Tilghman's Pier. The pier met its match with Hurricane Hugo. At right is an advertisement for Surfboards by Corky. This entrepreneur was making surfboards to order at 860 Folly Road in Charleston in 1963 before moving to Myrtle Beach. He may have been the first to blow his own foam (the process of mixing chemicals to create the core of surfboards) on the East Coast. (Above, courtesy of Keith Thompson; at right, McKevlin's Surf Shop.)

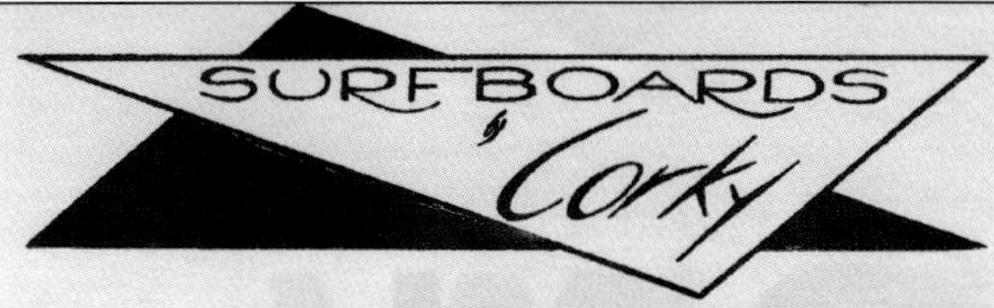

MYRTLE BEACH DIVERS & SUPPLY COMPANY
(Division of the Surfer Searcher Corporation)
Offices at 307 West Broadway
Myrtle Beach, S. C. Telephone: 803 448-5972
Wholesale - Retail - Jobbers

Personalized customized "Surfboards by Corky!"

Seven Day Delivery.

Polyurathane Foam Blanks made to order.

Expert Ding Repairs from $1.00

Diving & Surfing equipment rentals, air tanks filled.

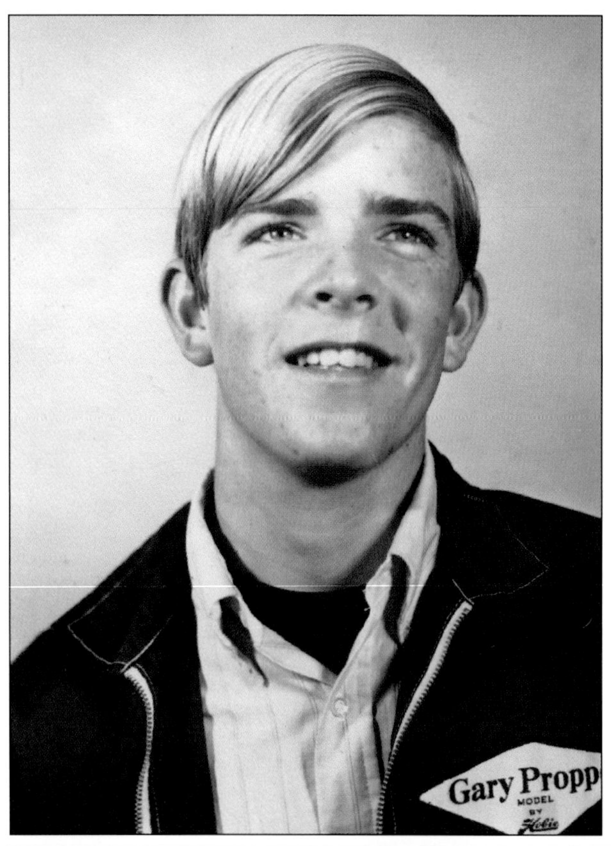

At left, showing off his choice of surfboard, a Gary Propper, Keith Thompson wears the Propper badge proudly on his club jacket. The Myrtle Beach Surf Club was started by Corky Hart and Danny West. The team sported matching jackets and were all photographed. The shots were displayed at club headquarters at the Myrtle Beach Diver Supply. Below, showing off their trophies from the 1968 South Carolina State Championship are, from left to right, Billy Gaither (third place), Allen Taylor (first place), and Keith Thompson (second place). (Both, courtesy of Keith Thompson.)

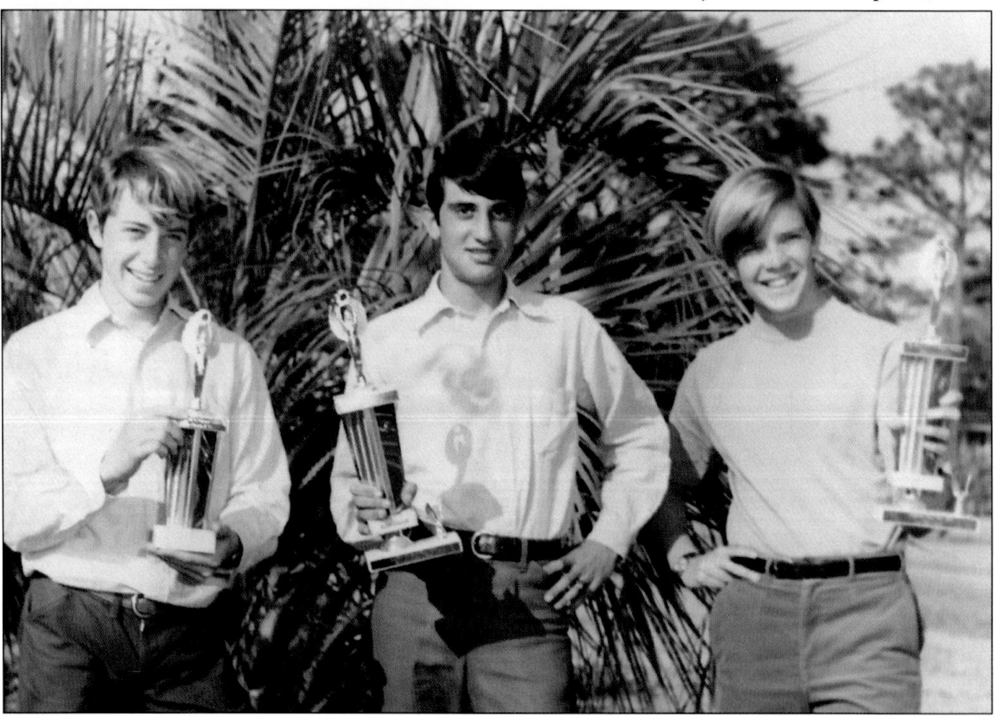

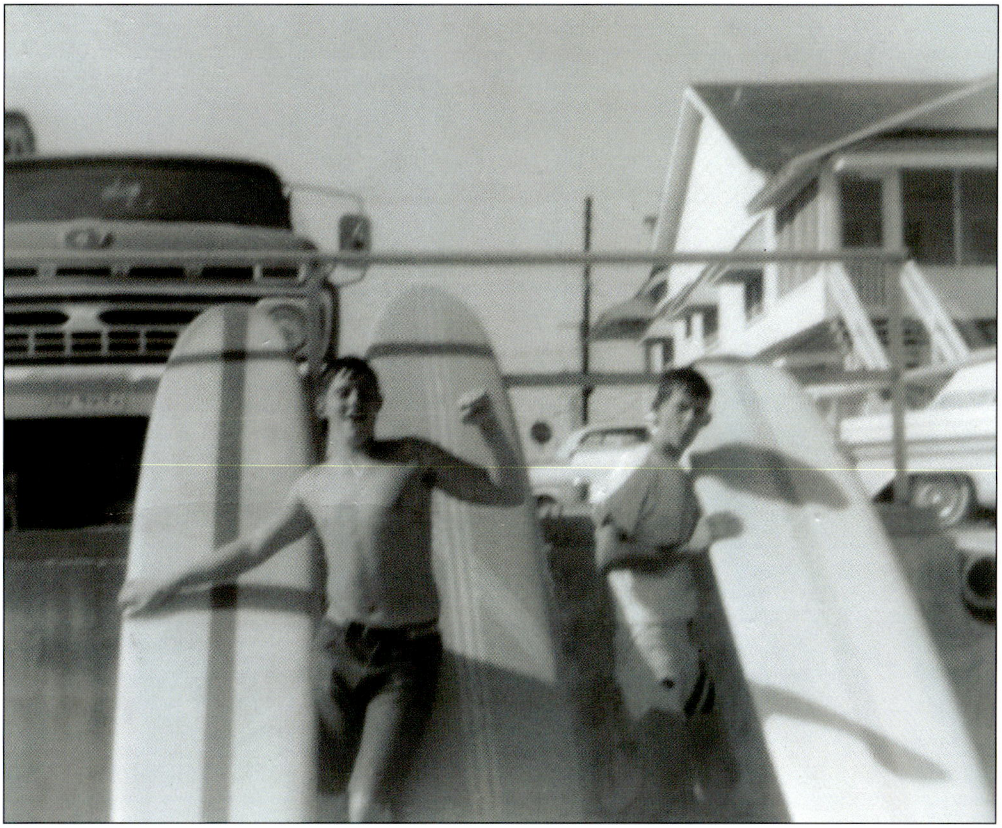

Garvin "Bozo" Huggins (left) and Mike White show off their favorite boards, a Velzy, a Mako, and a Hansen leaning against the parking lot wall at the Second Avenue Pier in November 1966. (Courtesy of Tim Holt.)

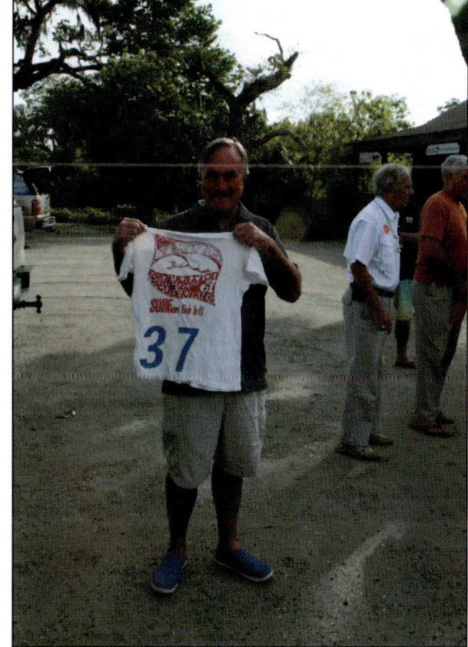

Conway brothers Billy and Tommy Benson made the news when they were tapped to compete in the semifinals of the 1967 World Championship in Puerto Rico. Winners would compete later that year in Peru. Billy Benson shows off his original competition jersey in 2015. (Authors' collection.)

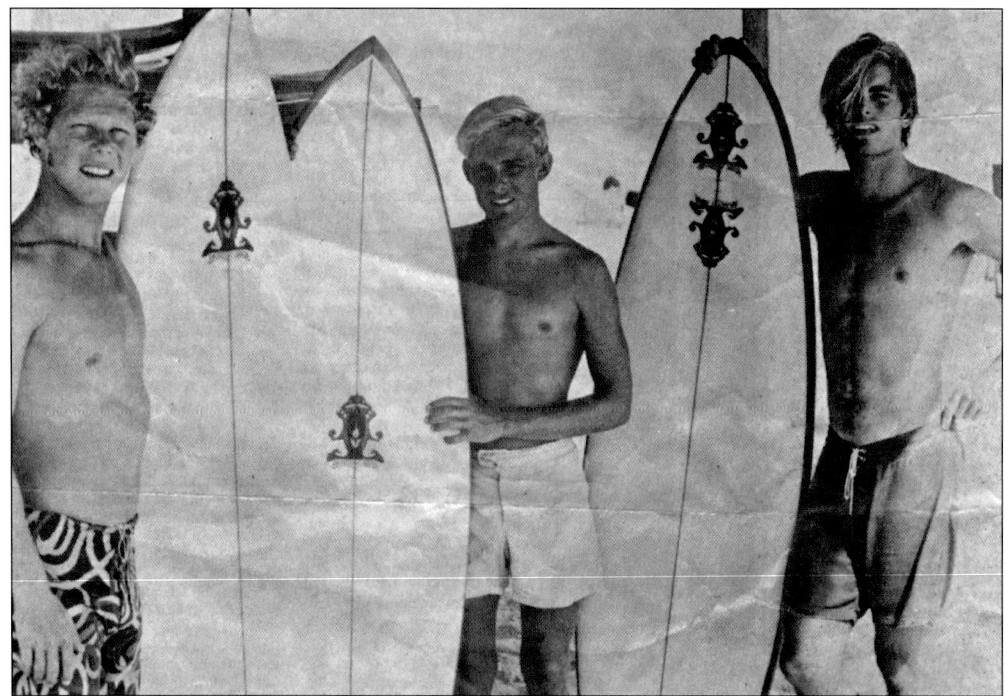

Above, Gary Propper (left) and Richard Dwyer (right) pose with Tommy Benson, manager of Vernon Pinner's Hobie Surf Shop in Myrtle Beach, in a photograph from the *Myrtle Beach Sun-News* in August 1970. Dwyer, a surfboard designer, and Propper, a professional surfer representing Hobie, enjoyed the waves in Myrtle Beach. They also liked the surfing crowd, saying they were a relaxed group—they just need more waves. Below, Tim Holt (left) and Tony Holmes find some waves at the Swash, at Twenty-Ninth Avenue in Myrtle Beach, in 1968. (Above, courtesy of Tommy Benson; below, Tim Holt.)

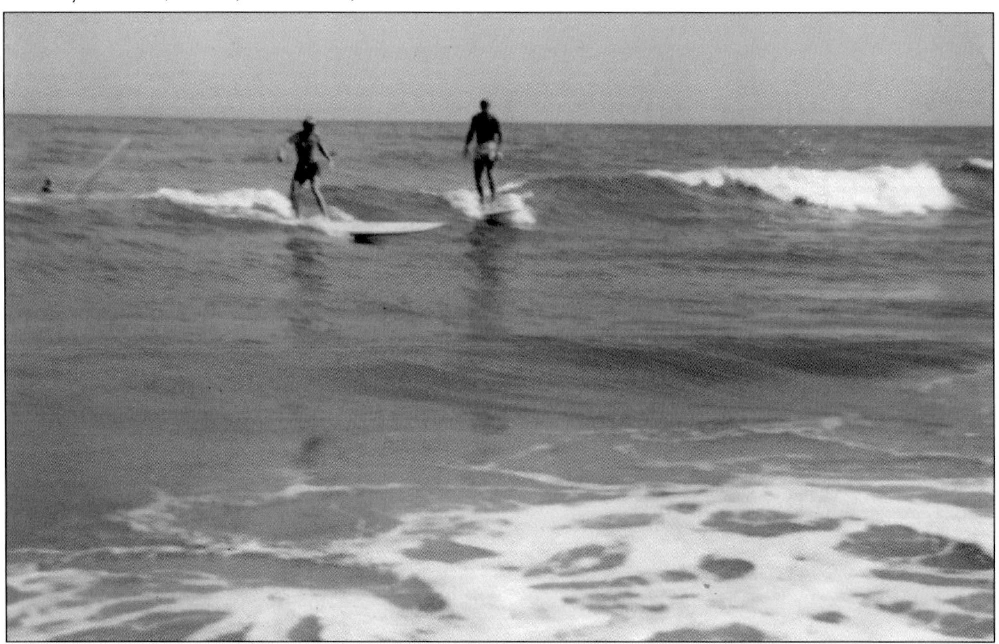

Ted Watts (pictured) began going to the beach at an early age. His brother Bruce (in the below, right) says that the boards were so heavy that he needed someone on the other end just to carry it, and Ted happened to be around. Ted, a former state champion, sees the influence of the ocean in his life every day. As a high-end custom furniture maker, he incorporates sea-life carvings into tables and cabinets. (Courtesy of Scot Benston.)

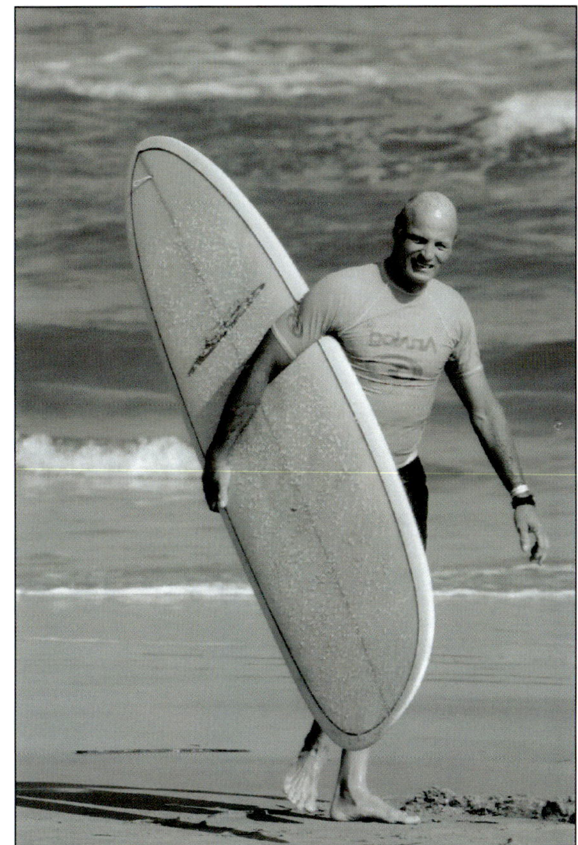

The brothers surf together today, not out of necessity but out of a mutual love of the ocean and a good solid friendship. (Courtesy of Scot Benston.)

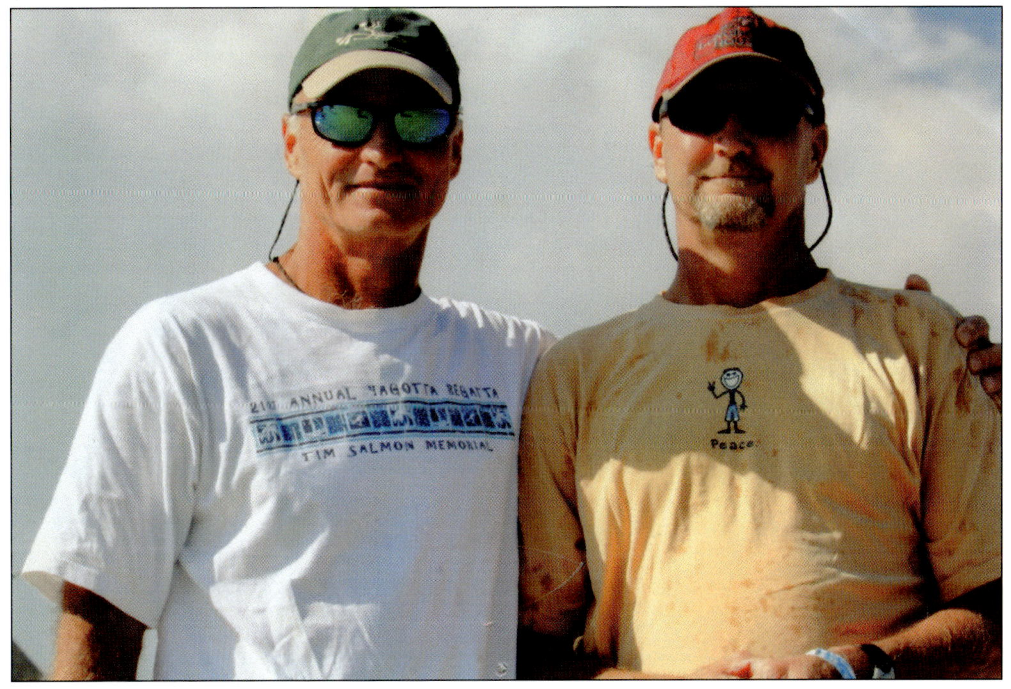

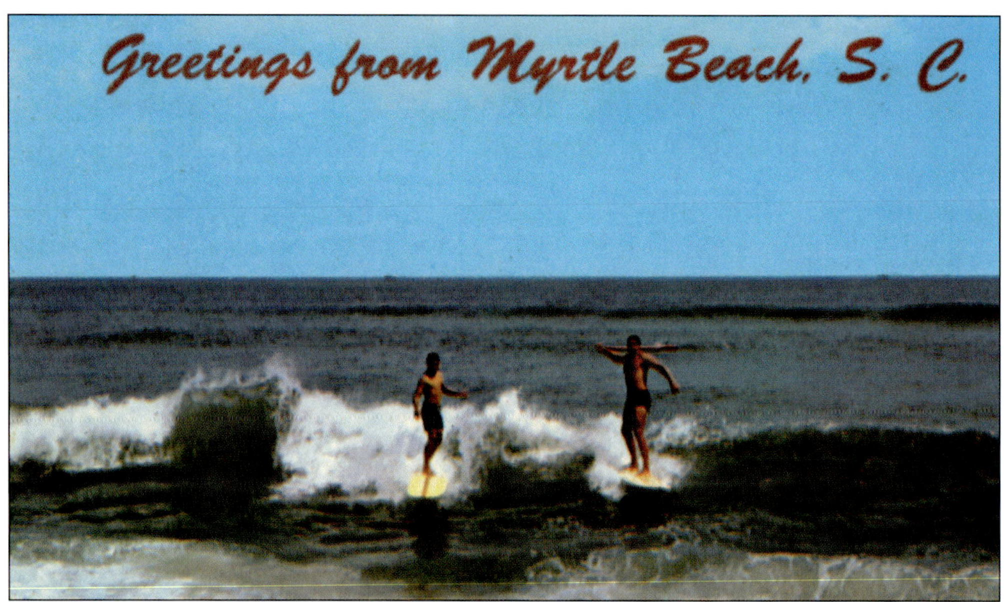

Randy Anderson must have been surprised when this postcard showed up in the tourist stores in Myrtle Beach. He is shown here at left on his yellow board *Tiki*. The photograph was taken in the 1960s at Forty-Second Avenue. (Courtesy of Randy Anderson.)

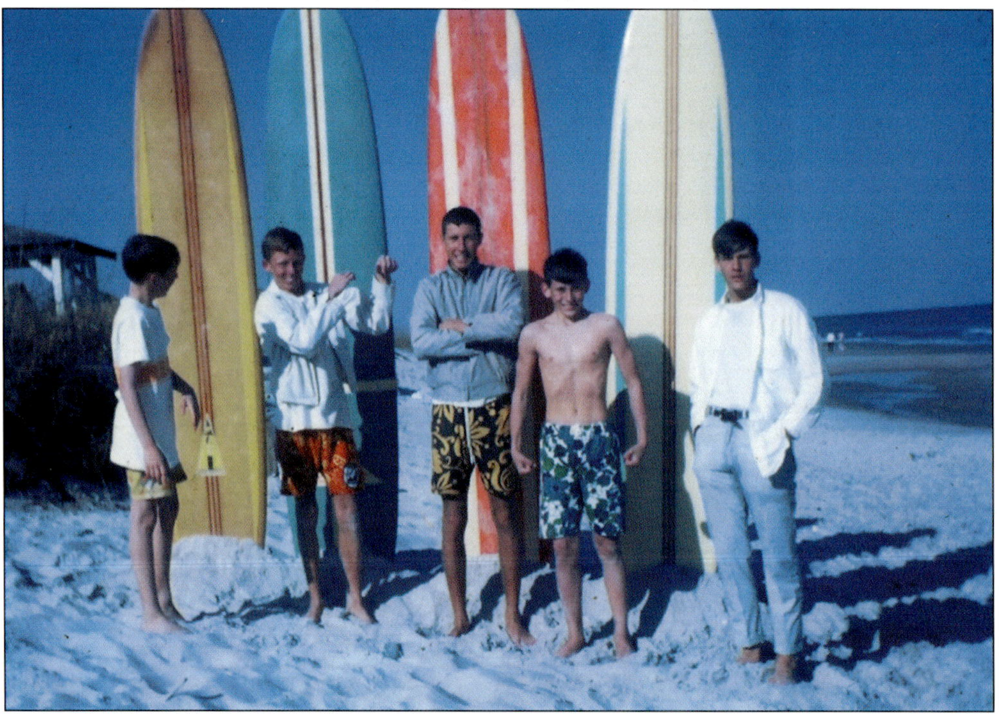

Usually, the closest a young surfer could come to his or her idol was a copy of *Surfer* magazine and the eight-millimeter films that one could order out of the back. One can tell that Danny West, second from left, and the Forty-Second Avenue crew had been studying the magazine photographs, as they strike a pose with their boards stuck in the sand behind them around 1966. (Courtesy of Tim Holt.)

Winter waves always looked good, but until one got the right equipment they were just eye candy. Brothers Tim (left) and Robert Holt got the best gifts a boy could ask for on Christmas Day in 1965. New baggies, Birdwell of course, and wet suit tops made their day. Guess where they were later that afternoon? (Courtesy of Tim Holt.)

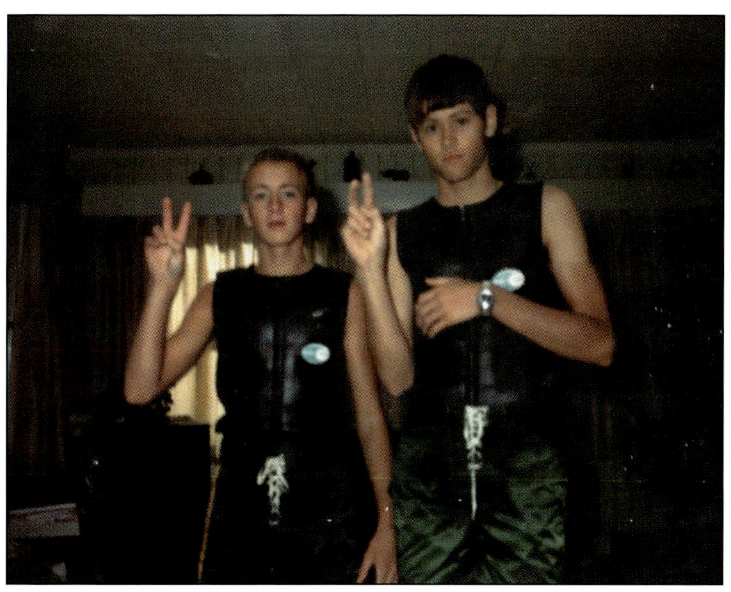

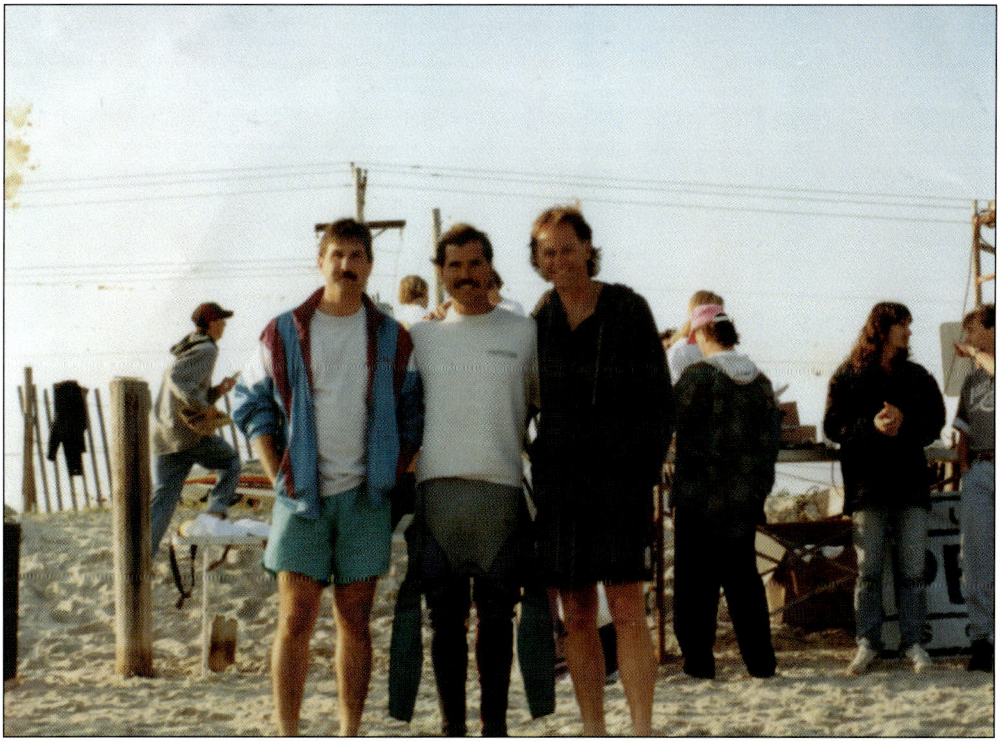

Fast forward a few years, and they are still out on the beach. Enjoying the contest atmosphere are, from left to right, John Bailey, Robert Hurt, and Tim Holt at Twenty-Ninth Avenue, Downwind Sails. The chance to reconnect with old friends and competitors is a big draw for contests and special events. (Courtesy of Tim Holt.)

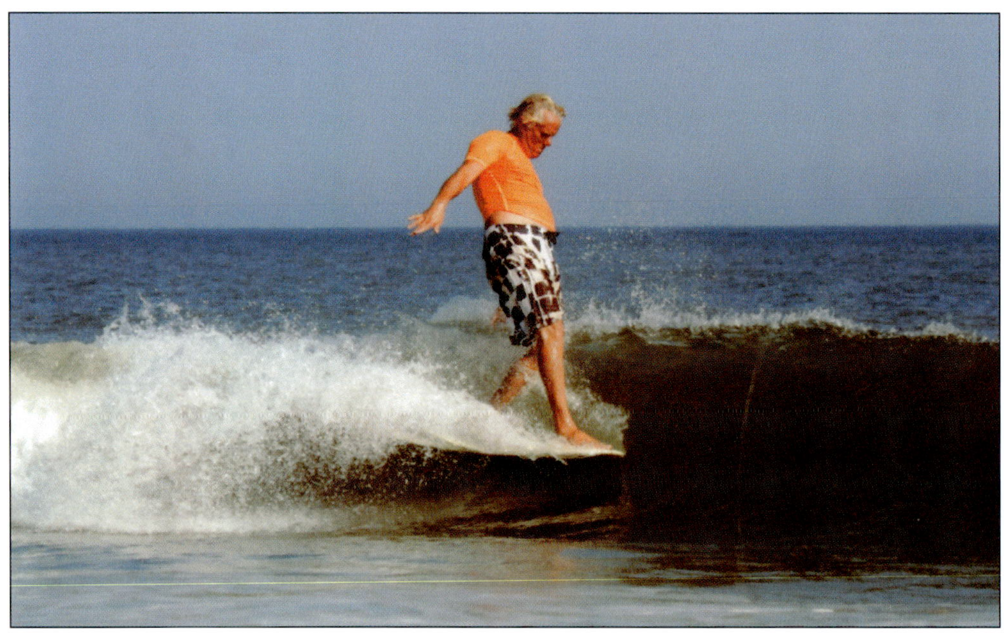

Bob Weaver is pictured here hanging five at Pawleys Island. Surfers still talk about this "goofy foot" beating all the professionals at the Record Bar Pro in Wrightsville Beach in the 1980s. The waves were macking, and he took on all comers. A true voice in the lineup, he kept things straight at the south end of Pawleys Island. He has instilled his sense of the sport in his sons, who are all forces to be reckoned with. (Courtesy of Scot Benston.)

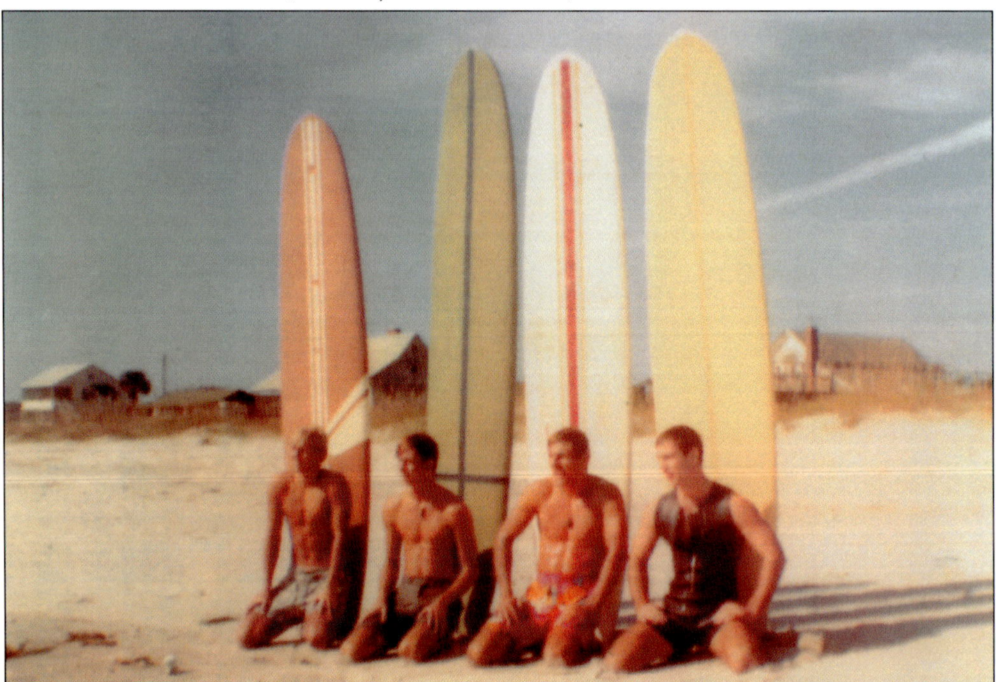

Looking like a page out of *Surfer* magazine, these boys of summer (from left to right) Danny ? , Larry Marlowe, Eric Harrison, and Craig Thomas pose with their boards on Pawleys Island around 1966. (Courtesy of Craig Thomas.)

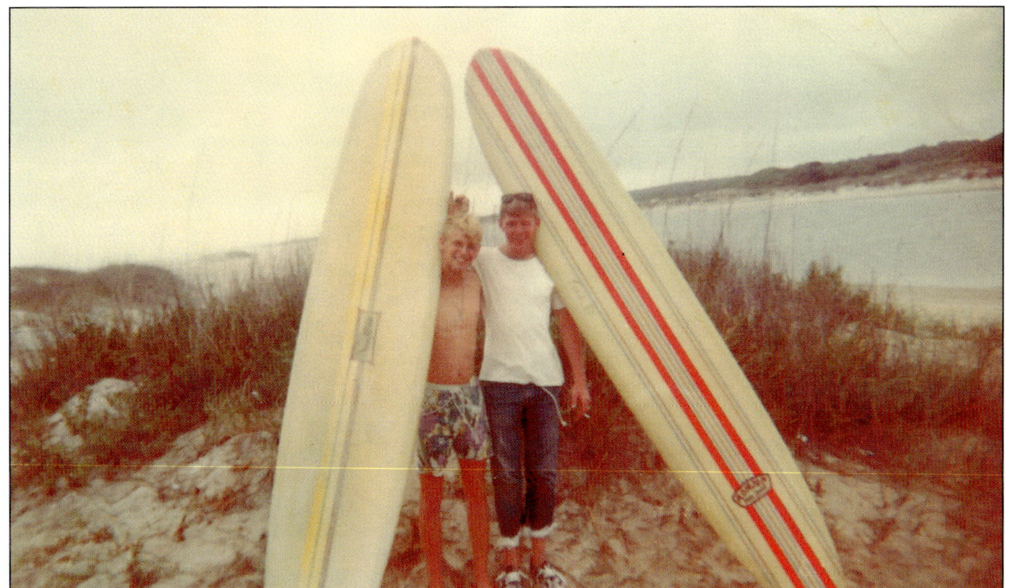

Rock Smith (right) poses with his Ron Jon and Wayne Billings with his Hansen at the Point at Garden City. Rock says he bought a balsa Jacobs Velzey in 1960 when he was 12 years old from Keith Salvo, who got it in 1959 from a local solicitor—it was the only board in town. (Courtesy of Rock Smith.)

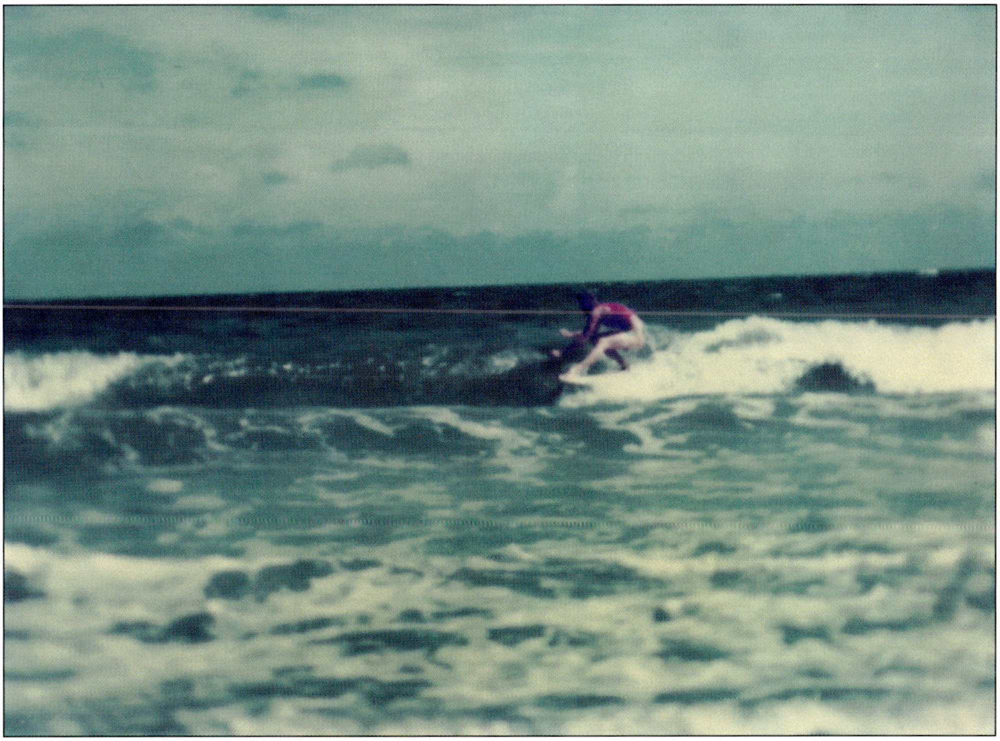

Tim Holt rides his Sunshine surfboard in a 1975 contest in Surfside. From 1972 through 1982, Tim rode for Claude Codgen, exclusively on Sunshine surfboards. (Courtesy of Tim Holt.)

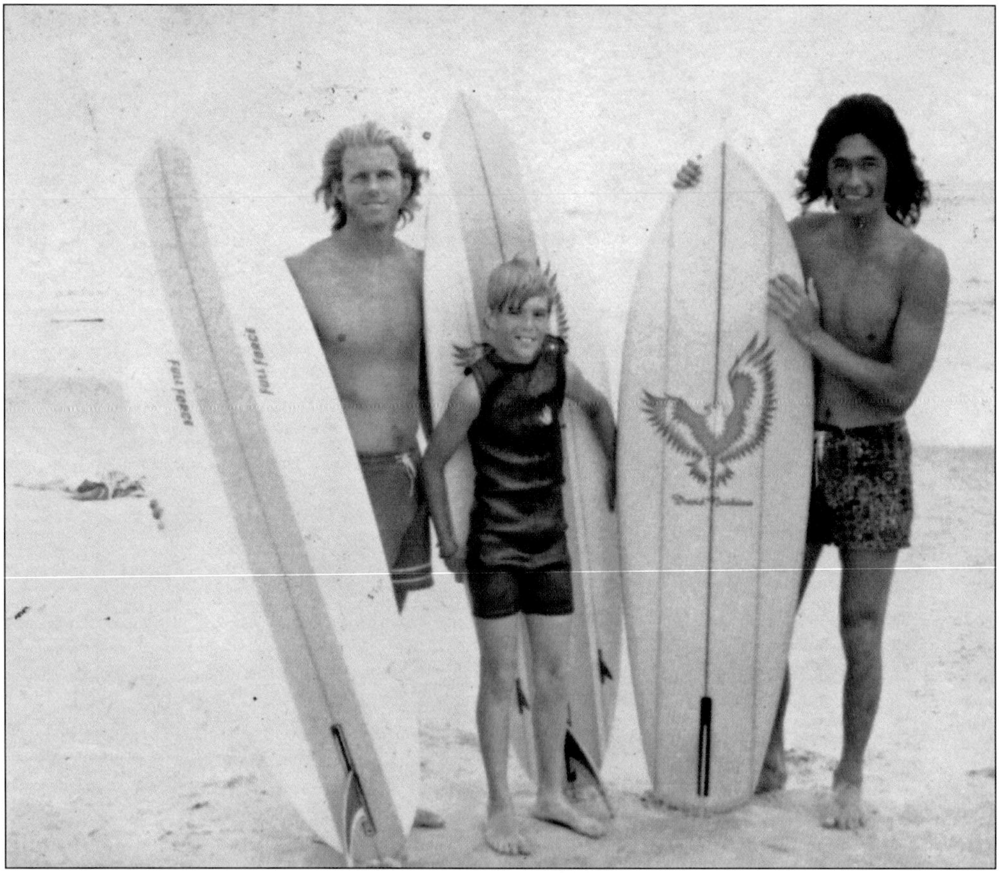

In 1971, local David Nuckles (center) got the chance to meet his surfing idol, David Nuuhiwa (right), when he was traveling through Myrtle Beach. Nuuhiwa graciously took the youngster and Charlie Baldwin (left) surfing with him. (Courtesy of David Nuckles.)

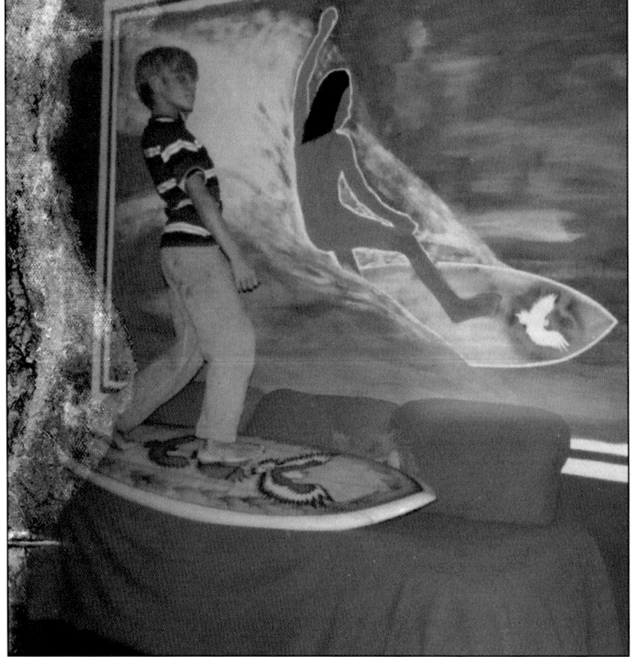

Nuckles (pictured) had a friend paint his bedroom wall with Nuuhiwa riding his trademark logo board. After a call to California, Nuuhiwa made a special board for Nuckles, which David treasured. In 1979, Nuckles represented the United States in the seventh World Surfing Championship at Mahoon Reef, South Africa. (Courtesy of David Nuckles.)

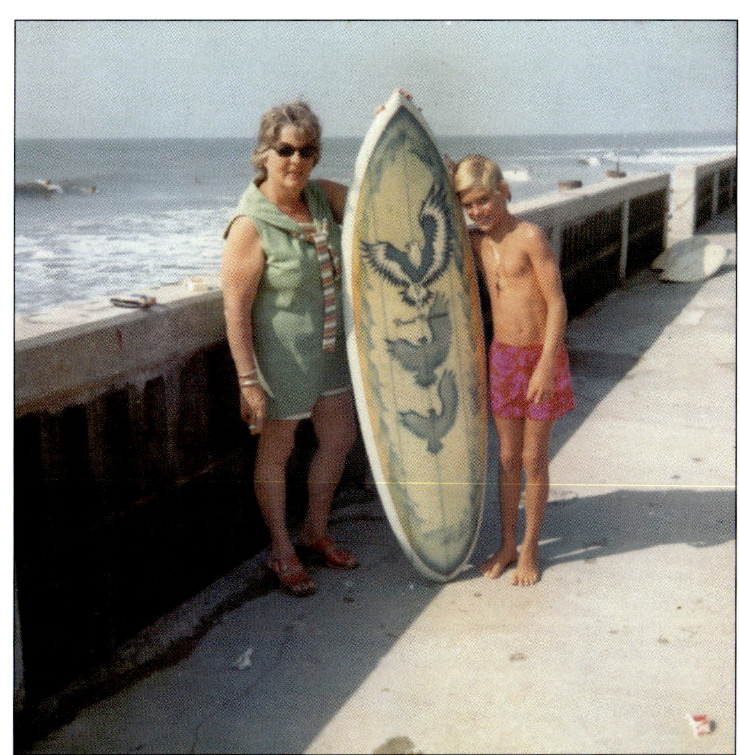

David Nuckles and his mom are shown with the surfboard that David Nuuhiwa made for him. Nuckles says he worshipped that board—he even slept with it. Nuckles's mom was unique on the surfing scene. Truly a surf mom, she supported her son's ambitions wholeheartedly, similar to surf families today. She was definitely an anomaly in the 1970s. (Courtesy of David Nuckles.)

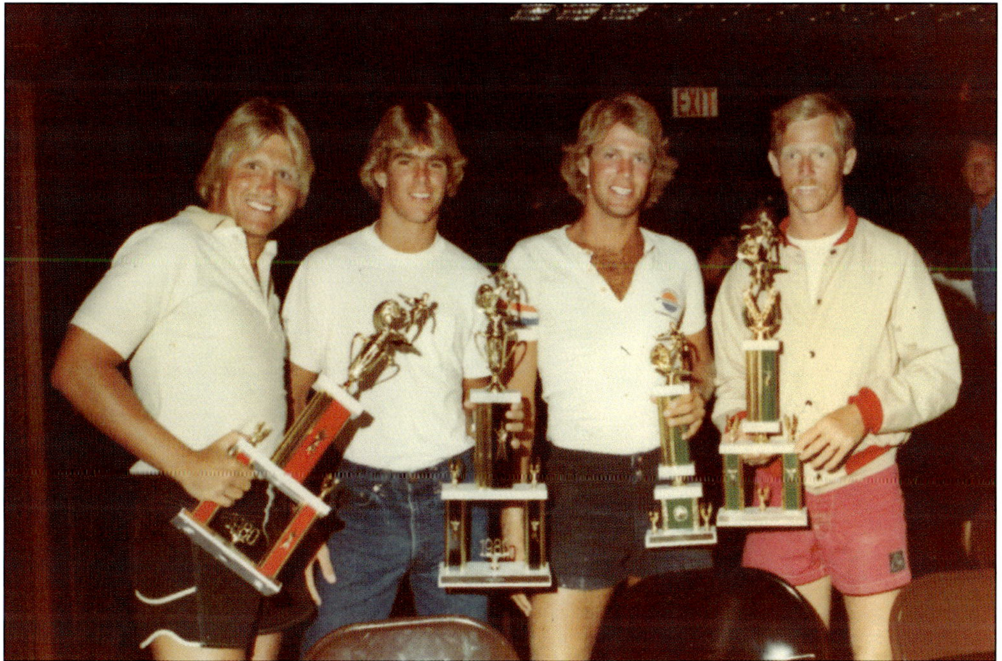

The winners of the Myrtle Beach Sun-Fun Pro-Am line up for a photograph with their trophies. From left to right are Wade Smith, David Nuckles, Mark McDaniels, and Danny West. The contest, held here from June 7–9, 1980, is a local tradition. (Courtesy of David Nuckles.)

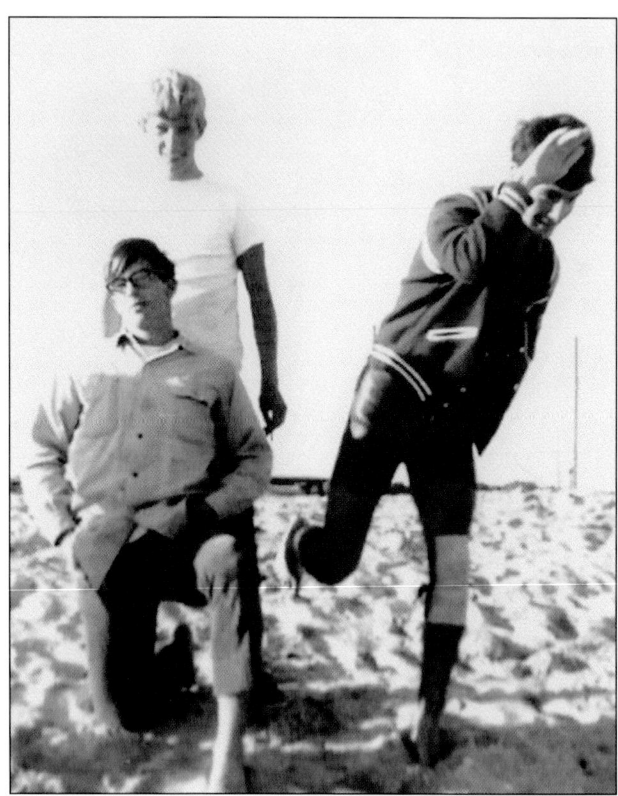

Tim Holt snapped this photograph of Ward Spillane (kneeling), Eric Eason (back left), and Steve Jordan in 1965 by the Garden City Pier. When he first encountered them, Tim thought that this group knew how to have fun. He managed to look them up whenever he was in Garden City. (Courtesy of Tim Holt.)

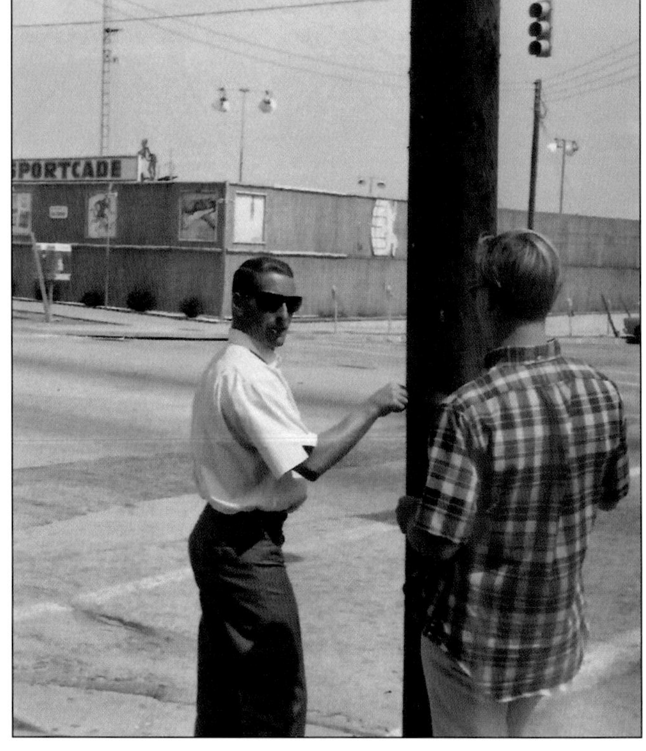

The Pendletons, a surf music band, blazed a trail up and down the East Coast in the 1960s, playing a new style of music to an ever-growing audience. One afternoon, grabbing a sandwich, they recognized Mickey Munoz walking down the street in Myrtle Beach. They quickly snapped a photograph of Munoz (left) with band member Greg Nutt. (Courtesy Frank Davis.)

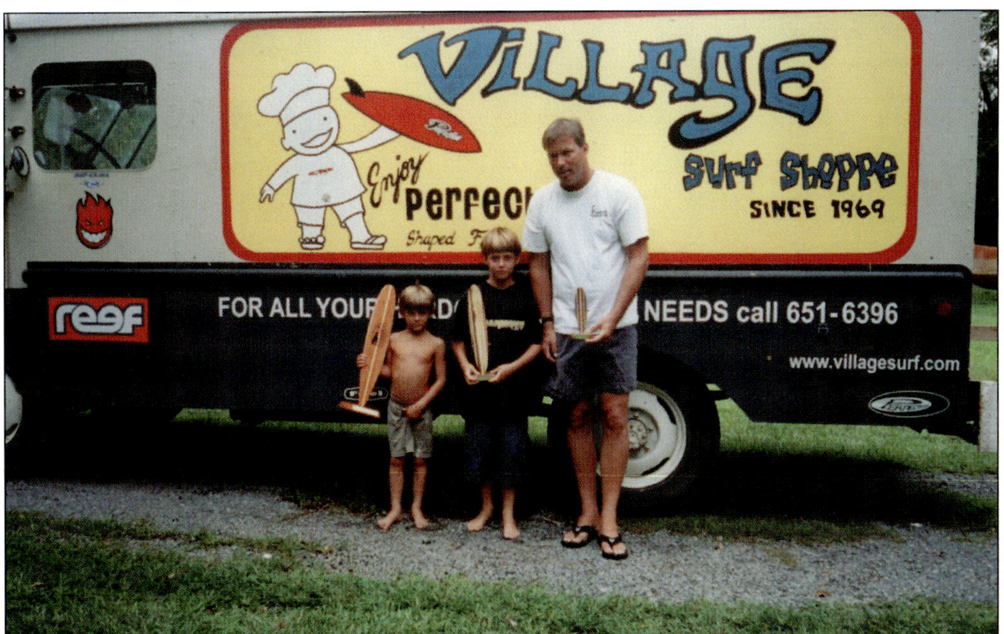

What a difference a few years can make. Seen above around 1999, Kelly Richards stands in front of the "bread truck" from the surf shop with sons Cole (left) and Cam (center); they are just back from the Buddy Pelletier Memorial Longboard Contest in Atlantic Beach. Five-year-old Cole got third, nine-year-old Cam won his age group, and Kelly got fifth place. Not many years later, around 2009, it seems he had sired a pair of champions. If someone making money is the criteria for a pro, Cam laughs, as he turned pro when he was 11, winning a check from Billabong. When he went up to get his check, he was so small they thought he was asking directions. He said, "No, ma'am, you owe me $200." (Both, courtesy of Kelly Richards.)

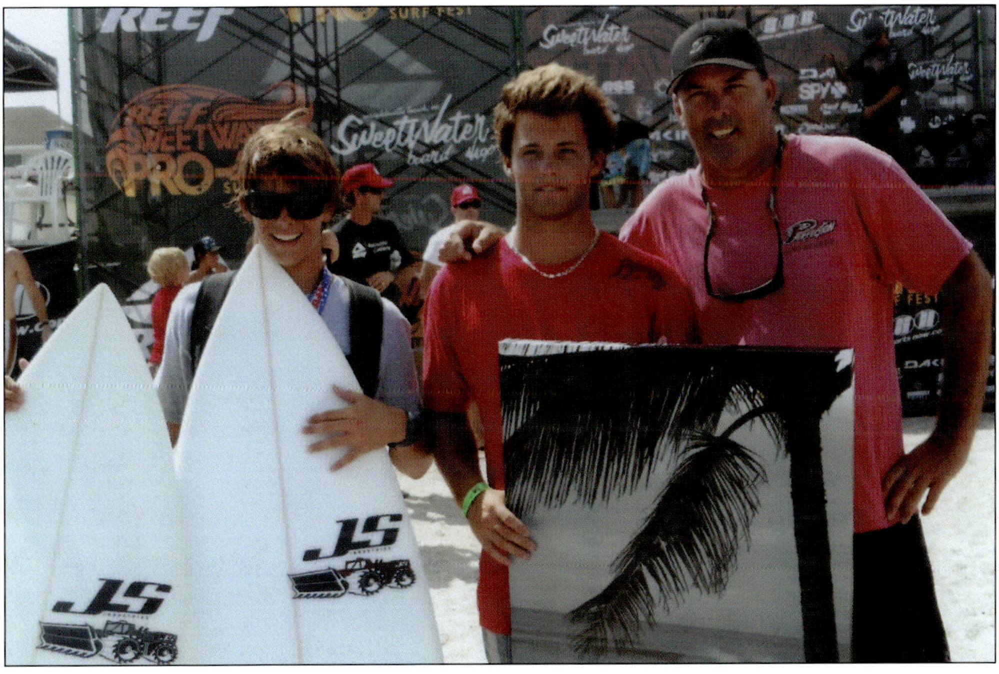

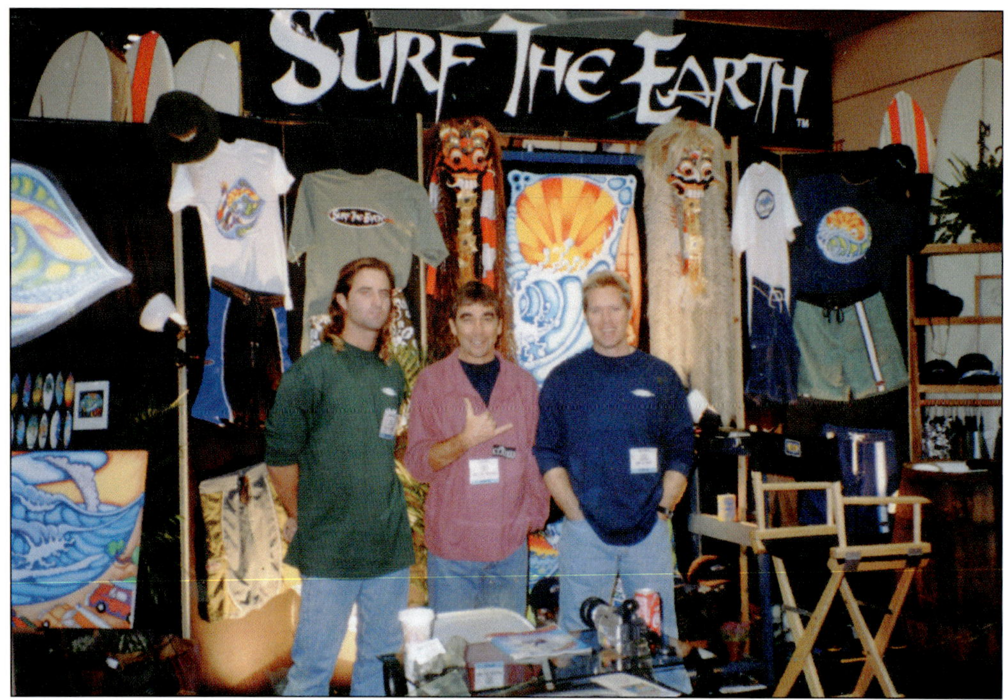

Scot Benston (right) came to Pawleys Island in 1989 and opened a screen-printing shop. People kept asking where he had surfed, so he made a T-shirt that showed all the locations and titled it "Surf the Earth." By 1992, his brand of Surf the Earth apparel was in over 500 surf shops. He is seen here at Surf Expo with Drew Brophy (left) and Gerry Lopez. Even though he spends much of his energy in ecotourism, he still runs the surf shop. (Courtesy of Scot Benston.)

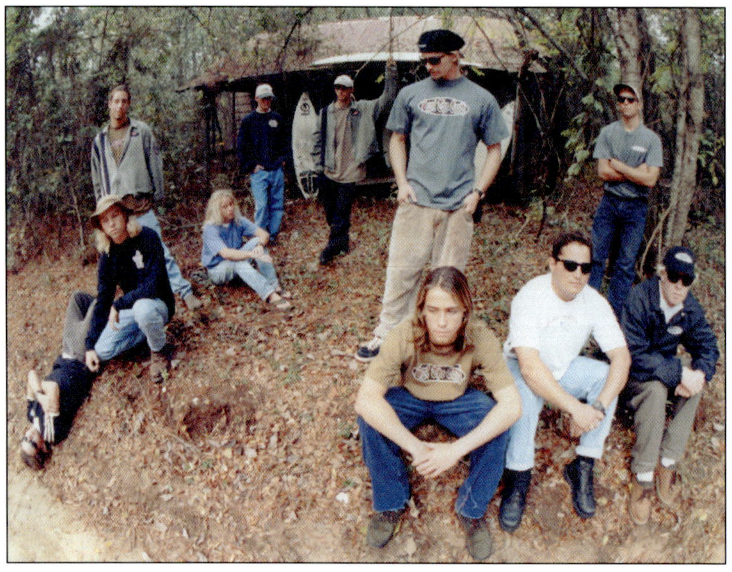

The Surf the Earth surf team is shown here at the hut in one of their iconic advertisements. Pictured from left to right are (seated) Jacob Stackley, Eric Molton, Coleen Hanley, Jonathan Owens, Dave Clifton, and Scot Hanske; (standing) Jim Whitney, Chip Adams, Robbie Fennel, Chris Brown, and Todd Youngblood. (Courtesy of Scot Benston.)

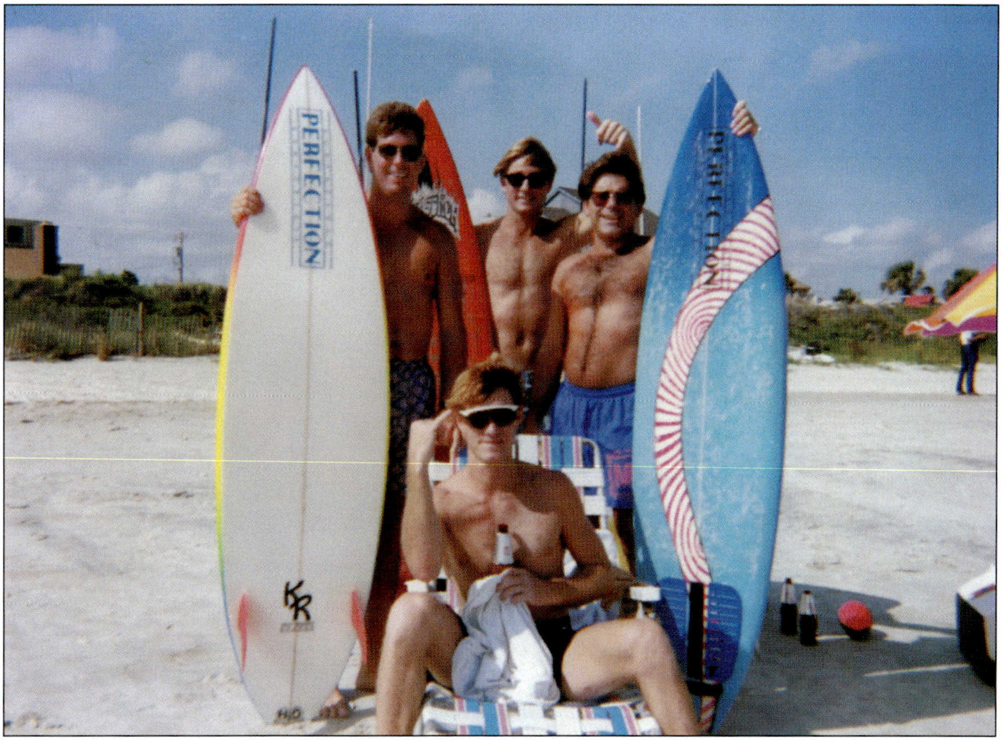

This group of Myrtle Beach surf legends in the making were captured chilling at Seventy-Second Avenue North in the 1980s. Pictured are (seated) Tommy Rainwater; (standing, from left to right) David Nuckles, Billy Rainwater (Tommy's brother), and Chuck Dawes. (Courtesy of Village Surf Shop.)

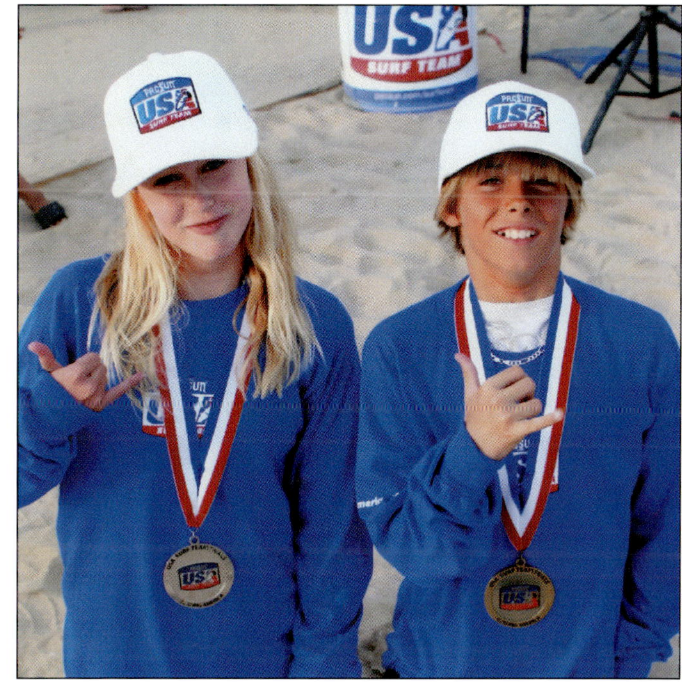

Keenan Lineback (left) and Cam Richards show some class on being named to the United States team at Huntington Beach. Keenan, age 14, and Cam, age 12, were two of the youngest to make the team. (Courtesy of Kelly Richards.)

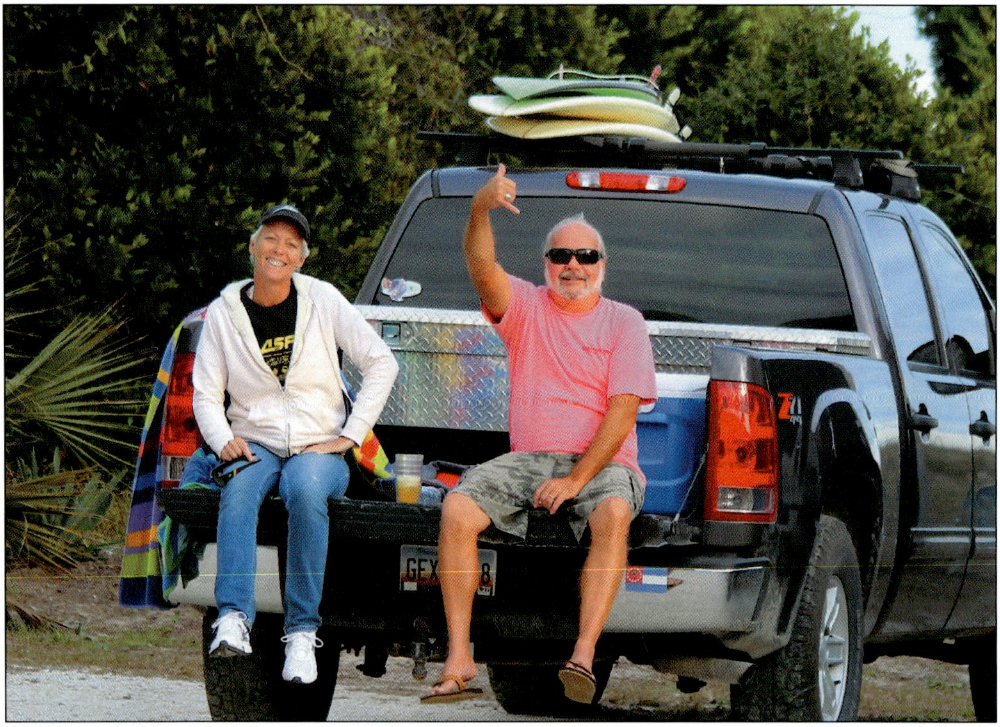

In 1990, Terri (left) and Denny Green (right) made a conscious choice to mentor young surfers. As former directors of the Eastern Surfing Association and now directors of the American Surfing Federation, they teach the etiquette of the lineup and provide the knowledge to raise the level of skill of up-and-coming Grand Strand surfers. (Courtesy of Denny Green.)

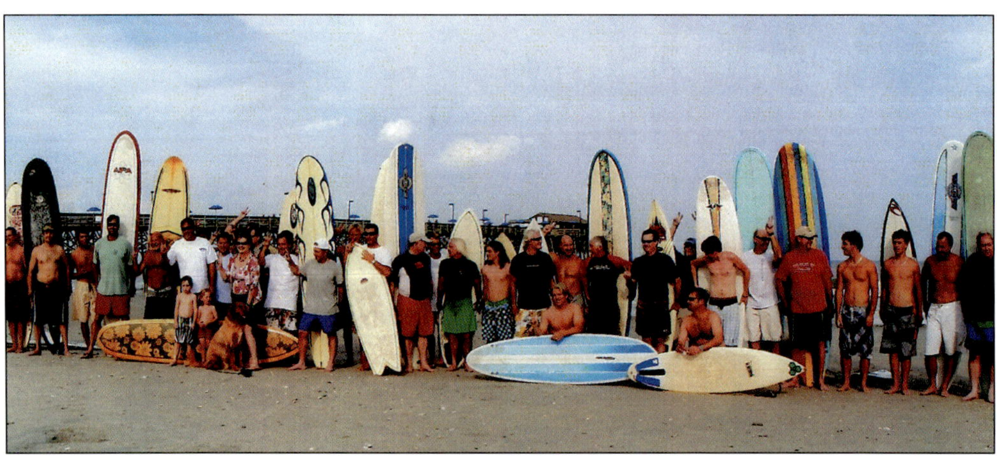

Nothing creates a legend better than having the respect of peers. The tradition of honoring fellow surfers when they pass is called a "paddle-out." This group assembled at the Garden City First Street access for a paddle-out to honor Eric Eason. Eason was the original owner of the Village Surf Shop and passed away in 2008. (Courtesy of Kelly Richards.)

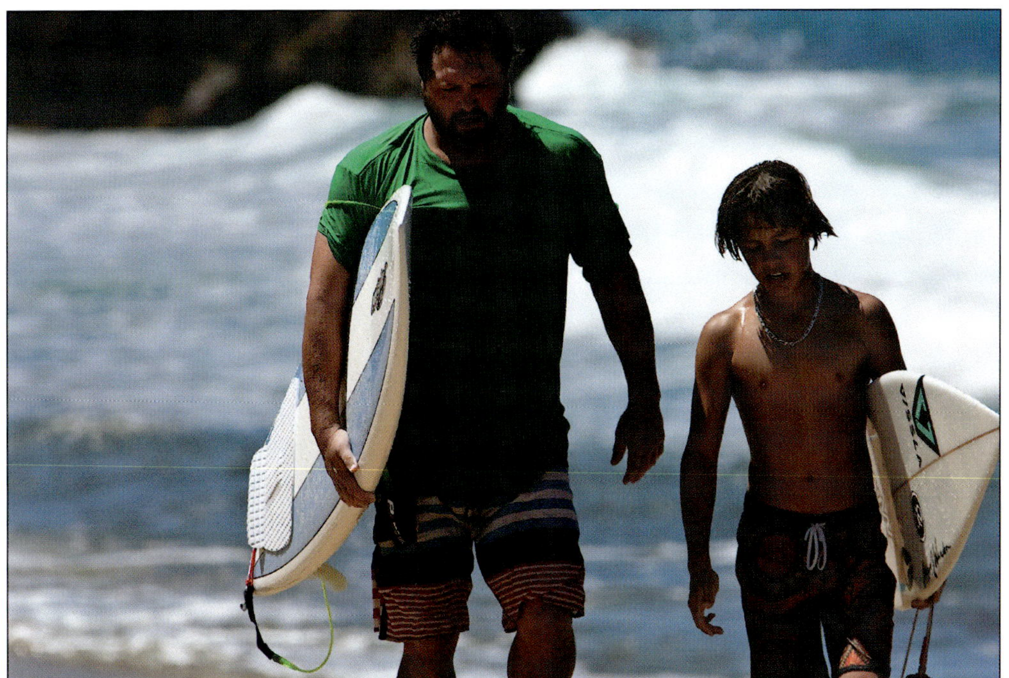

Stoney Cantor, a superb East Coast champion and US Championship contender takes a quality moment with his son Micah. Stoney started surfing at Surfside Beach when he was 10 years old. In 1994, he nailed every contest that year, including the South Carolina State Championship. (Courtesy of Stoney Cantor.)

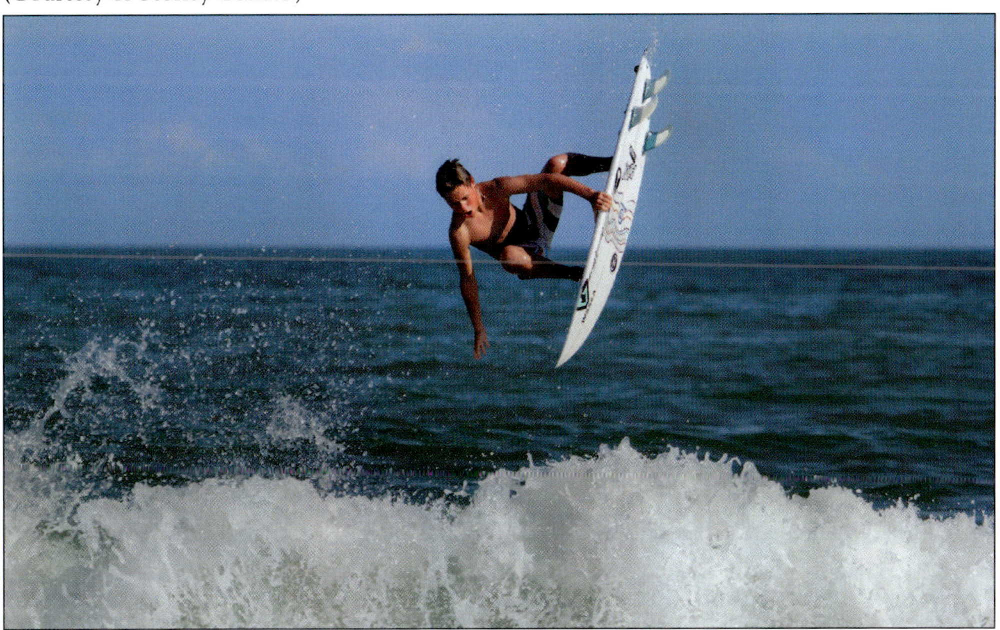

Stoney has had Micah on a board since he could walk, and it shows. At age 13, Micah was the youngest to win the Men's Open at both the East Coast Championship and the Atlantic Surfing Championship. "We're looking for Micah and Luke Gordon to enter the World Surf League Junior Pro Series and maybe the World Championship Tour," Stoney says. (Courtesy of Kent Ficklin.)

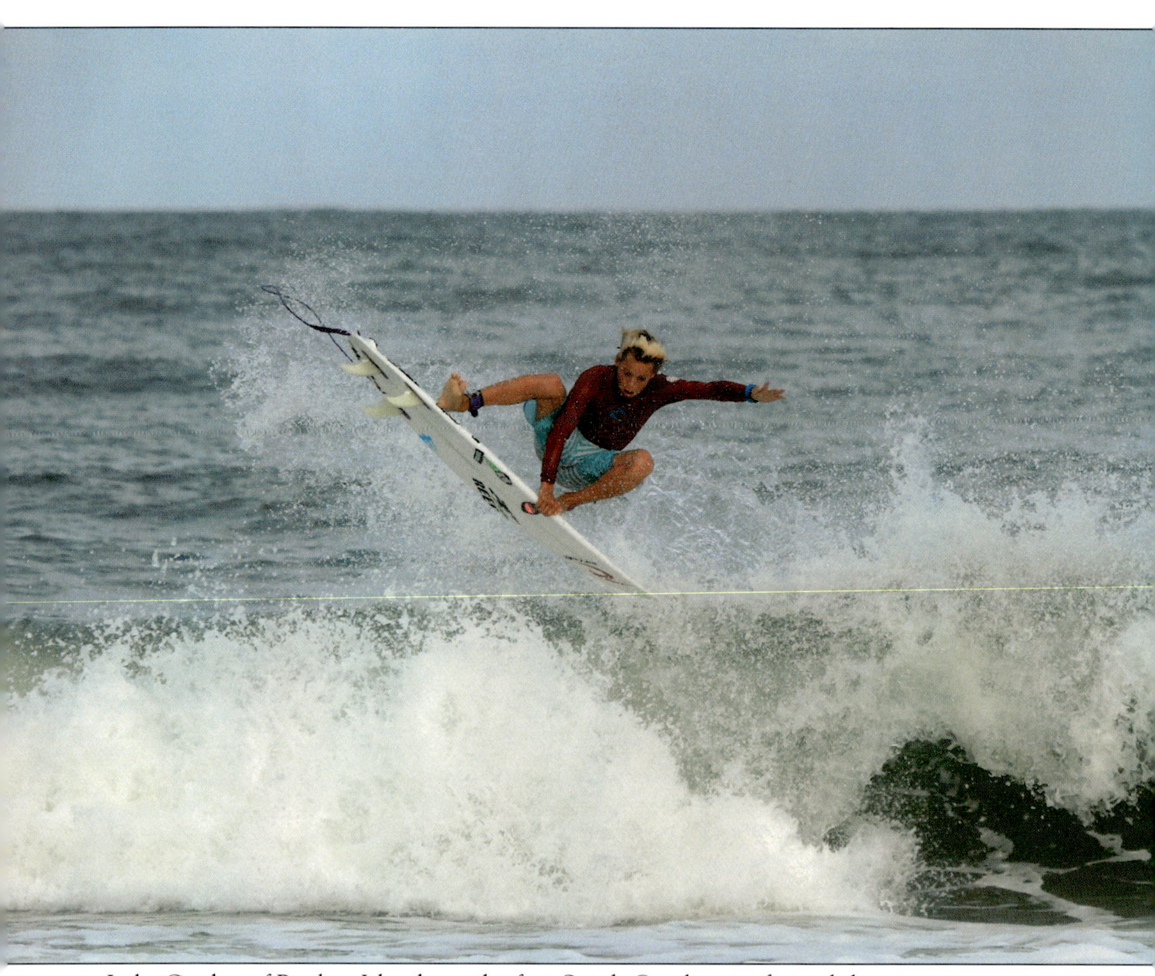

Luke Gordon of Pawleys Island was the first South Carolina surfer and the youngest ever to win the marquee pro division at the O'Neill Sweetwater Pro-Am contest. The first man-on-man contest in his career, he had always dreamed of being chaired up the beach, so winning this contest was a dream come true. (Courtesy of Ken Ficklin.)

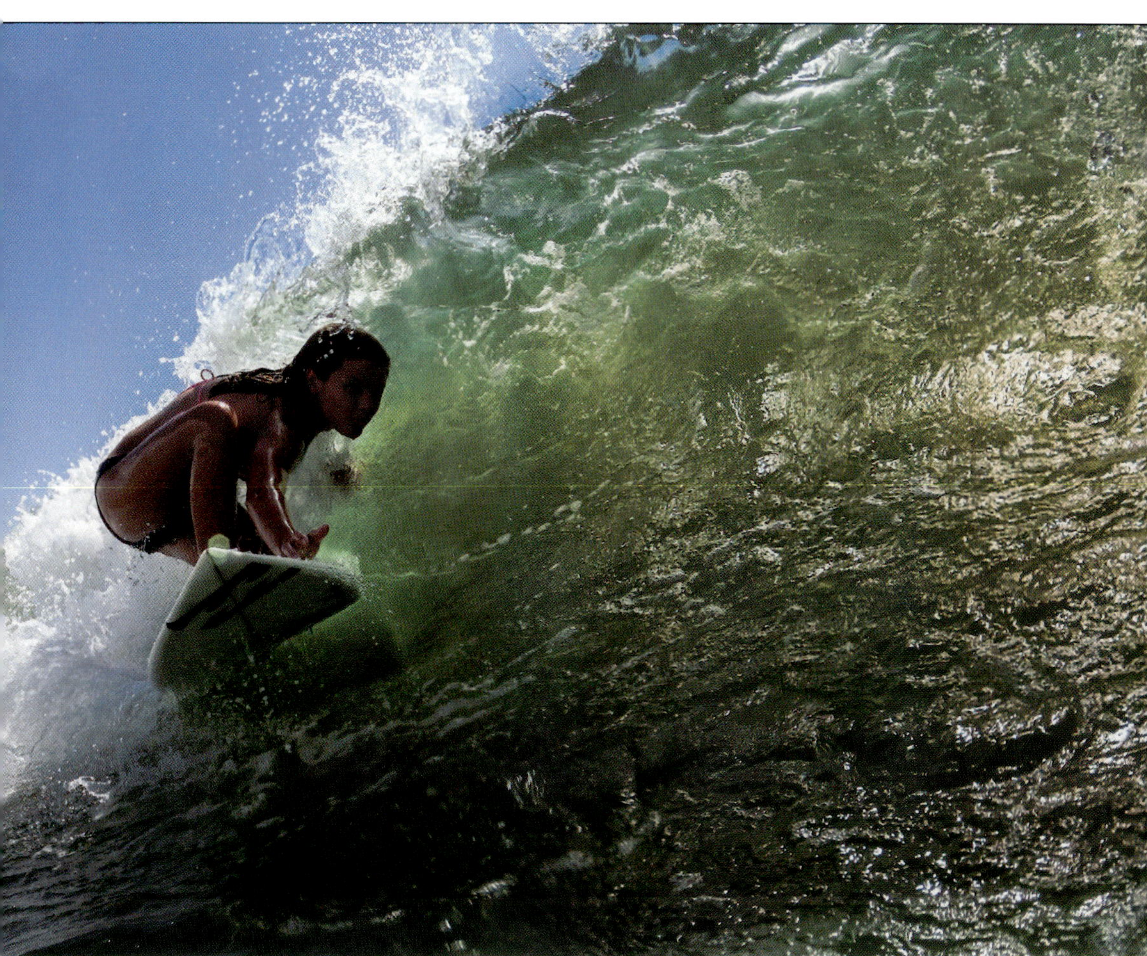

Emory McClary is one of the hottest young women surfing today. At age 16, she surfs for Billabong, the US team, Nimbus GSS, and Village Surf Shop and is someone to watch. In this shot, one can see her smooth free-surfing style in crystal green Myrtle Beach waves. (Courtesy of Kent Ficklin.)

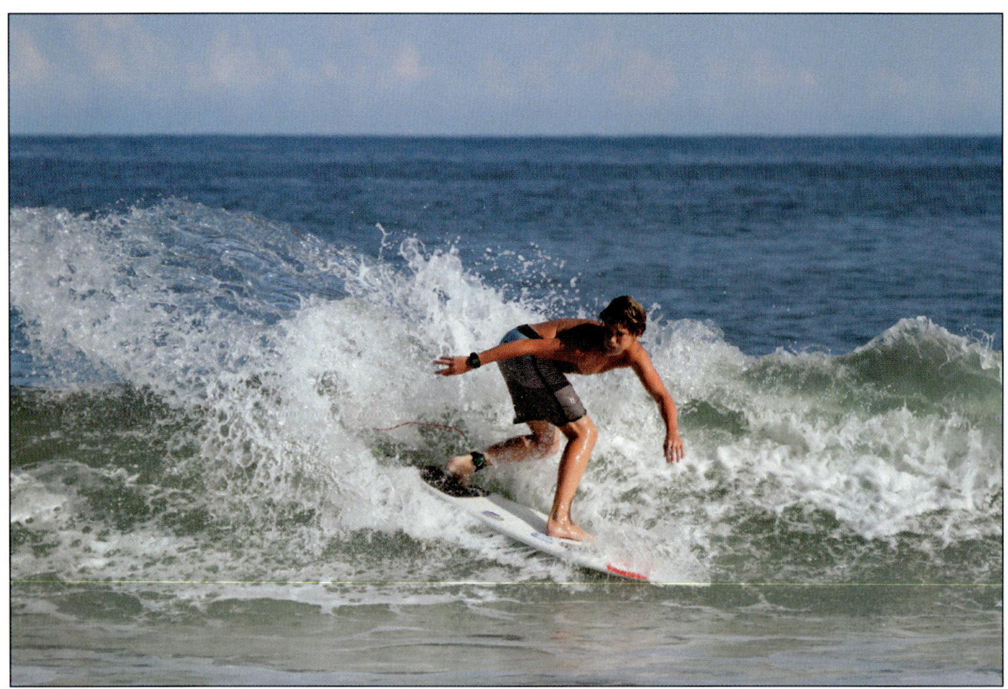

Shane Evans, a Surfside Beach native, has only been surfing about three years, but that has not stopped him from picking up slots in the winner's circle at local contests. In this photograph, he is free-surfing the Garden City Pier. (Courtesy of Ken Ficklin.)

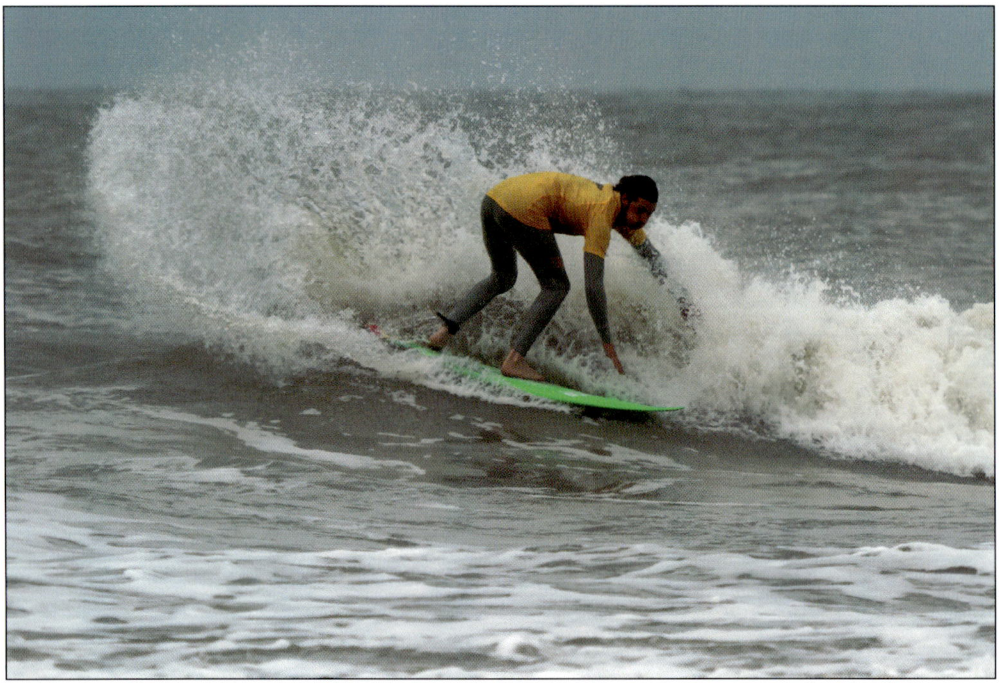

Shawn Clark, shown at the ASF contest in Garden City, is one of the up-and-comers in the Myrtle Beach area. When he is not touring with his company, H2O Adventures, he is out there ripping up the surf and winning contests. (Courtesy of Kent Ficklin.)

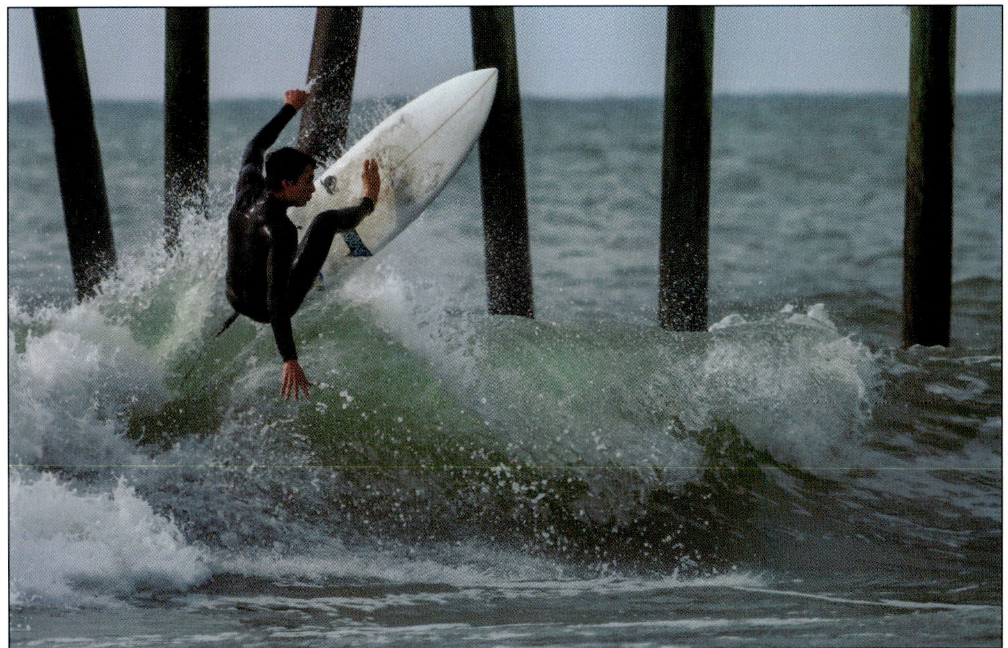

A talented surfer from Garden City, Tyson Miller attends the University of South Carolina, but he comes home to surf any chance he can get. Riding for Village Surf Shop, Nimbuss GSS, Lost, and Oakley, he is racking up contest wins and is certainly someone to keep an eye on. (Courtesy of Kent Ficklin.)

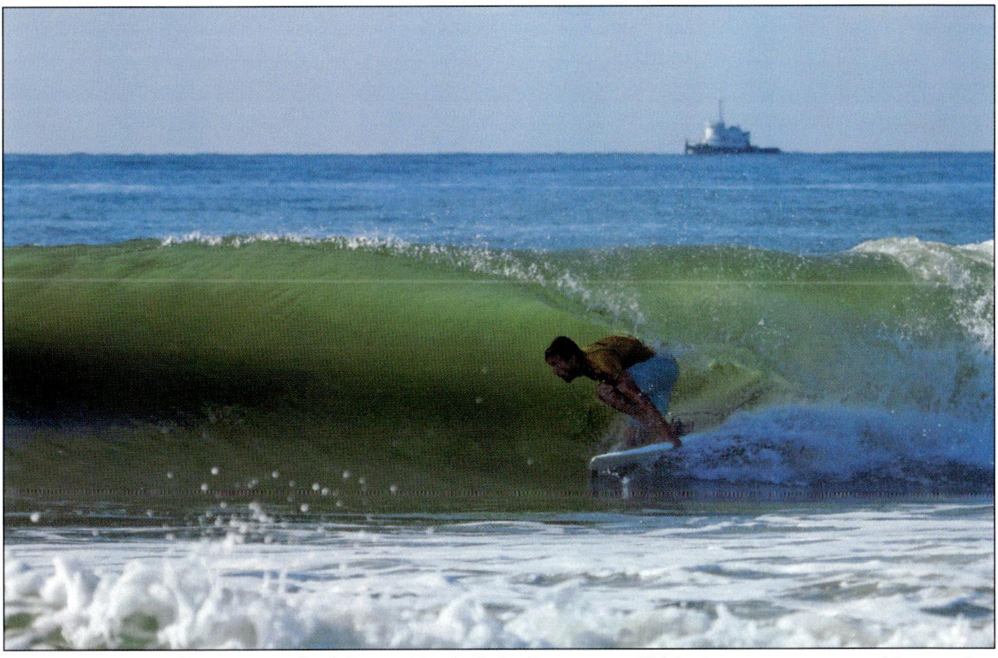

Here is Spencer Benton at the Native Son's Salt Games in 2015. An interesting sidebar to his excellence in surfing is his football career. He started as a kicker for Myrtle Beach High School and moved on to the same position at Clemson University in 2008. He later signed with the Dallas Cowboys. (Courtesy of Kent Ficklin.)

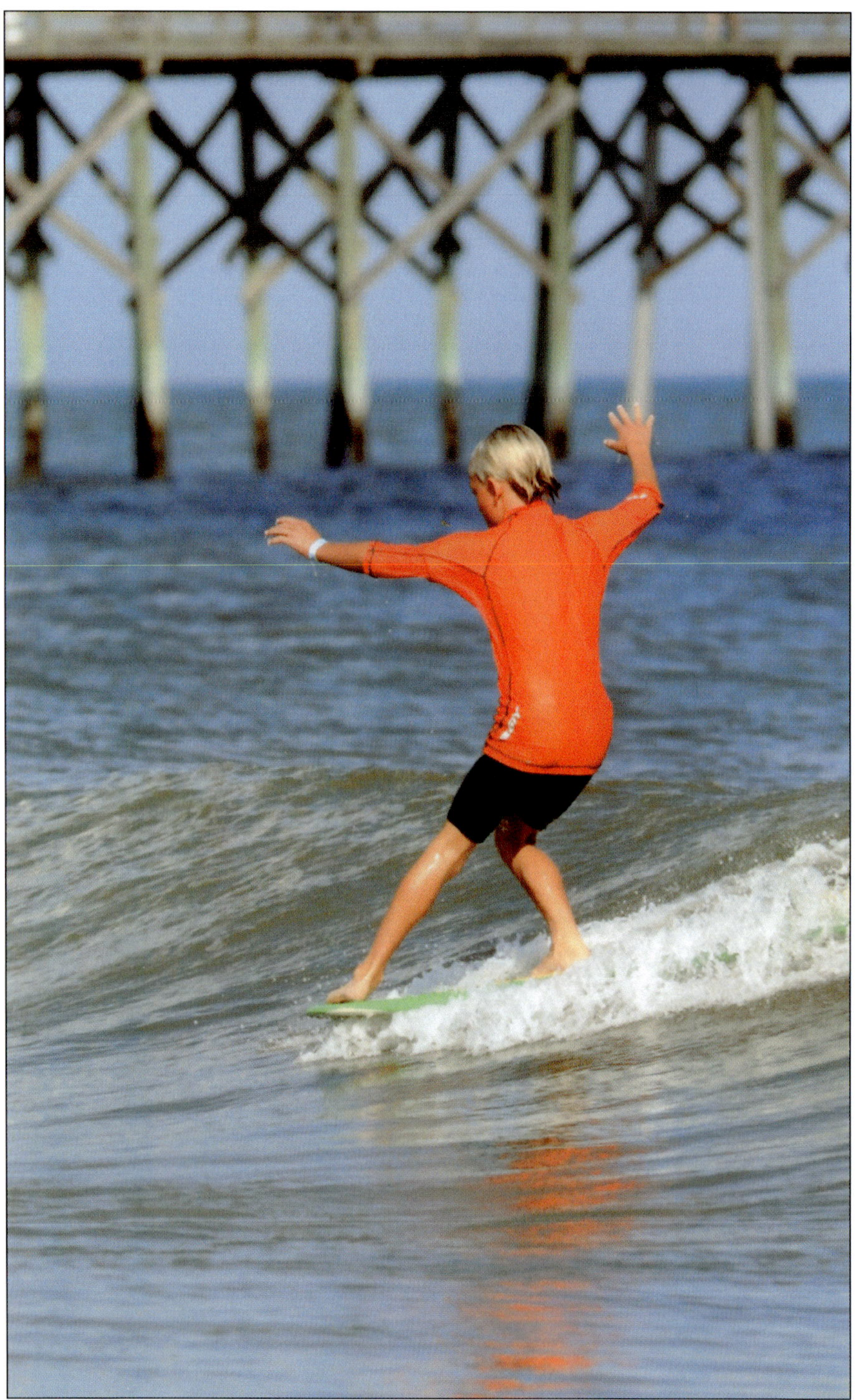

There is a beauty found in the grace and power of a surfer. The fluid form and use of the wave is always inspiring. Using the gifts of Mother Nature to the fullest is the highest and best use of one's talents. Luke Gordon shows us his grace, power, and form, proving that a wave does not have to be huge to be poetry in motion. (Courtesy of Stoney Cantor.)

Two

Charleston

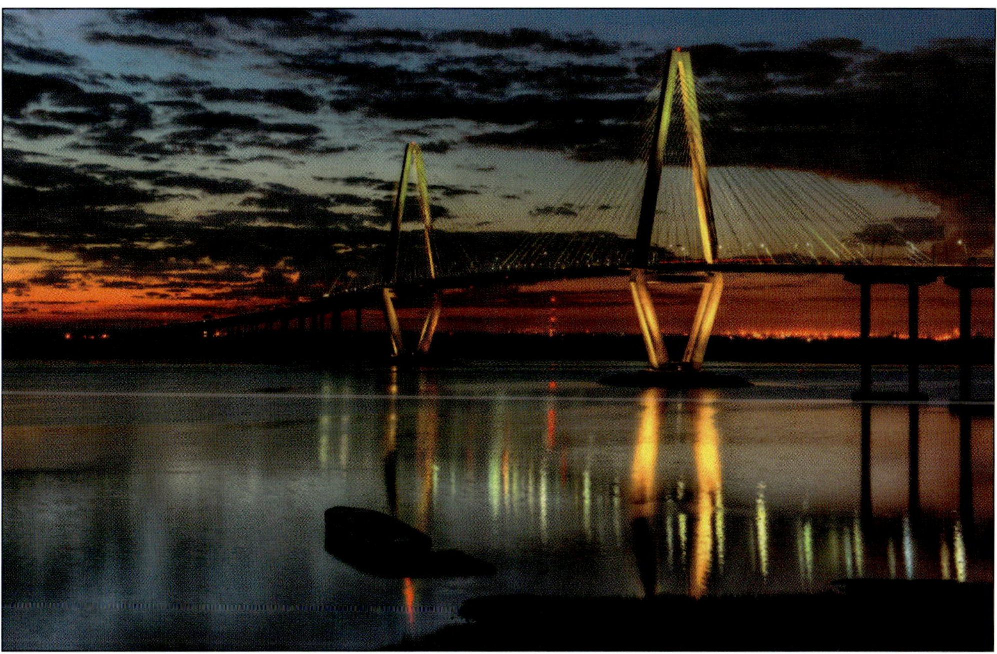

There are a few beaches between Pawleys Island and Beaufort. Barrier islands dot the coastline, each with its particular topography, accessibility, and wave characteristics. Accessible only by boat for centuries, ferries and streetcars opened the islands north of the city. As soon as bridges were constructed, dance pavilions sprang up on Isle of Palms and Folly Beach. Beachgoers quickly found their favorite spots. Graduating from floats to surfboards, locals began to conquer their breaks, quickly adapting to wave changes made by shifting sands. The Isle of Palms and Sullivan's Island, north of the city, and Folly Beach, due south of the harbor, are the dominant areas today. (Courtesy of Paul Mulkey Sr.)

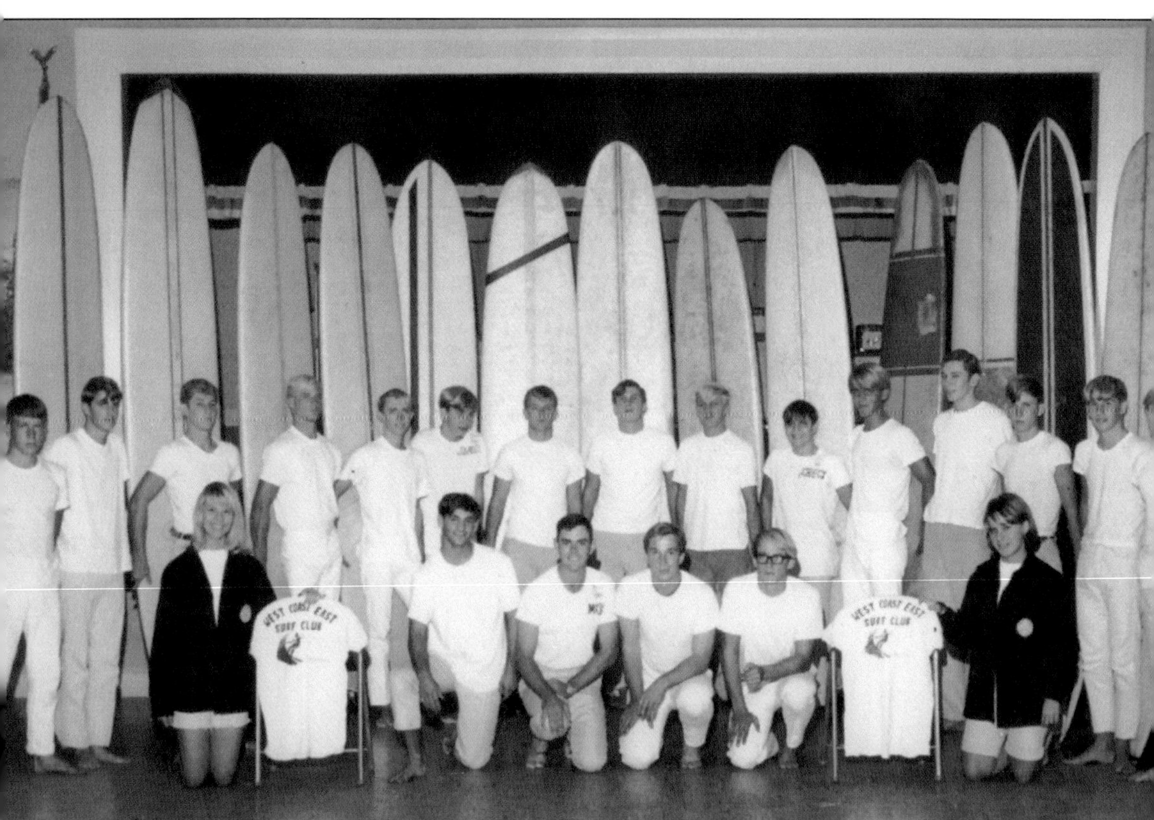

The West Coast East Surf Club 1965 members include, from left to right, (first row) Brenda Tucker, Rick Fichtman, Mike Taylor, Greg Nutt, Randy Nutt, and Kim Nutt; (second row) Chip Yarnell, Mike Jenks, George Steele, Ronnie Shephard, Frank Davis, Rusty Schwartz, Steve Means, Greg Holliday, Jack Tripp, Bob "Chico" Pachico, Jim Humphries, Allen Barnett, Foster Folsom, Dewey Mauldin, and Danny McMillan. (Courtesy of Frank Davis.)

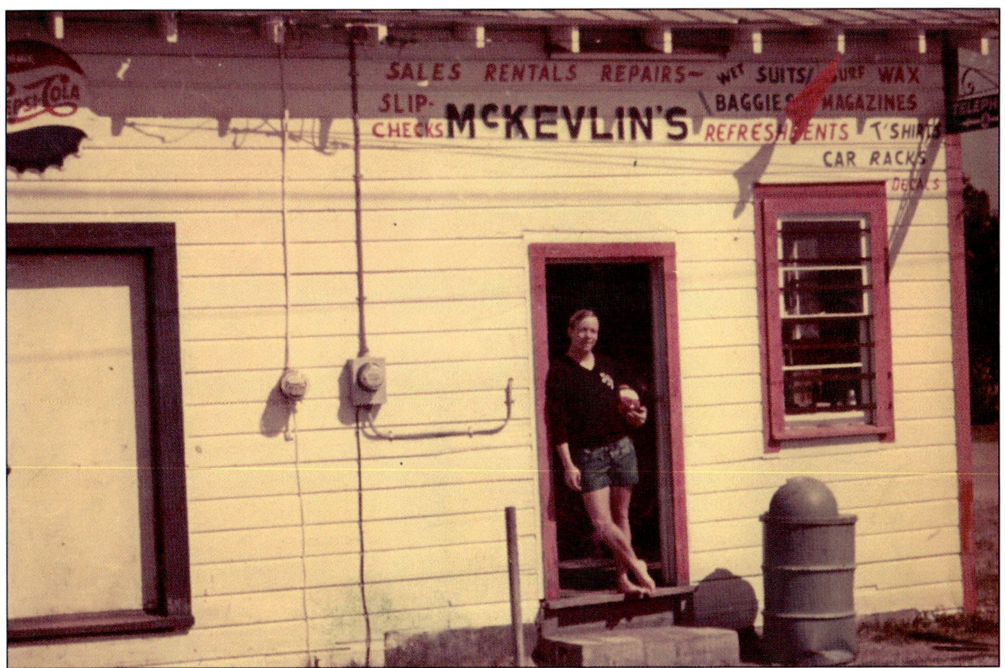

The original McKevlin's Surf Shop, shown here, opened in the back of the bowling alley on Folly Beach. The shop celebrated its golden anniversary in 2015. McKevlin and sons Teddy (pictured) and present owner Tim have piloted the business through many changes. They are one of a handful of shops across the country to remain in business in the same hands for 50 years. (Courtesy of McKevlin's Surf Shop.)

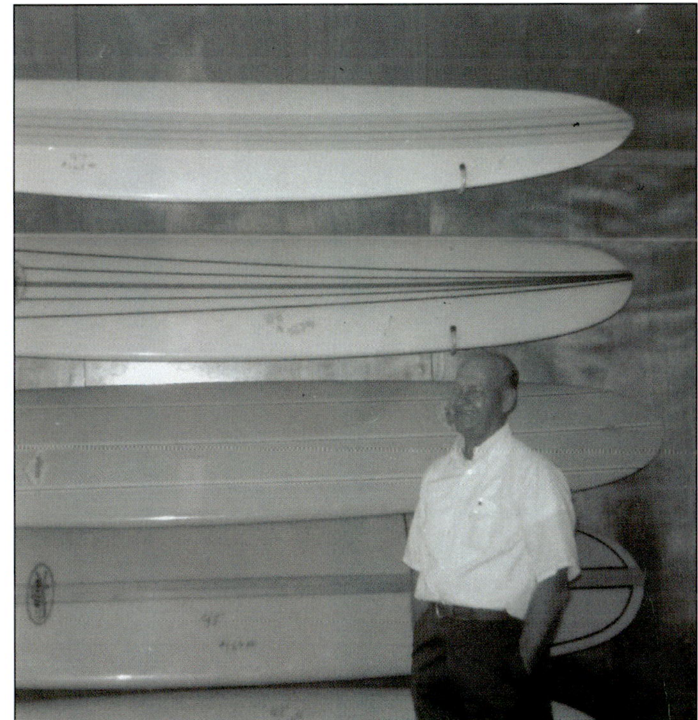

"Mr. Mac," as Dennis McKevlin was known to generations of surfers, began with a bowling alley on the corner of Center Street and Arctic Avenue. It was just across the street from the arcade and amusement park, Smoak's Rent-a-Float, and the famous Folly Beach Pier. The carnival atmosphere of the area brought in fun-seekers from all over the Charleston area, and Mr. Mac was there to help them with their surfboard purchase. (Courtesy of McKevlin's Surf Shop.)

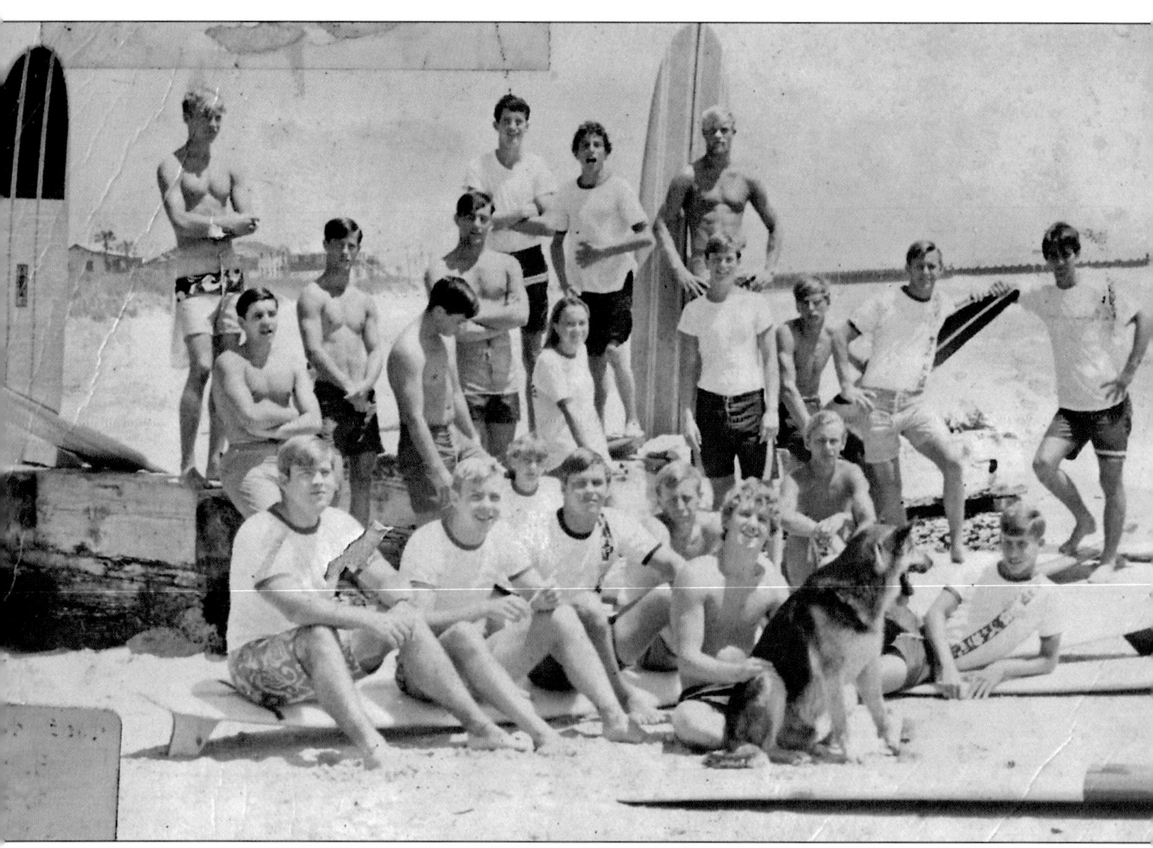

Members of the West Coast East Surf Club relax on Folly Beach's Second Street in 1966. From left to right are (first row) George Steele and Chief the dog; (second row) Terry Hennet, Ted McKevlin, Greg Holiday, Dave Hebden, Hubert Jones, and Dewey Mauldin; (third row) Bob "Chico" Pachico, John MacDonald, Darrel Wagner, Rick Fichtman, unknown, Kim Nutt, Jackie Peters, Eddie Benton, Bugsy Chevrier, and Jim Humphries; (fourth row) Jack Tripp, Ed Andrews, Dean Monk, and Ronnie Shephard. (Courtesy of Dean Monk.)

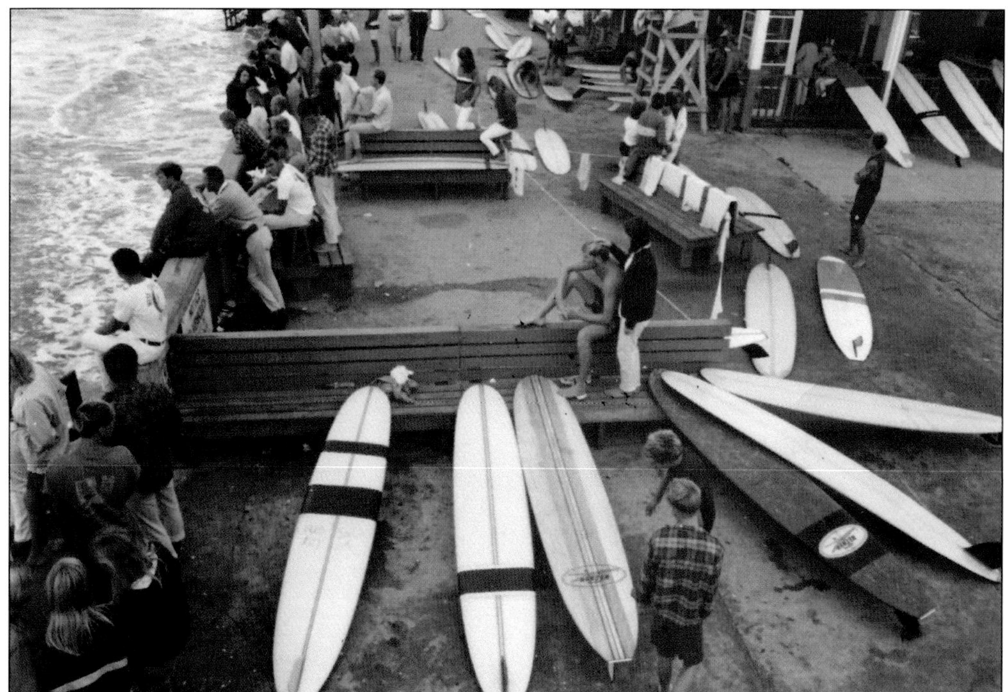

Mikey Knight (front) and Dean Monk check out a Hansen balsa surfboard in the foreground of this contest photograph. It was January 8, 1966, and the first annual Invitational Surfing Meet was under way on Folly Beach. The newspaper reported 95 entries from across the Southeast showing up to surf the 40-degree water. (Courtesy of McKevlin's Surf Shop.)

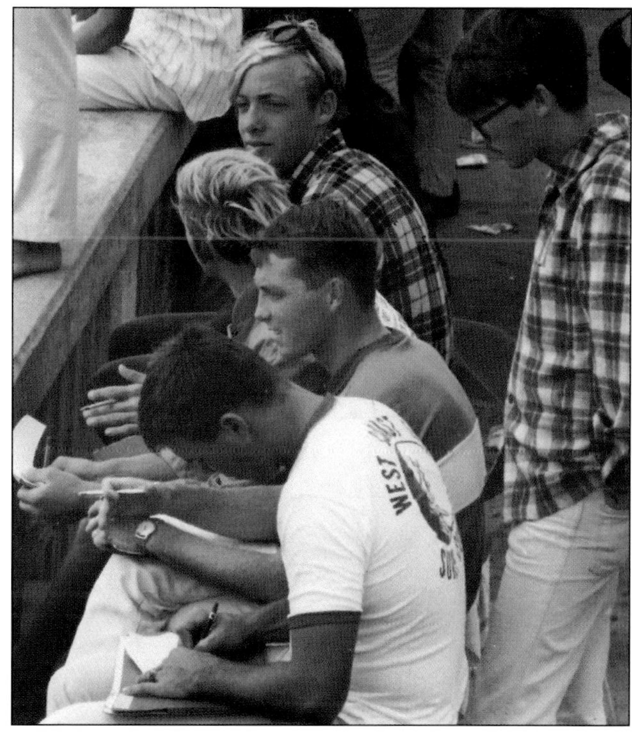

When asked about the conditions, Bugsy Chevrier, shivering, was quoted as saying, "No, it's not too bad. I've been in colder water." Black rubber suits were also a hot topic. Tom Proctor, a Carolina Coast club member, went on to explain the theory behind wet suits. While the newspaper concentrated on people in the freezing water, blonde Ted McKevlin, facing the camera, oversees the judging panel. (Courtesy of McKevlin's Surf Shop.)

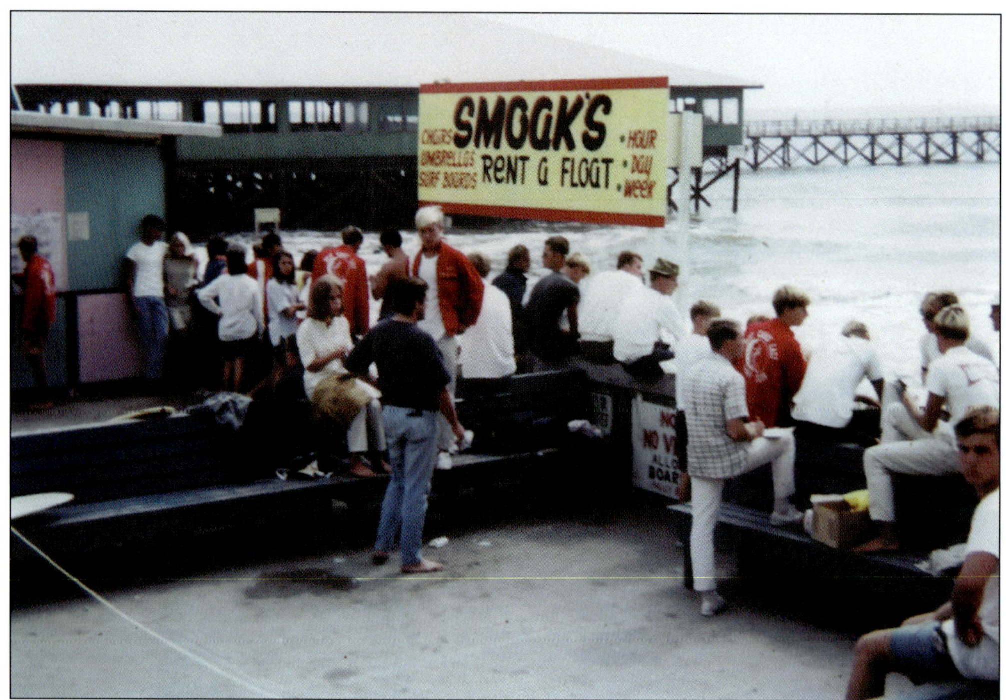

George Steele explained to reporters that most Folly surfers owe their knowledge of the sport to "Sarge" Bowman of the Air Force. Ray Holliday agreed: "I remember when he first started coming down to the beach, he'd be the only one in the water with a surfboard. Now if you don't have one, you're left out." Carl Beckman was quoted saying that three years prior if one mentioned surfing, people would think it was crazy—now they come running. A sports store owner admitted that while a few people had inquired about boards, the steep price of $115 put them off. "I'm not sure about future prospects," he said. (Both, courtesy of McKevlin's Surf Shop.)

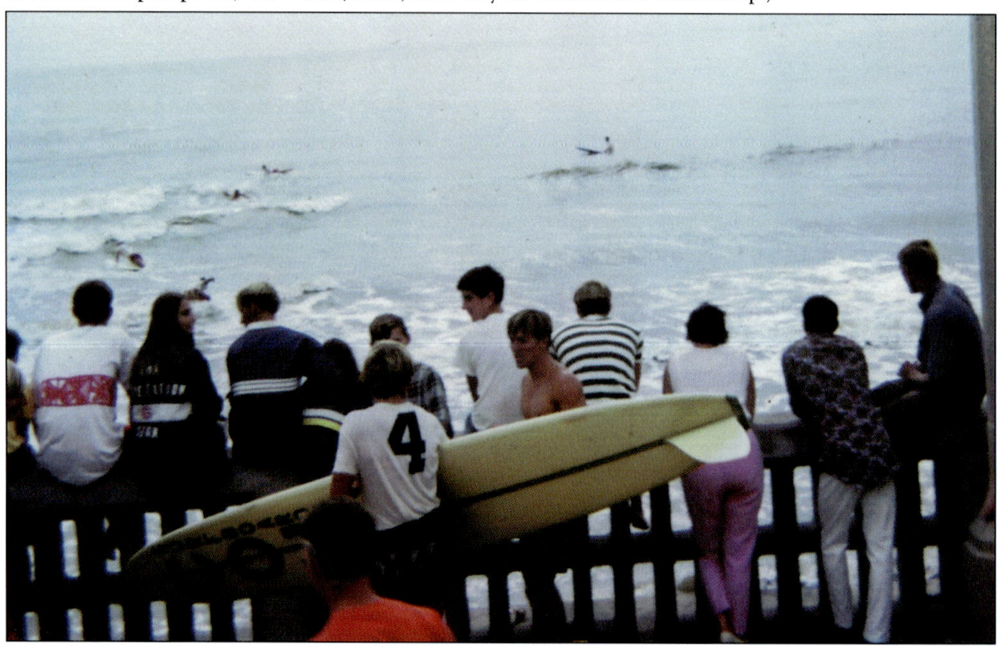

Bugsy Chevrier is pictured here in his competition shirt during a contest during the 1960s. The talented artist and carver was one of the few people who could back up his claim of having attended Woodstock. During the movie *Woodstock* (and the album of it), one can hear him being paged to the medic tent. (Courtesy of Philip Chevrier.)

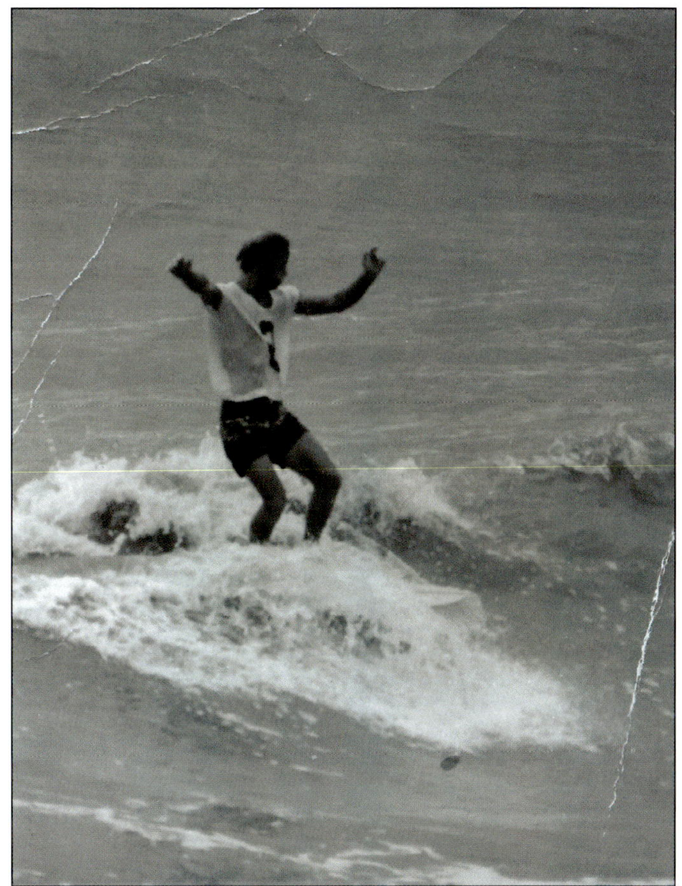

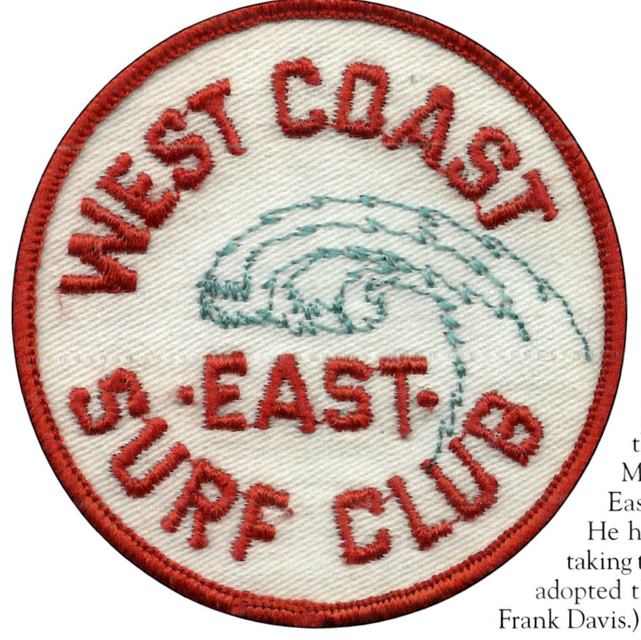

Frank Davis, an early West Coast East club member and part of the Pendletons, a surf music band, says that Rick Fitchman had come up from Miami, where the original West Coast East Surf Club had been disbanded. He had a box of patches left over, and taking the path of least resistance, the locals adopted the name and patch. (Courtesy of Frank Davis.)

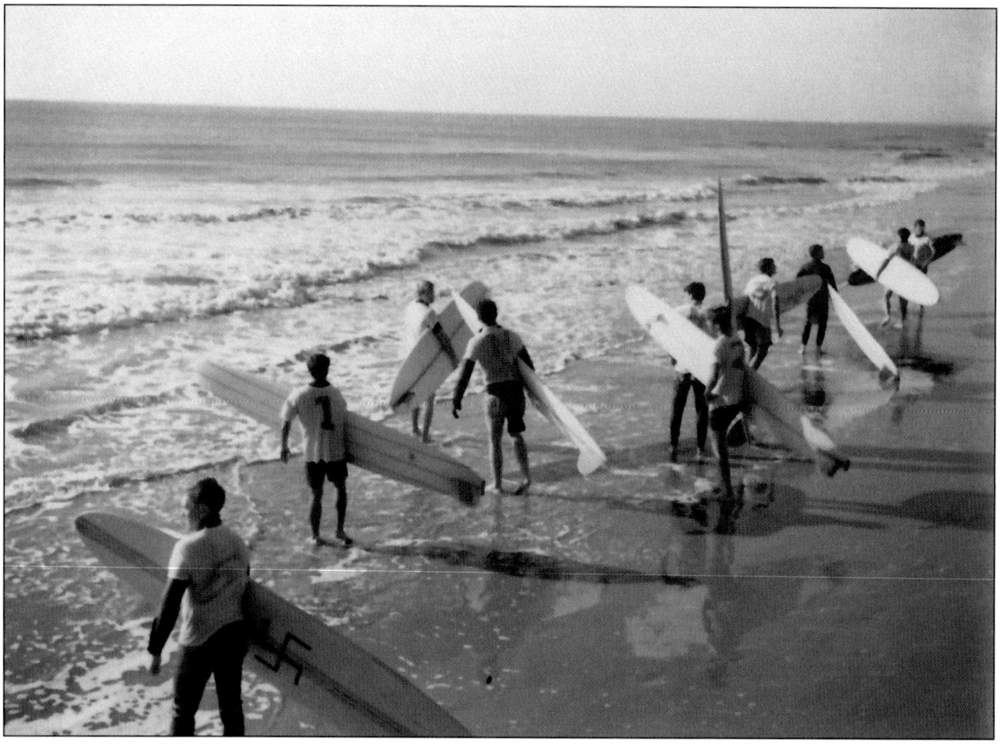

Contestants line up to enter the water in the first heat of the West Coast East's first annual Invitational Surf Meet at the pavilion on Center Street. After the contest, competitors ran to a burn barrel and wrapped in blankets to get warm. A far cry from the comfort of modern wet suits, the suits were just making their way to the East Coast during the 1966 contest. Below, the area's first surf music band, the Pendletons, entertained up and down the East Coast from Miami, Florida, to Virginia Beach, Virginia. Pictured are (kneeling) Randy Olsen; (standing, from left to right) Frank Davis, Jim Humphries, Greg Nutt, Dan Aurellio, and Randy Nutt. (Both, courtesy of Frank Davis.)

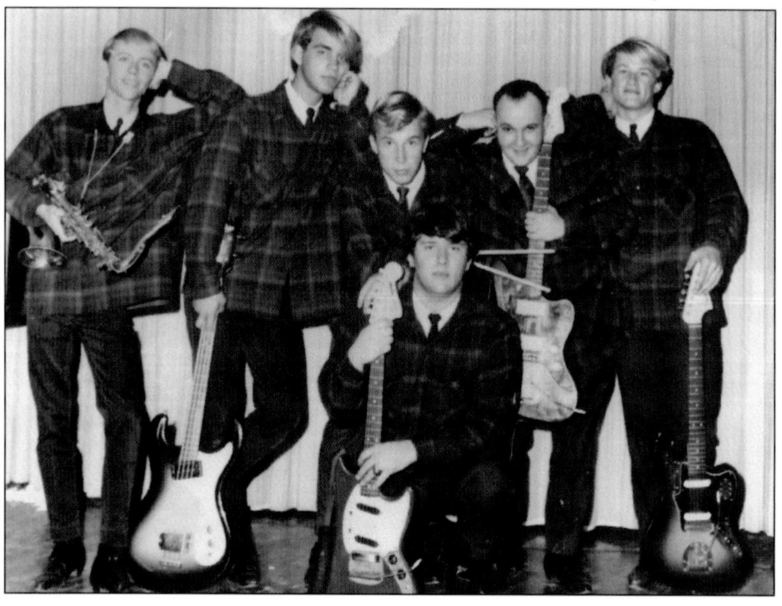

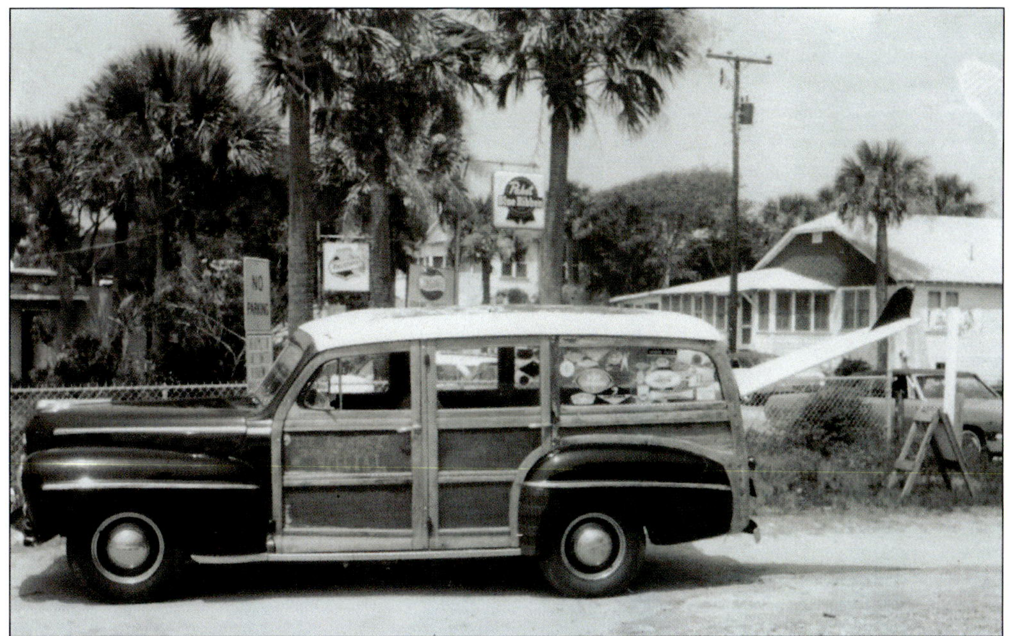

Woodie wagons similar to the one here owned by Jack Tripp on Folly Beach in the early 1960s became the emblematic surf vehicle. Made popular in surf movies, woodies are now collectible classic cars and much sought after. Restoration is a big business, and woodie clubs and museums can be found across the nation. (Courtesy of Jack Tripp.)

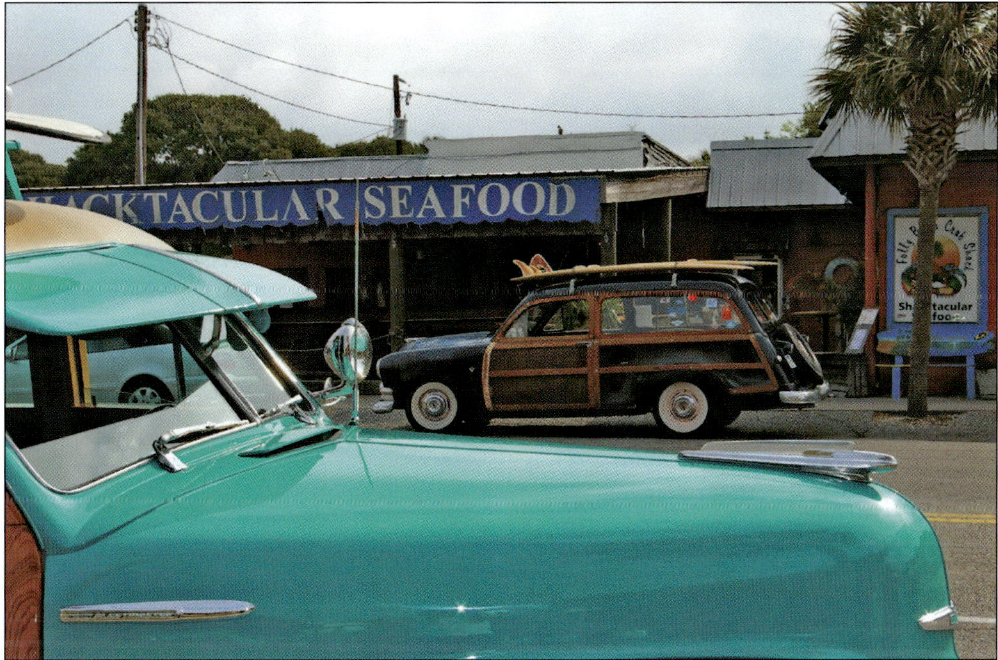

A woodie car show, Wagons on the Edge, held in conjunction with the 2006 Eastern Surfing Association's Mid-Atlantic Region Surfing Championship at The Washout on Folly Beach, drew many cars from around the Southeast. Positioned throughout the commercial district on Center Street, the cars drew much interest. (Authors' collection.)

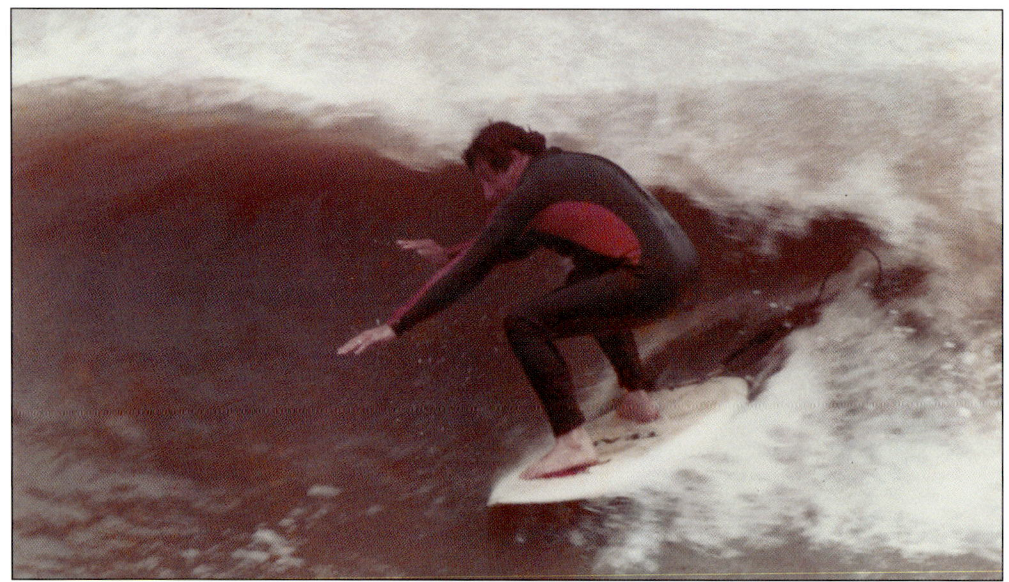

August 1971 brought rough seas to the Carolina coast as Hurricane Dora blew by 250 miles offshore. A situation that cautions small crafts to keep to nearshore waters is a clarion call to surfers looking for a boost in wave conditions. Local surfers at Folly Beach enjoyed their share. Dean Monk catches a wave at Twelfth Street on Folly Beach as the storm approaches. (Courtesy of Dean Monk.)

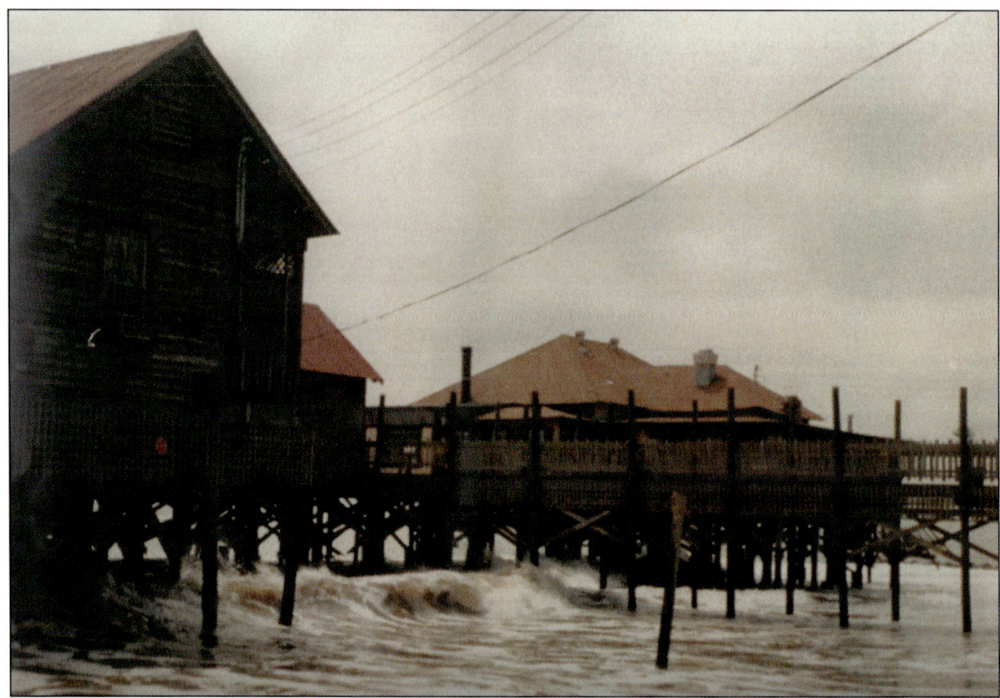

Surfers have seen wave forecasting make enormous strides since the 1960s. Coupled with the Internet, smartphones, computers, and surf cameras, people can check the waves from their desks. Sometimes, all the gadgetry is not necessary, as shown in this photograph of homes on Third Block West on the day before Hurricane Hugo struck in September 1989. (Courtesy of Dean Monk.)

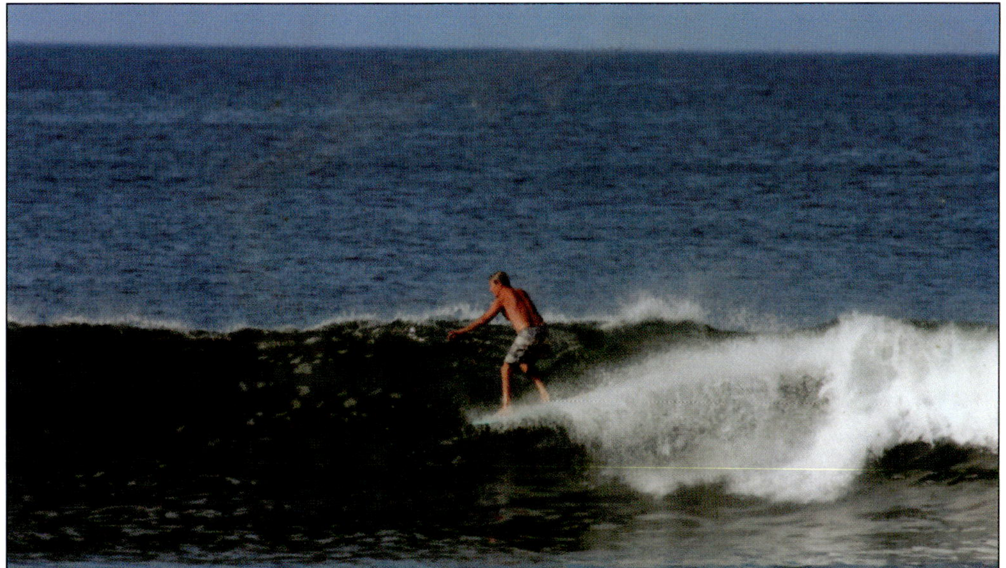

Hal Coste charges on a head-high wave in storm surf in the late 1960s. An original member of the Carolina Surf Club, he has been instrumental in bringing the club back to life with a mix of new and original members. (Courtesy of Hal Coste.)

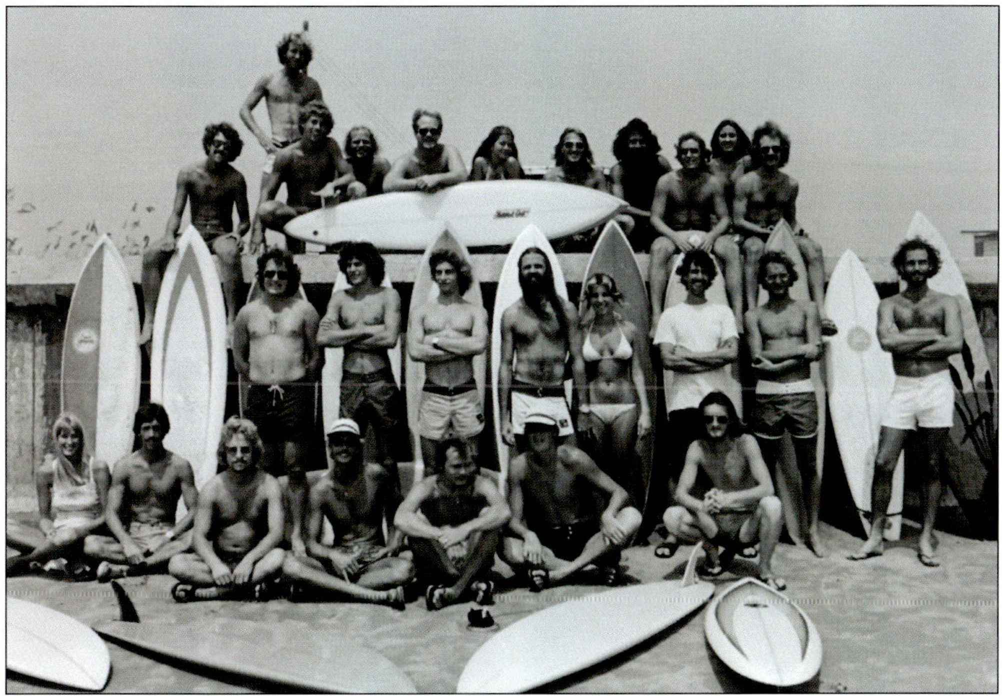

Natural Art surfers pose on Folly Beach in 1979. From left to right are (first row) Judy Godley, Norman Godley, Mark Morgan, Chip Smith, unidentified, Ed Budolf, and Hank Bauer; (second row) Ken Morgan, unidentified, Mark Patella, Mike Amerson, unidentified, Johnny Martin, Richard Green, and Reid Anson; (third row) Harry Erickson, Glenn Tanner (standing), Greg Elliott, Pete Burbage, Rick Koger, Boo Norton, Mike Buttle, Lindy Corley, Alfred Atkinson, Tina Jordan, and Howard Davis. (Courtesy of Richard Green.)

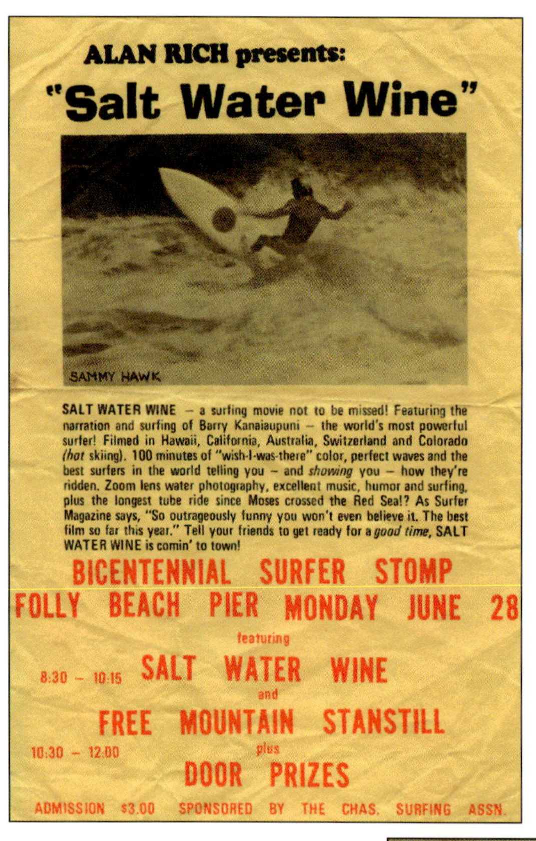

This handbill advertises the Bicentennial Surfer Stomp held at the Folly Beach Pier in 1976. Movies were projected on the pavilion's outside wall. The Charleston Surfing Association formed to fight for a surfer's rights on Folly Beach. Beginning as early as 1966, the newspaper started to report the police chief's concern over swimmer's safety, wanting to restrict surfing areas, then moving toward outright surfing prohibition on Folly Beach. (Courtesy of Glenn Tanner.)

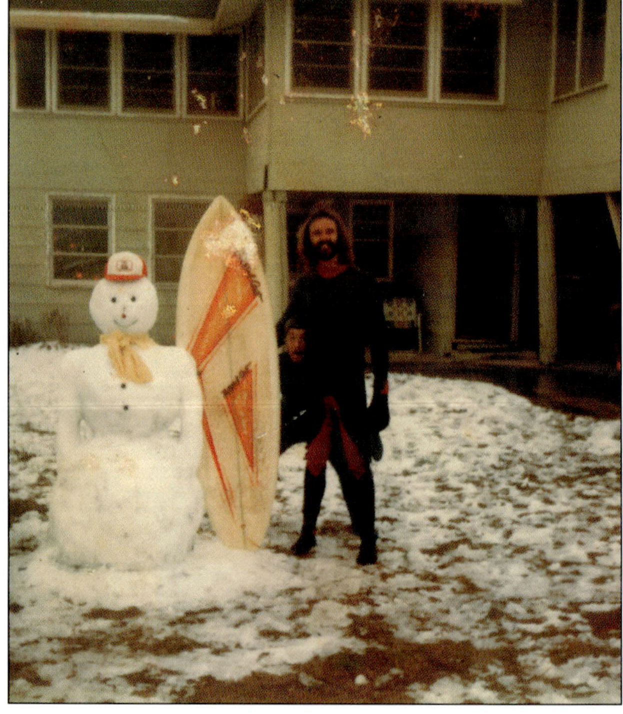

Whatever this white stuff is, it is certainly not sand. A dapper snowman shows off his board as Mike Garrett (left) and Mike Amerson mug for the camera in 1979. Their wet suits were perfect protection against the unusual weather. (Courtesy of Mike Garrett.)

Speaking of dapper, the Southern South Carolina chapter of the Eastern Surfing Association presents their 1974 competition team for the all important Easterns, a contest that pits the best of the best in the organization against each other. Heading to North Carolina are, from left to right, (first row) Glen Tanner and Cathy Walker; (second row) Donnie Smith, Al Logan, Greg Elliot, and Stephen Fletcher. (Courtesy of Glenn Tanner.)

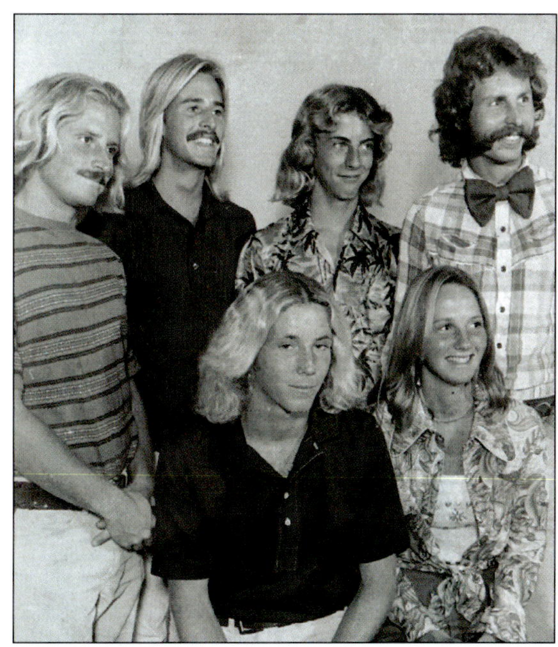

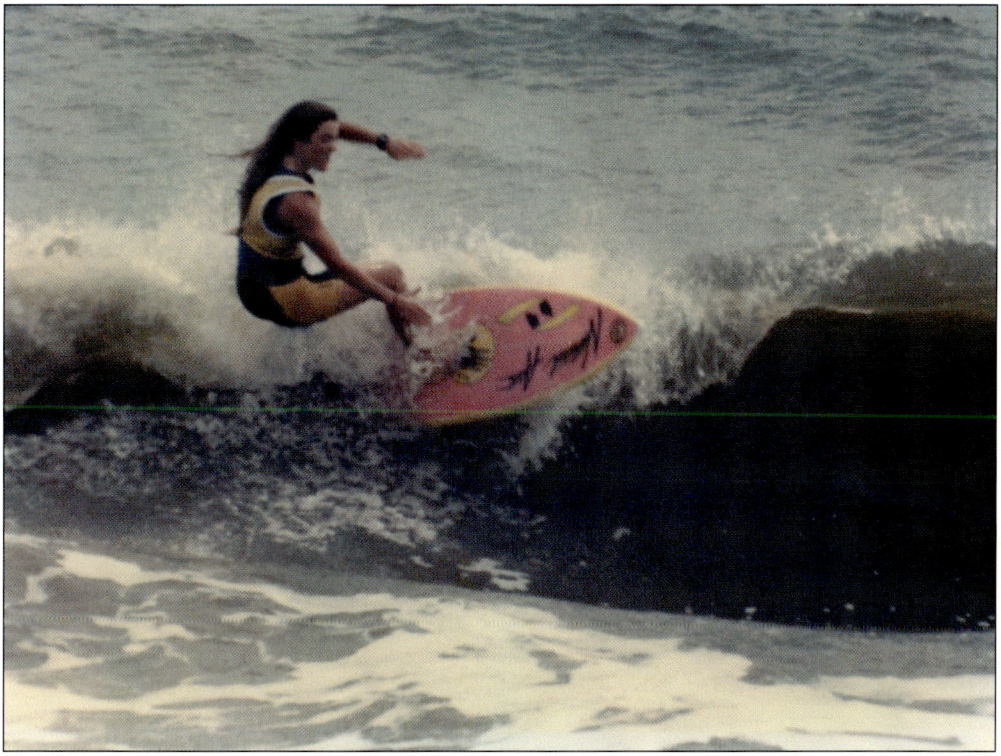

Competing since 1982, Terri Tanner won the 1988 Junior Women's division of the invitation-only East Coast Championship at Cape Hatteras. In 1992, at the Lighthouse in Cape Hatteras, she was awarded the "Hottest Wave" trophy of the entire contest. As a competitor, she was awesome. As a mom, married to fellow surfer Glenn Tanner, she has nurtured a family of talented surfers. (Courtesy of the Tanner family.)

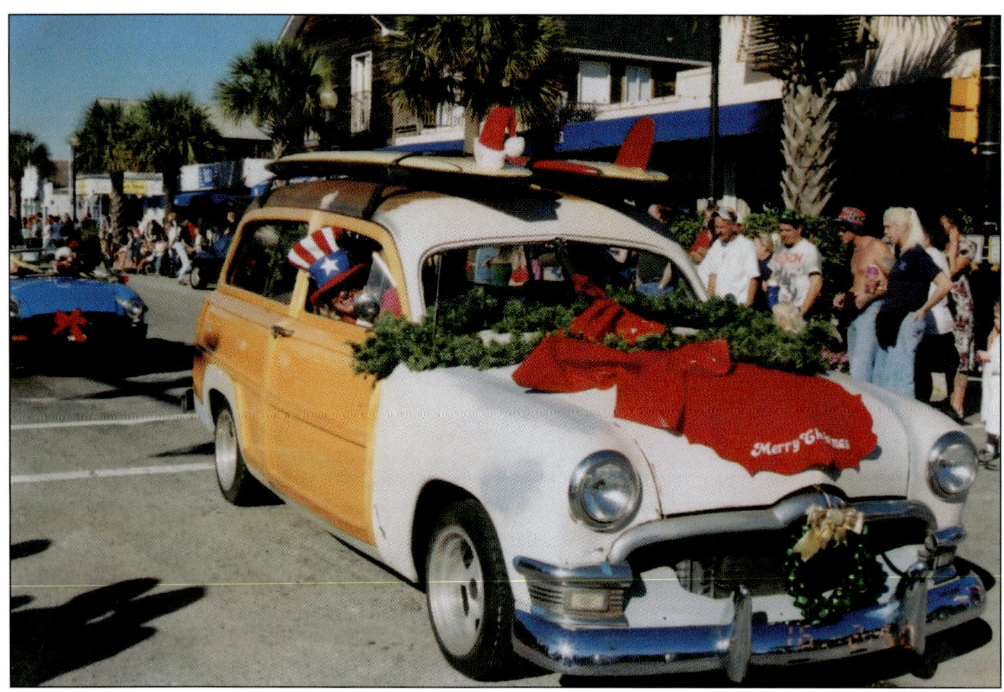

Bill Jones (above), a passenger in the authors' woodie, joins the fun at the infamous Folly Beach Christmas Parade. One caution: grab a place on the sidewalk early. Having only one road on and off the island, the beach closes from the time the parade assembles through the duration of the festivities. One highlight of the parade is the precision surfboard drill team. The group, hastily assembled each year from shop customers, was the brainchild of Bill Perry and Betty Sue Cowsert, owners of Ocean Surf Shop. They have their choreography down as they "wave" down Center Street. (Above, authors' collection; below, Ocean Surf Shop.)

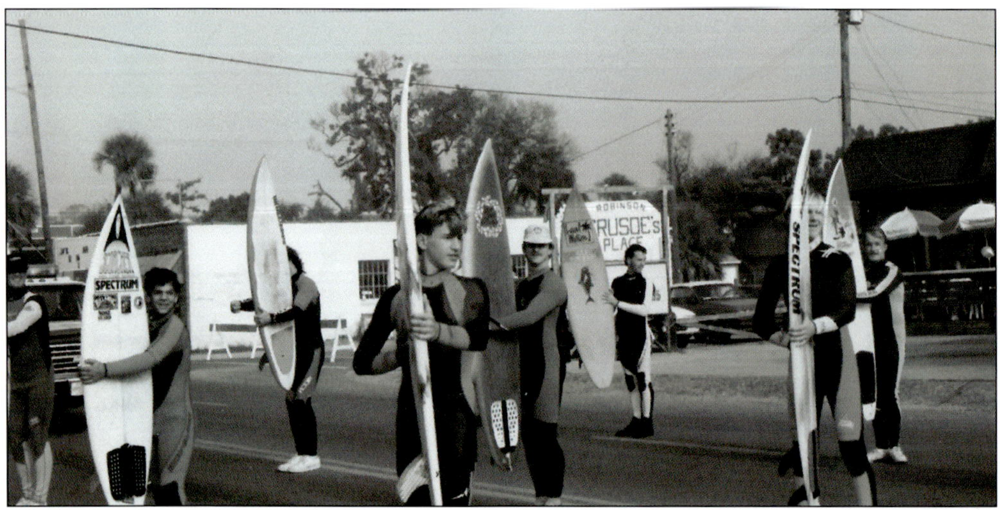

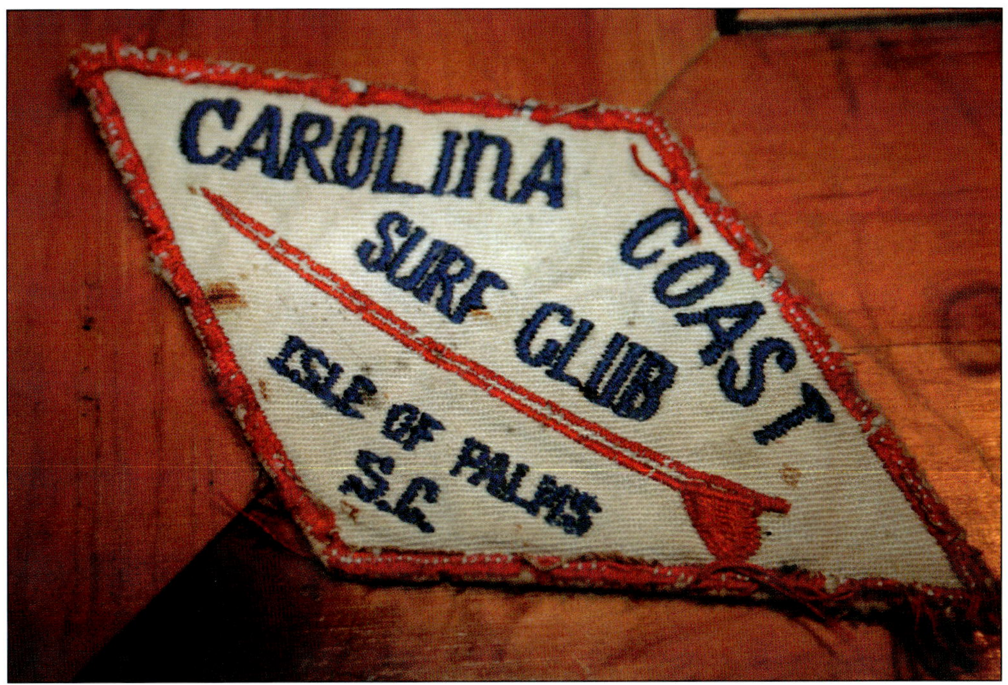

Van Crist saved his original patch from the Carolina Coast Surf Club. Each year, the revived club holds a three-day reunion in front of the Windjammer on the Isle of Palms. Pictured below are, from left to right, (seated) Charlotte Witte, Sparky Witte, and Jimmy Carroll; (standing) Philip Chevrier, Larry Jacobs, Steve Rhea, Diane Southerland, Charlotte Coste Collias, Hal Coste, Robin and Stevie McNeal, Eulie Middleton, Sally Price, Richard Middleton, and Jimmy McNeal. (Above, courtesy of Van Crist; below, Hal Coste.)

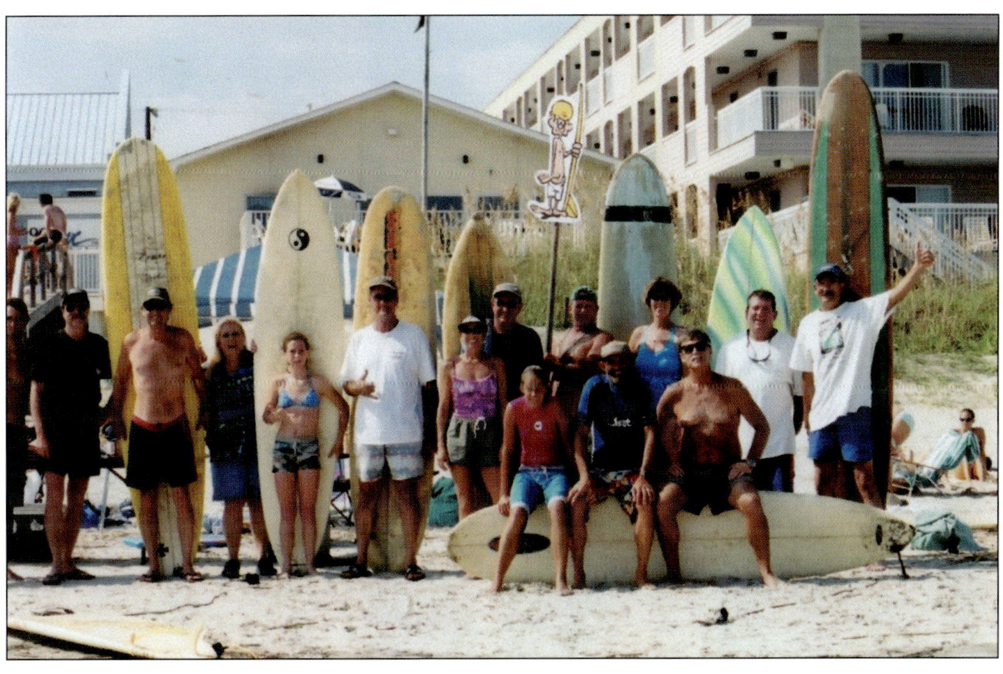

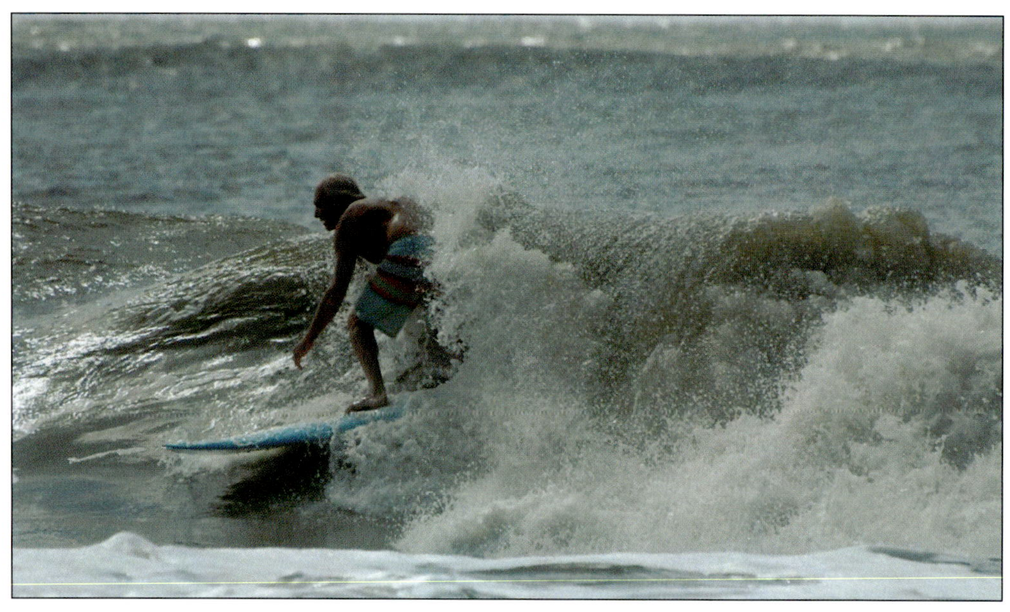

Rick Anson came to Charleston from San Diego, California. He remembers Dewey Mauldin, whose family opened Dewey's Surf Shop on Center Street on Folly Beach in the 1960s, moving in next door, dragging big boards into the house. Intrigued, he and his brother Reid started surfing in 1968 when Rick was in sixth grade. A veteran of the Eastern Surfing Association's winner's circle, he is seen above at Folly Beach. Charlie Guss is shown below grabbing some air. People can spot an East Cooper surfer who has come of age at The Washout. (Courtesy of Paul Mulkey Sr.)

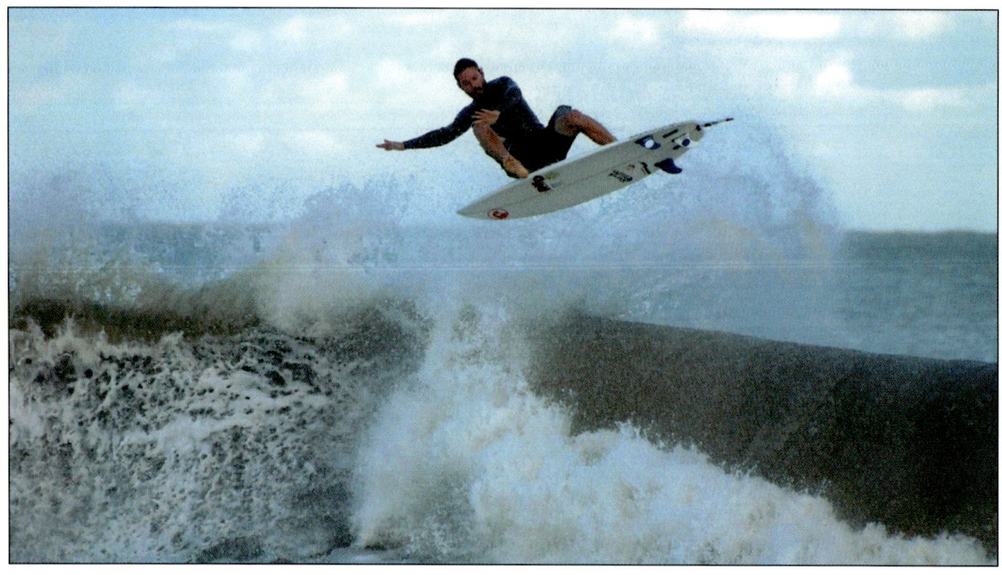

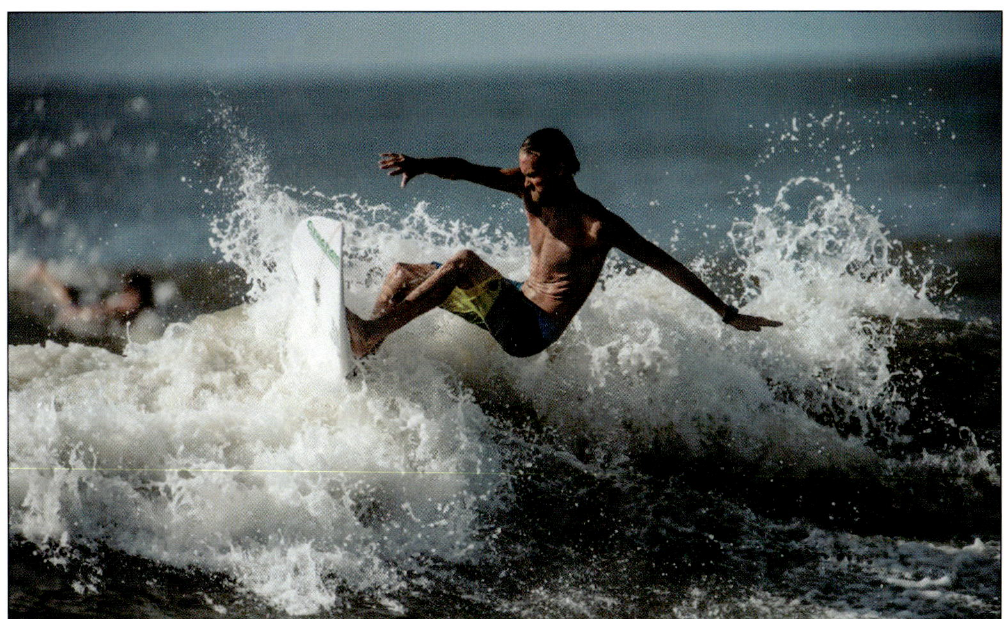

Anthony Osment started surfing at age 11 with his grandmother bringing him to the beach. He says for him it was like a drug; he was hooked and never looked back. Traveling endlessly looking for waves, he eventually competed professionally. Surfing to him is like family: even if there are years between meetings, there is always a bond. He plans to pass the love of the sport to his daughter Lilah Rose. (Courtesy of Paul Mulkey Sr.)

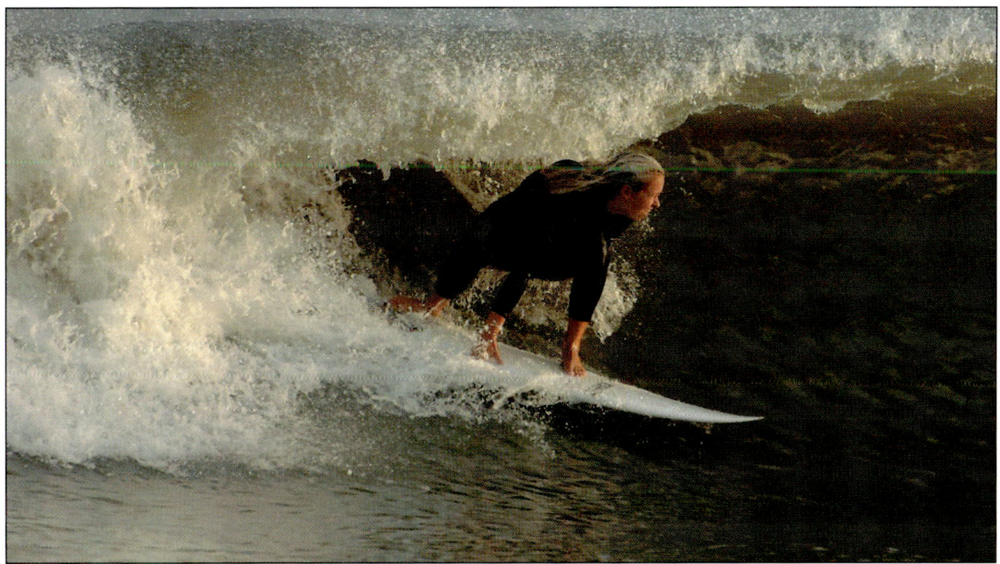

The past 12 years have been eventful for Grace Muckenfuss. Her first board, a five-foot-six Sol Shapes by Kai Dilling, started her on a road that began at The Washout and now has her calling Snapper Rocks, Australia, her favorite break. (Courtesy of Paul Mulkey Sr.)

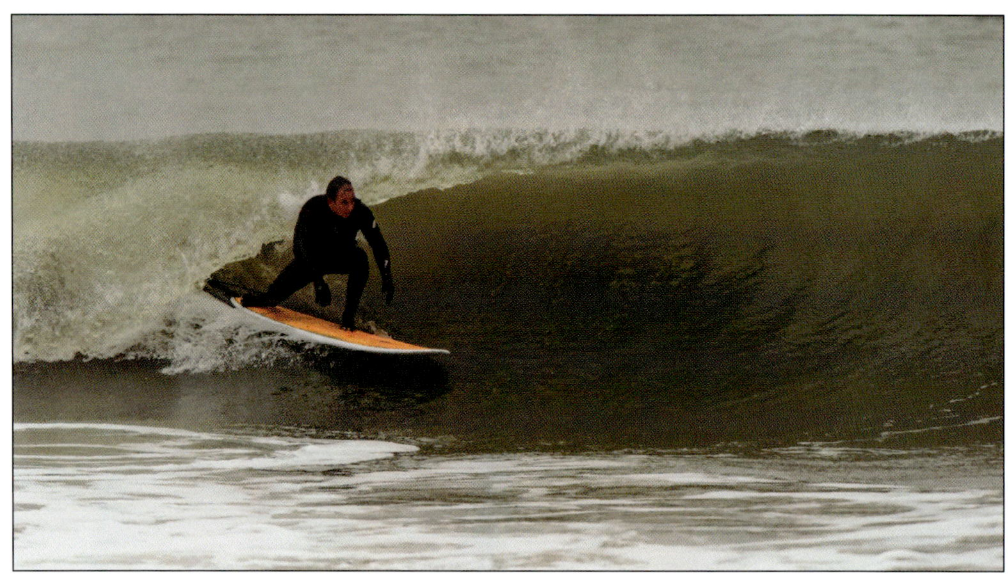

Glenn Tanner has enjoyed a phenomenal career in competition, going as far as winning the US Championship and just about every title along the way. He is a natural athlete with the agility and grace that defines the phrase. A McKevlin's team rider for decades, he just seems to get better with age. He is shown above on a 40-degree windchill day on Folly Beach. Chad Hilton, below, almost has to show identification when he comes to Old Man's on Folly Beach. The Charleston native started surfing short boards in 1993 at Sixth Street and progressed up the beach until he was good enough for The Washout. Why the move to longboards? At the end of the day, he says, it is all about fun and consistency. (Both, courtesy of Paul Mulkey Sr.)

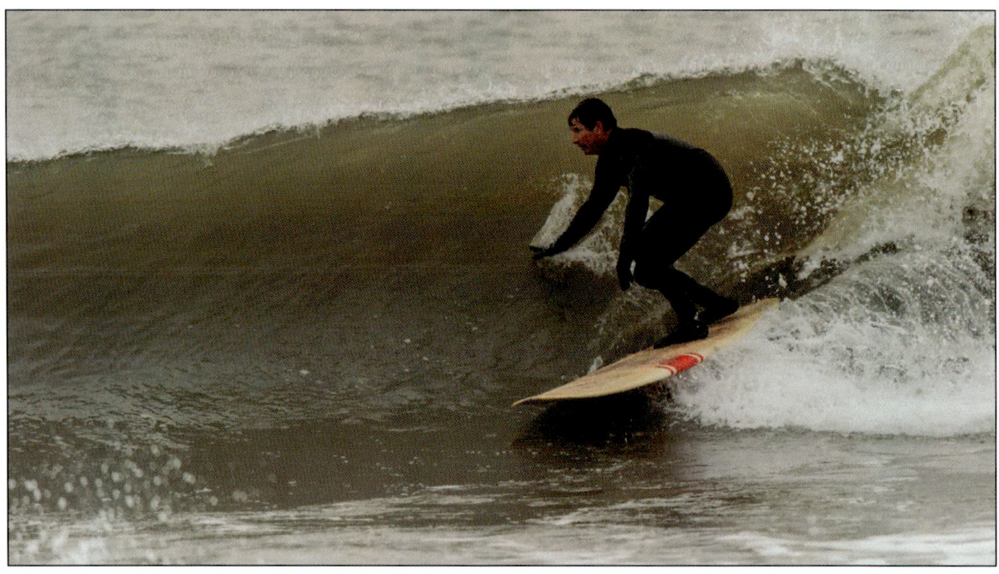

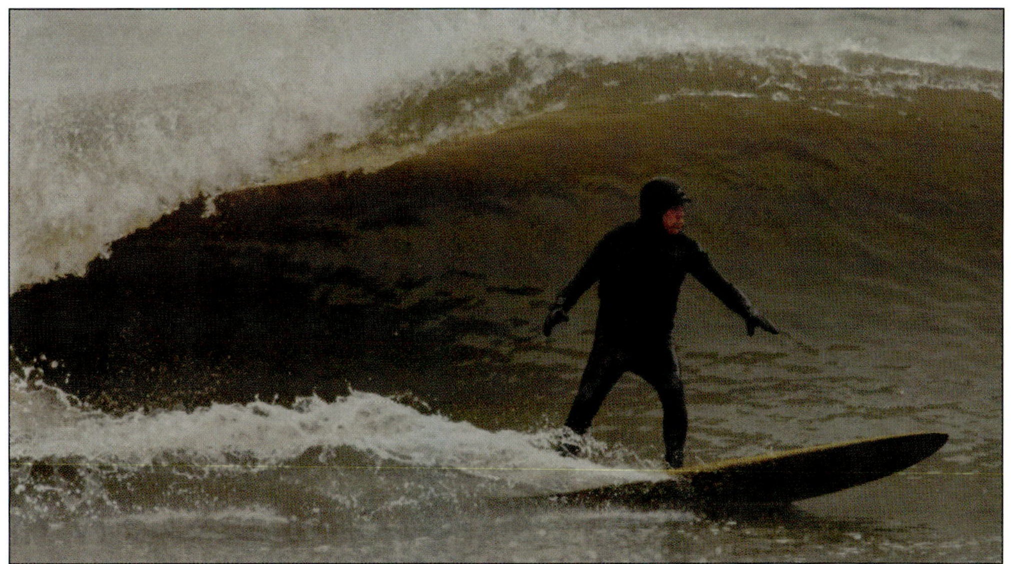

Foster Folsom grew up on Folly Beach and has been surfing the waves since the early 1960s. He is shown here at The Washout, running like he stole that wave. He splits his time between his two home breaks: Folly Beach and Nova Scotia. He has come full circle, starting his surfing career as ding repairman for Mr. Mac. Now, he is back at it for Tim. (Courtesy of Paul Mulkey Sr.)

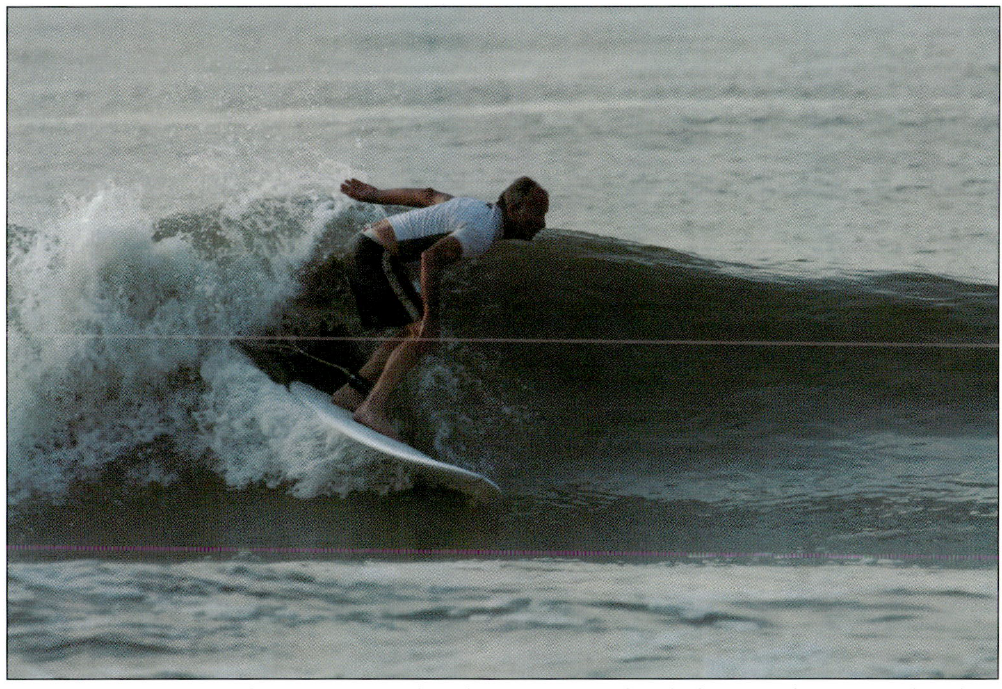

At age 12, Jimmy Dowds was an Army brat learning to surf on lush tropical Hawaiian beaches. What an eye-opener it was when his father retired to the Isle of Palms in 1966. The easy waves were actually just right for Jimmy, and there were plenty of boards to borrow. He is a proud member of the Equator Club. He figures by now he has paddled the circumference of the earth at the equator. (Authors' collection.)

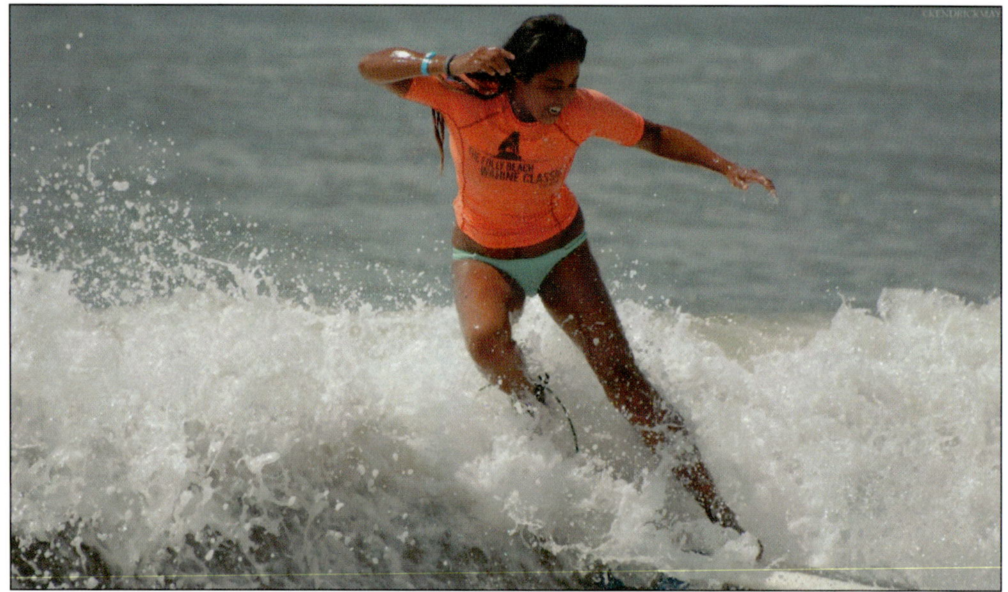

Perng Chen Hutson started surfing in southeast Florida, trying every weekend until she got it. A decade ago, she started working at McKevlin's Surf Shop, and the rest is history. She loves how the job allows her to immerse herself in the surf culture: meaning when there is surf, she is already at the beach. Hutson is pictured at the 2015 Wahini Contest. (Courtesy of Paul Mulkey Sr.)

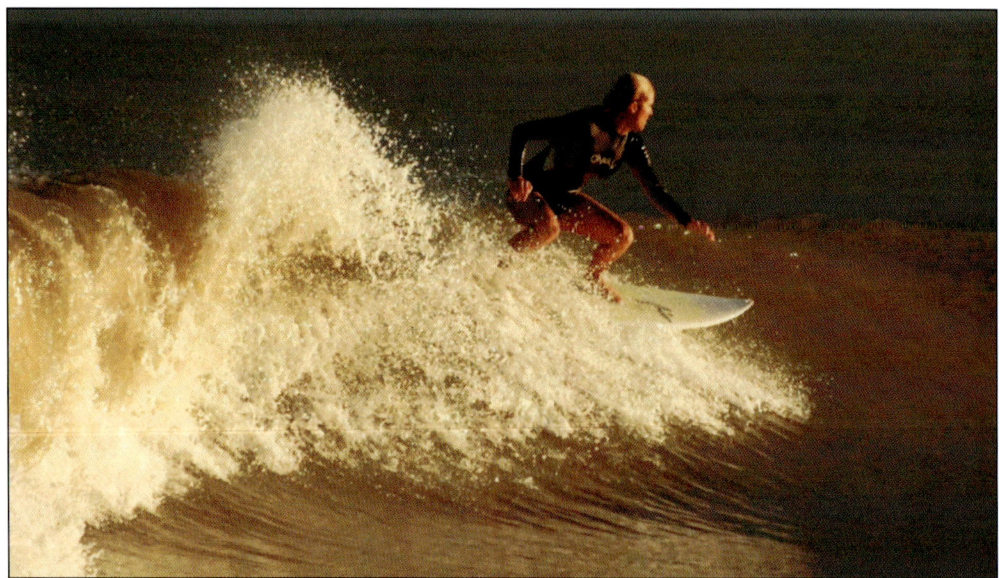

Dawn Relyea Holcombe's great-grandfather built a house on Folly Beach's eighth block, where she grew up playing in the surf. Norman Godley loaned her a three-foot-six kneeboard when she was 14 years old, and she was hooked. Her favorite spots are Twelfth Street and The Washout (pictured). Dawn has been surfing for 37 years, and the thrill, she says, is as strong as ever. (Courtesy of Kendrick Mayes.)

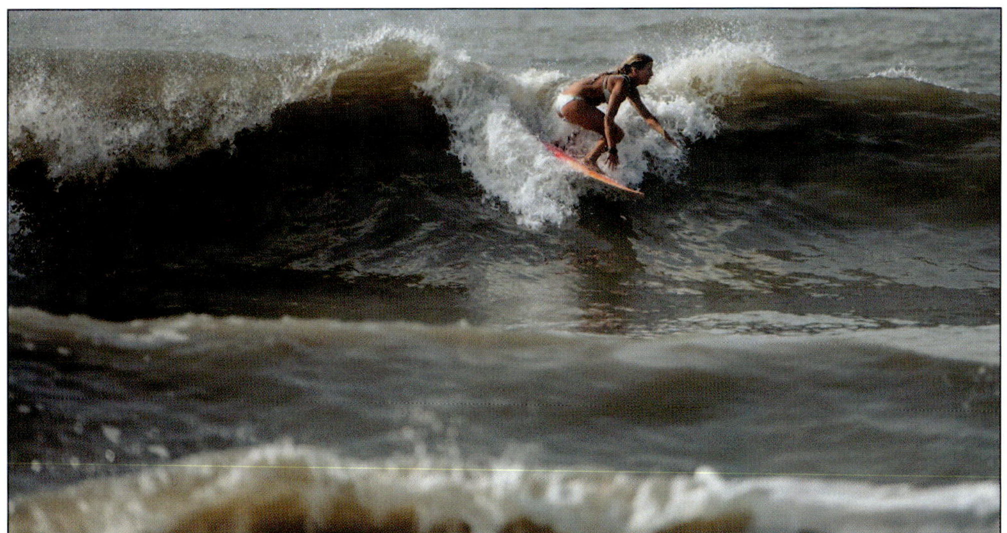

One can tell Jenny Brown learned to surf hard. Her charging style puts most guys to shame. Starting out surfing for Surf the Earth in Pawleys Island, she has dominated local, regional, and East Coast meets within the Eastern Surfing Association for years. She concentrates these days on yoga, her own surfing, and teaching groms, the next generation of surfers. (Courtesy of Paul Mulkey Sr.)

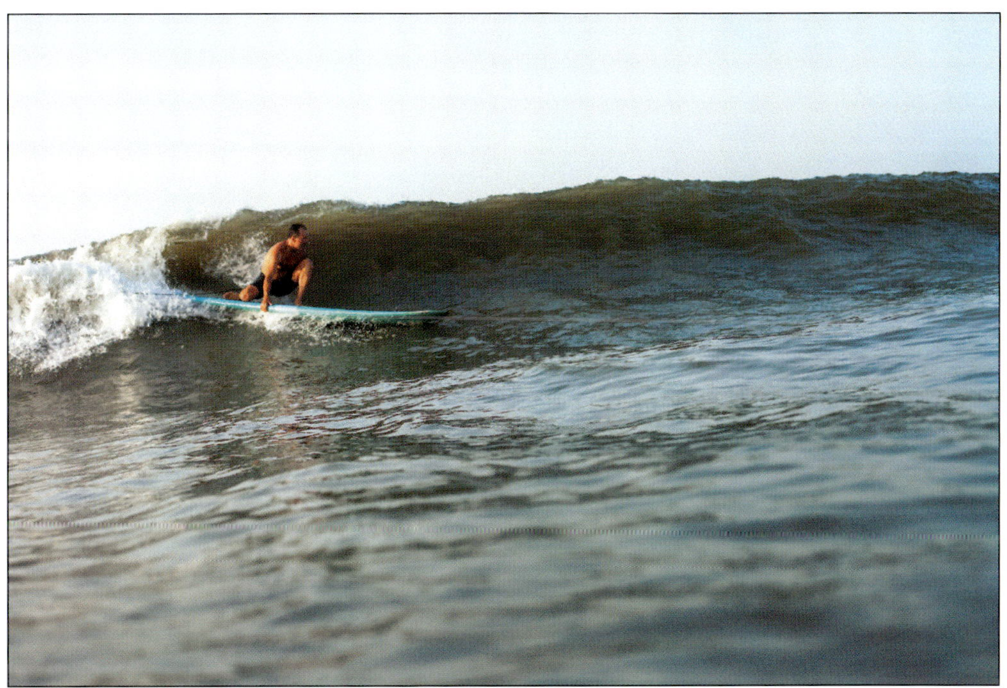

Rocky Hayes proves one can come full circle. Dragging home a 10-foot wooden board out of a trash pile, he started surfing at age 12. Hayes gradually moved to smaller, lighter boards, but as he has grown older he is back to his old tricks on a 12-footer. He says he can catch anything, anywhere, much to the frustration of the lineup. (Courtesy of Patrick Willey of *Two Feet and Classy*.)

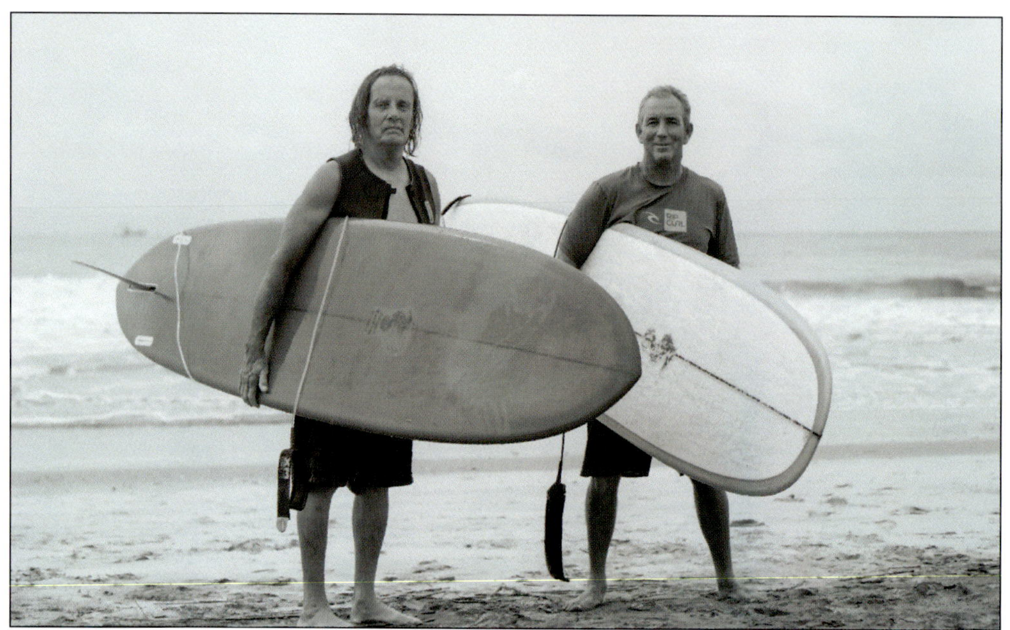

Foster Folsom (left) and former US champion Glenn Tanner take a break from the surf at Old Man's on Folly Beach. This photograph was taken during filming for the local surfing movie *Two Feet and Classy*. The film premiered at the inaugural Carolina Surf Film Festival in 2014. (Courtesy of Tanya Boggs Photography.)

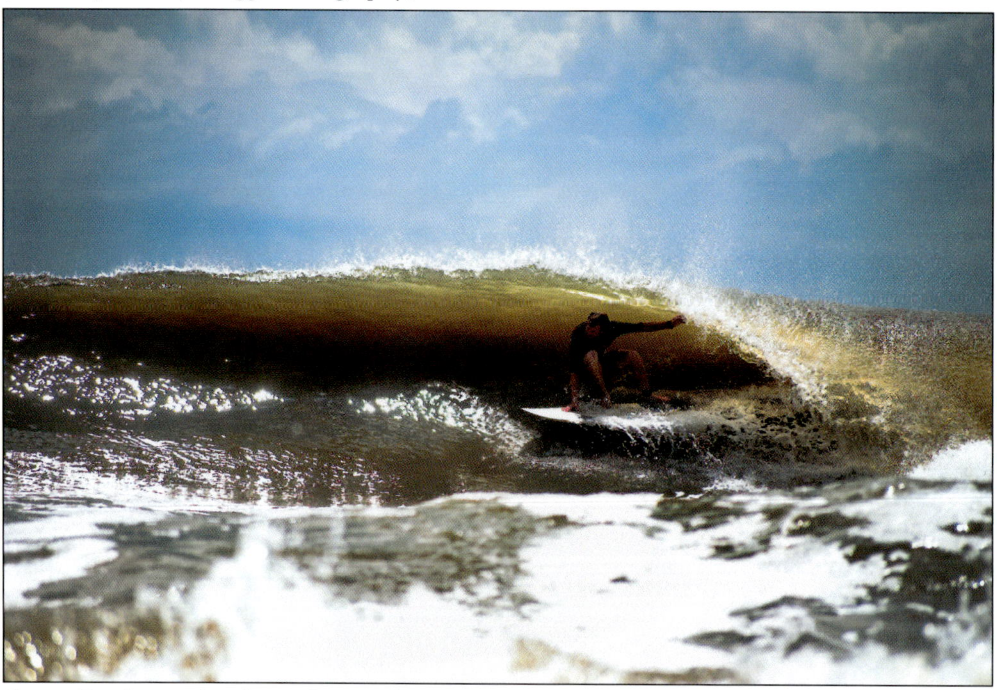

Center Reed starts his day with a quick trip to The Washout looking for any opportunity to surf or any sign of potential waves later in the day. The luxury of setting his own schedule means if the waves are there, he will be too. Here he is in Hurricane Bertha surf in 2014. (Courtesy of Lindsey Lee Graham.)

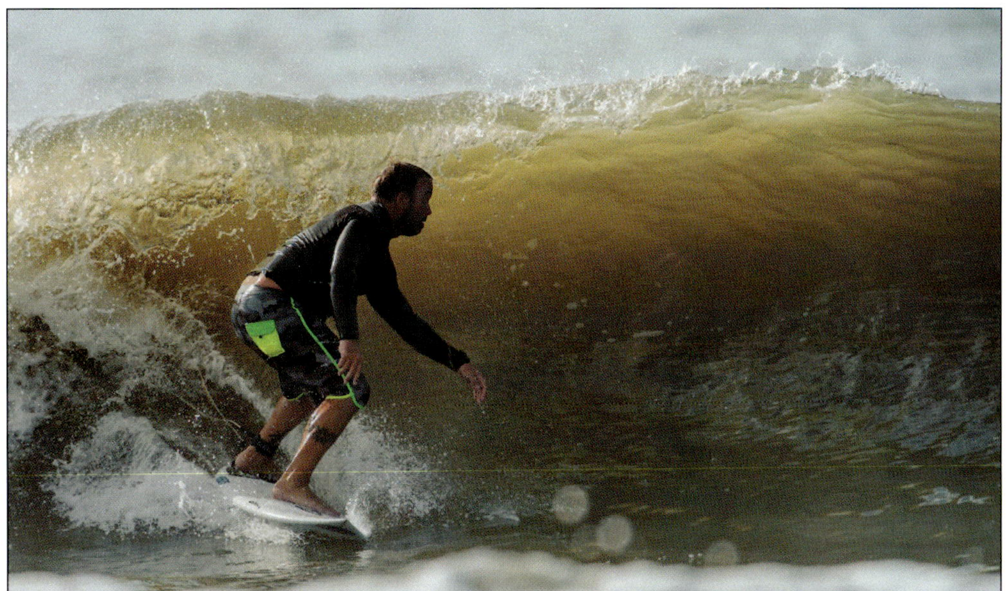

Dave Dixon, ripping at The Washout, started surfing at age 15 in Tampa, Florida. He would travel two hours to get to his break at Whitey's above Sebastian's. Moving to Charleston, he began competing up and down the East Coast and California. Sponsored by Roberts Surfboards, this local powerhouse calls The Washout home, but he loves Witches Rock, Huntington Pier, and Oxnard Shores in California. (Courtesy of Paul Mulkey Sr.)

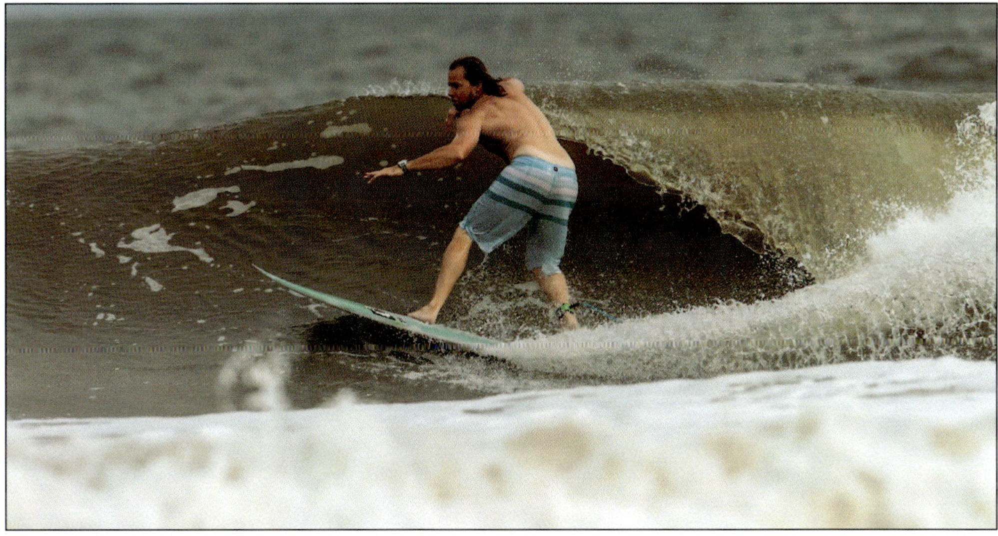

Harlie Stevens was a fixture on the Charleston surf scene for years. After taking a break, he is back, and nice warm water with smooth swells are all it takes to lure him to Folly Beach. As one can see, he has not lost his touch in the least. (Courtesy of Paul Mulkey Sr.)

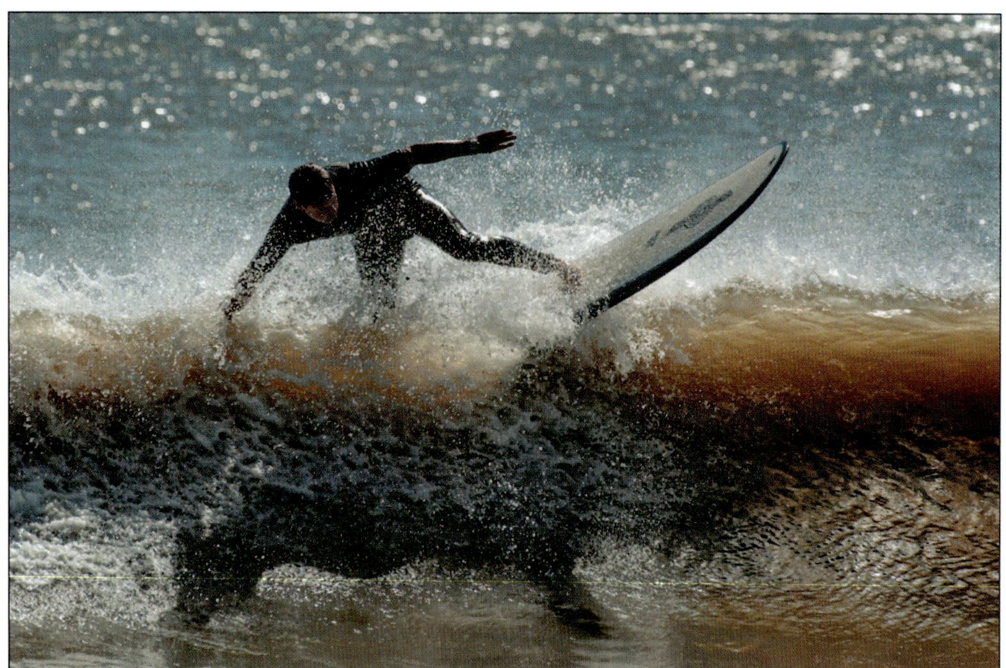

Watching the surfers on Pawleys Island in the early 1980s, Bates Hagood thought they looked pretty happy, and they got the girls, which seemed pretty cool to a 12-year-old. After surfing his way through the College of Charleston, he hitchhiked and surfed across the globe. Now as manager of Ocean Surf Shop, he has come back into the fold, into his community of surfers on Folly Beach. (Courtesy of Lew Harford.)

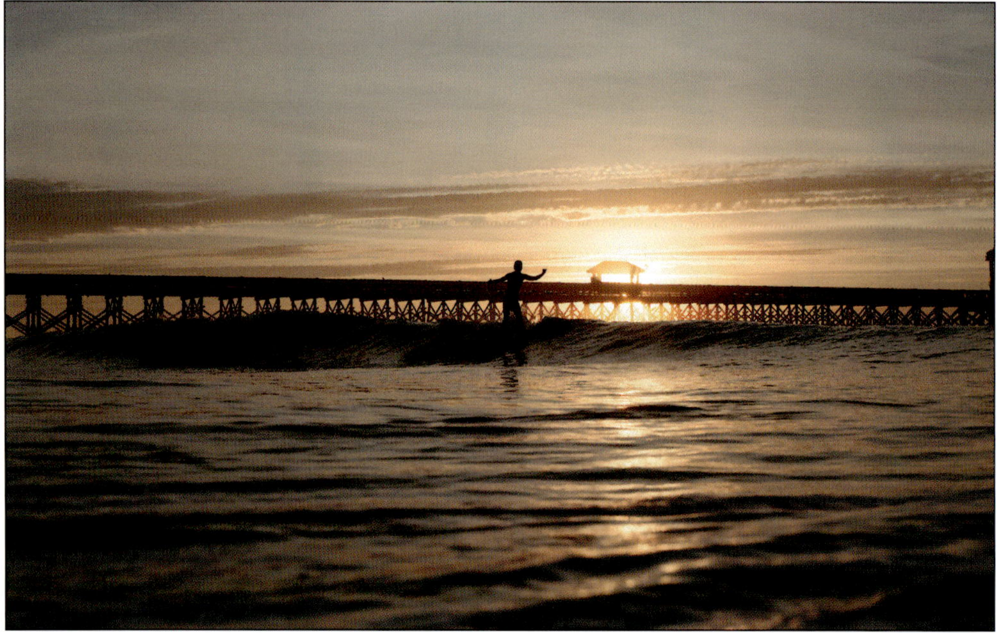

There is never a doubt where to find Damaris Tarrant if there is any swell at all. She will be down at the Folly Beach Pier, no matter the weather, grabbing any wave she can. With a no-holds-barred longboard style, she can dominate. (Courtesy of Patrick Willey of *Two Feet and Classy*.)

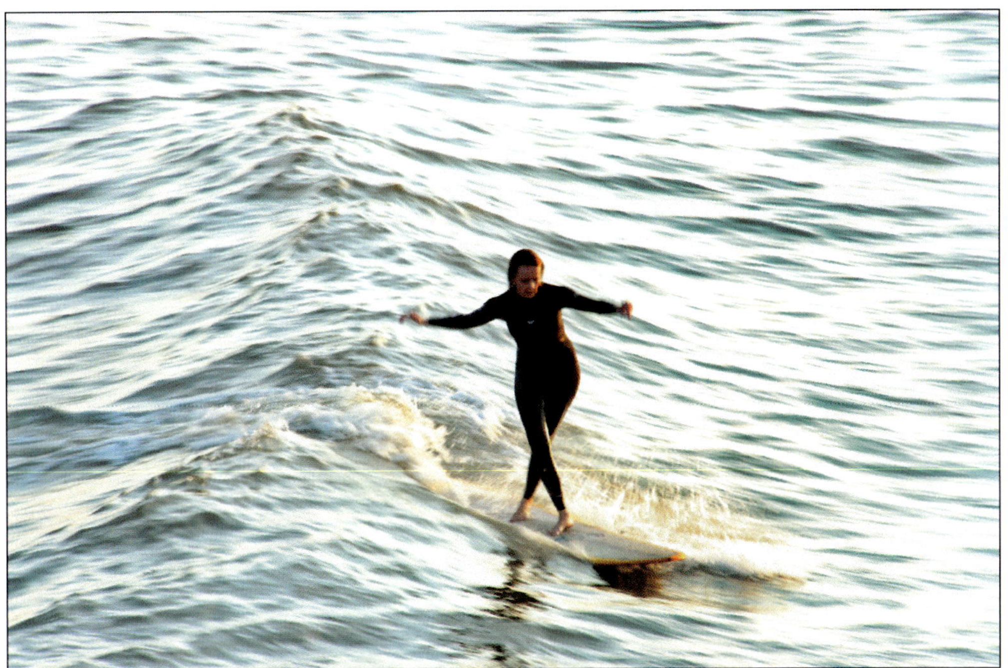

Above, Patti Noe glides on this wave at the Folly Beach Pier. Not beginning her surfing life until 1996, she was hooked, even meeting her husband, Alfred, on a wave. Entering her first Wahini contest, she was taken aback with having a block of The Washout only for her surf sisters. This energy led her to head the contest in 2013. She is still in awe of the event's vibe. She has decided that when she is an old lady surfer if she is not at Wilderness in Puerto Rico, one will find her in the lineup at The Washout because the stoke is the best thing there is. Below, Hampden Thomas, a new Wahini, is seen in the 2015 contest. (Above, courtesy of Lindsey Lee Graham; below, Andy Thomas.)

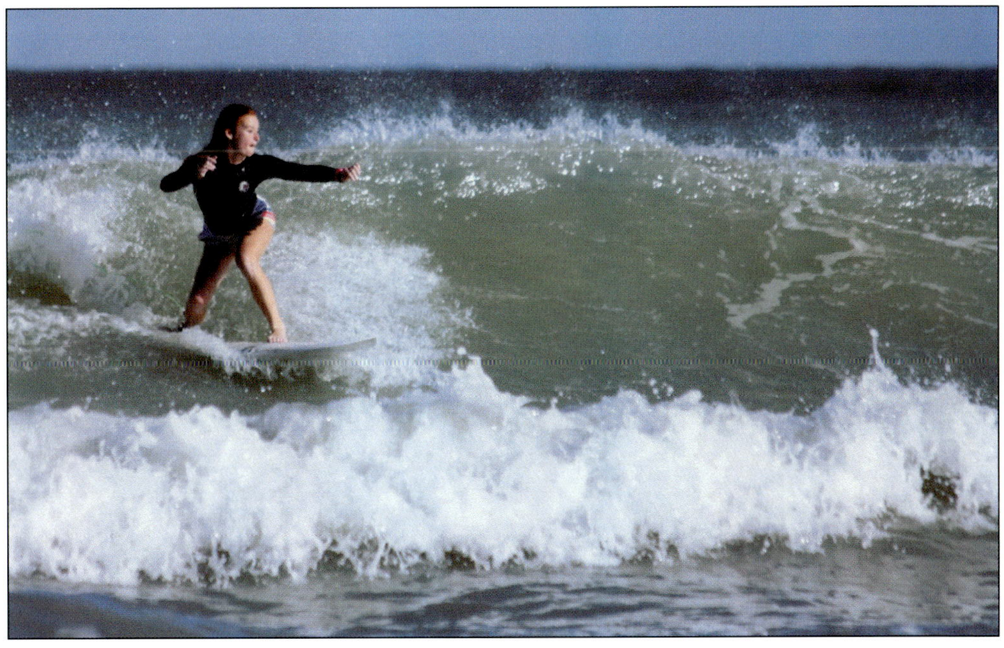

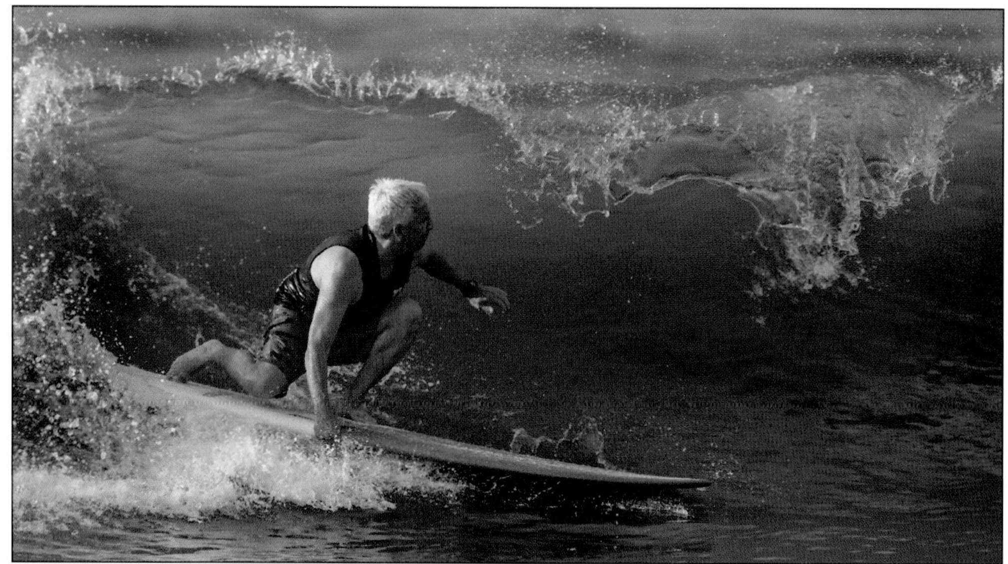

Paul Martin grew up catching rides to surf Twelfth Street on Folly Beach, and those 42 years of experience certainly show in the smooth style he has developed. He bought his first board from Mr. Mac when he was 13 years old for $25, a five-foot-ten Surfboard Australia. A shaper since 2005, he finds it gives him an awesome connection to the art of surfing. He recently rebuilt his 1951 Pontiac "tin woodie," which he packs with his boards when heading to the break. (Courtesy of Paul Mulkey Sr.)

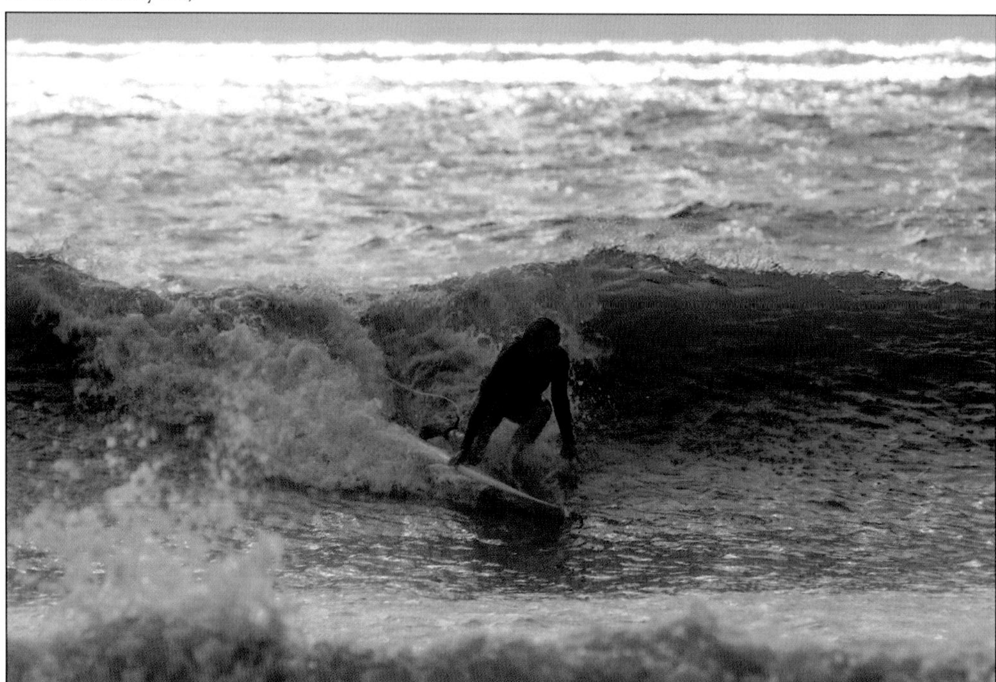

Lisa Michaels left her corporate job to spend every hour available surfing. If there are waves at Folly Beach, people will find her there. Lately, she has been concentrating her time in Central America, where the consistent waves and warm weather make up for all those days as a suit. (Courtesy of Paul Mulkey Sr.)

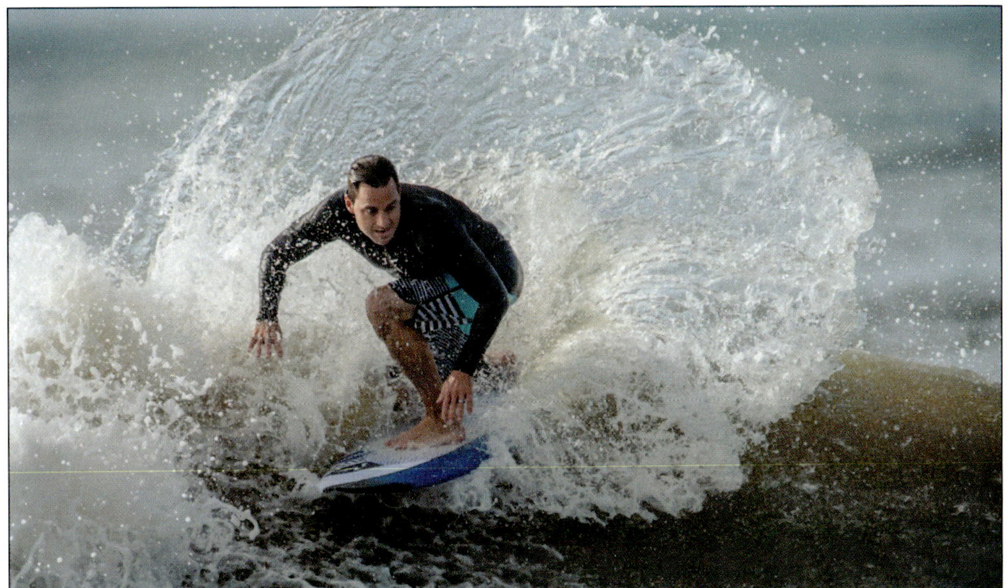

Blue Spivey was 10 years old when he spied a surfboard in his neighbor's garage. He tried it and was hooked for life. A world surf traveler, he favors breaks in California for their accessibility and sheer number of waves. Also, as the center of the surf industry, there are always friends' couches to borrow as well. (Courtesy of Paul Mulkey Sr.)

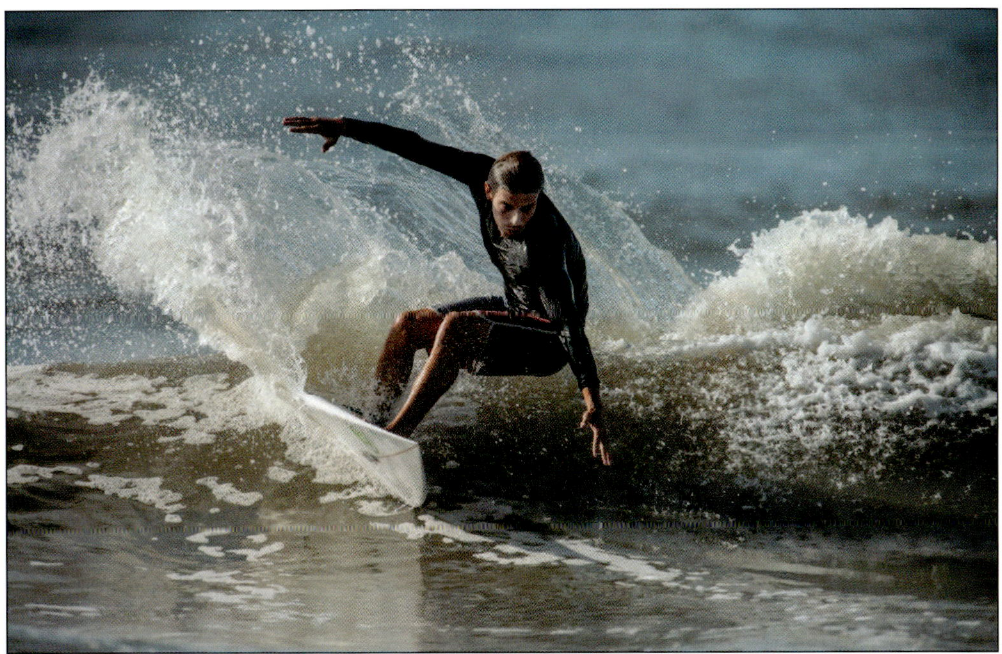

Tommy Bolus got his son Dawson up on a board when he was 10 years old, and Dawson never looked back. Now 22 years later, he has favorite breaks around the world, housed in countries like Bali, Mexico, and El Salvador. Dawson loves to travel, learning the language and culture wherever he goes. He enjoys passing on his knowledge of the sport. In his down time, he is an avid reader of Hesse and Camus. (Courtesy of Paul Mulkey Sr.)

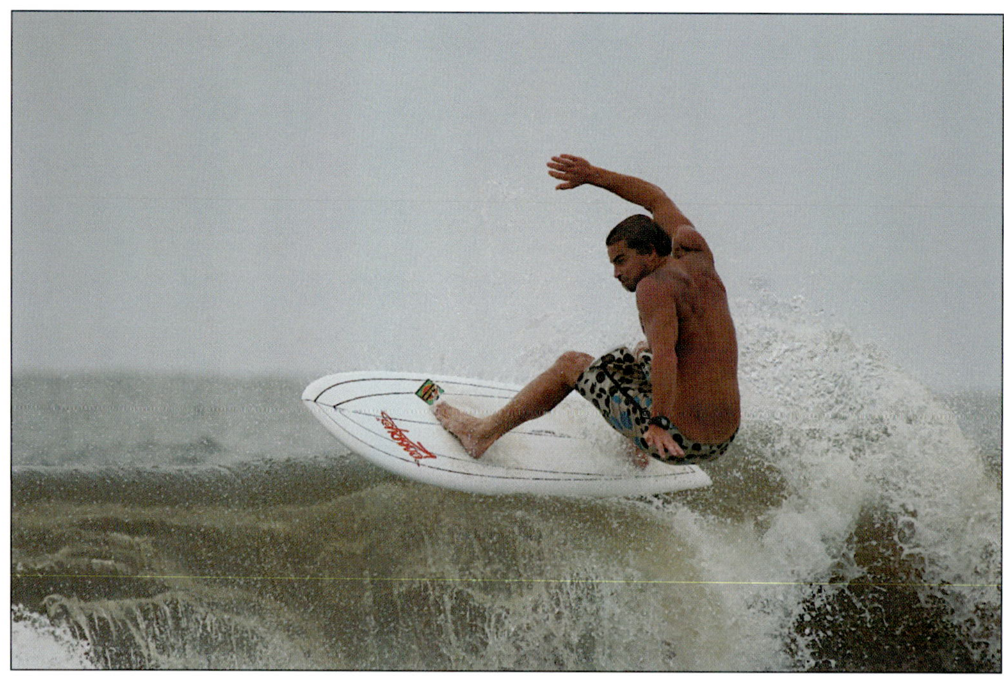

Chris Brown began surfing in Pawleys Island. Part of the Surf the Earth team, he has powered his way through waves on two continents. A true waterman, he works, plays, and even used to live on the water. As a research vessel captain for the South Carolina Department of Natural Resources, he is still at it and surfing whenever he can. (Courtesy of Moira Gill.)

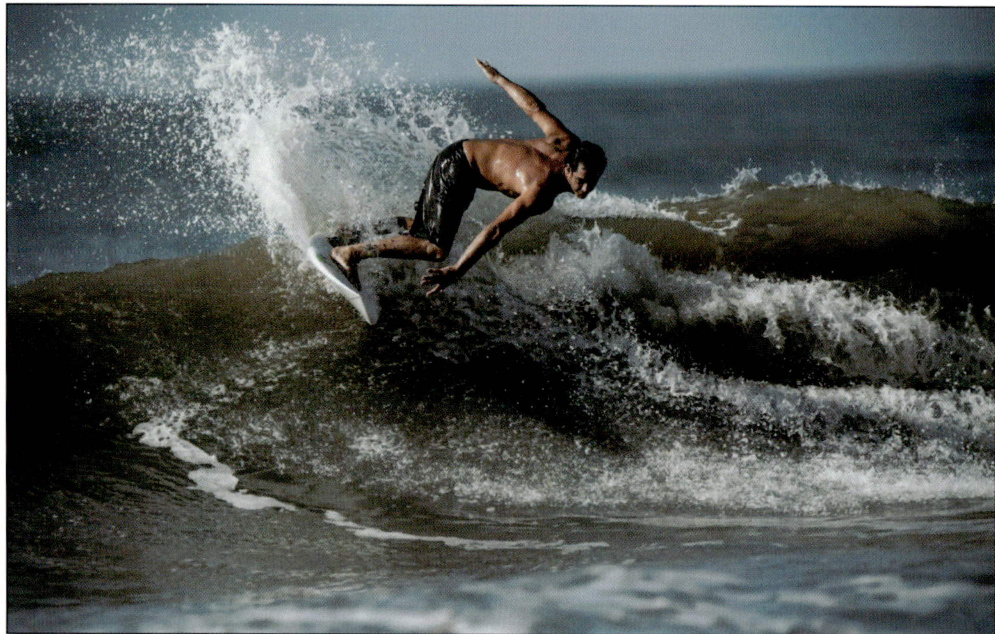

Chris John is a local, but one would not guess it seeing him dominate the lineup. People can see a little Indo in his style, surfing there after college in the cold waters of Santa Cruz. The marine biology graduate is a standout surfer and a true waterman. When not surfing the waves, he is a seafood entrepreneur working with local high-end chefs. (Courtesy of Paul Mulkey Sr.)

Three

Hilton Head Island

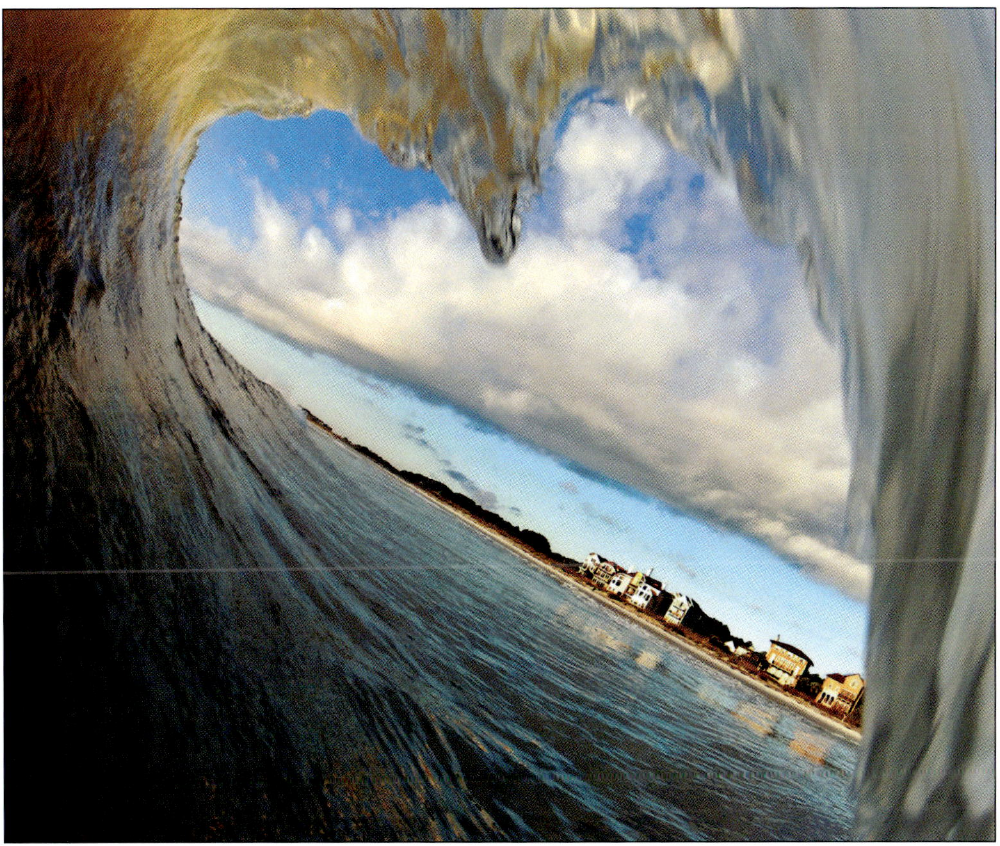

Hilton Head Island is not usually associated with waves, but there is an active surfing community staking out the beaches on the island. When conditions are right, there are a few spots with sweet waves. Back in the 1960s, there were only a handful of locals with boards. With the opening of Sea Pines Plantation in the early 1970s, a large contingent of surfers from Charleston moved down and opened up the sport. Beaufort was home to many military families during the 1960s, and as in other parts of the state, the sport benefitted from the surfers in their midst. The Hunting Island Surf Club was a presence in the area in the mid-1960s. (Courtesy of Jesse Cadman.)

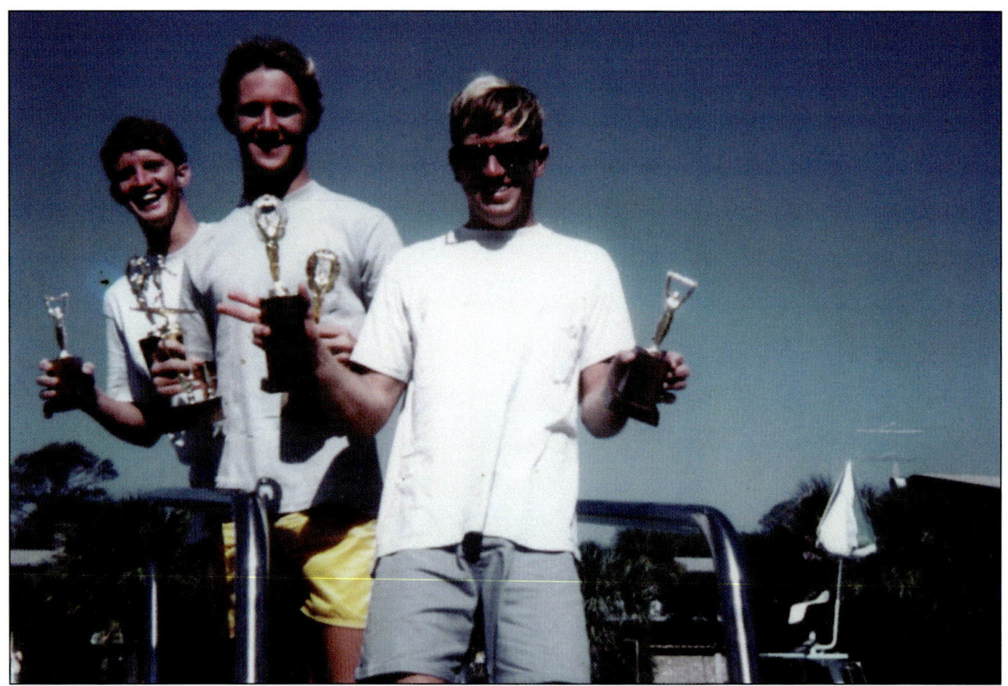

These Charleston surfers, Eddie Andrews (left), Bugsy Chevrier (center), and Chip Yarnell, were excited to travel to Hilton Head for a surf contest in the 1960s. When they arrived, however, they were disappointed to find no waves. Waiting around all day on the off chance that a swell would materialize, they were the last surfers standing when the contest was cancelled. They were rewarded with trophies for their patience. (Courtesy of Phillip Chevrier.)

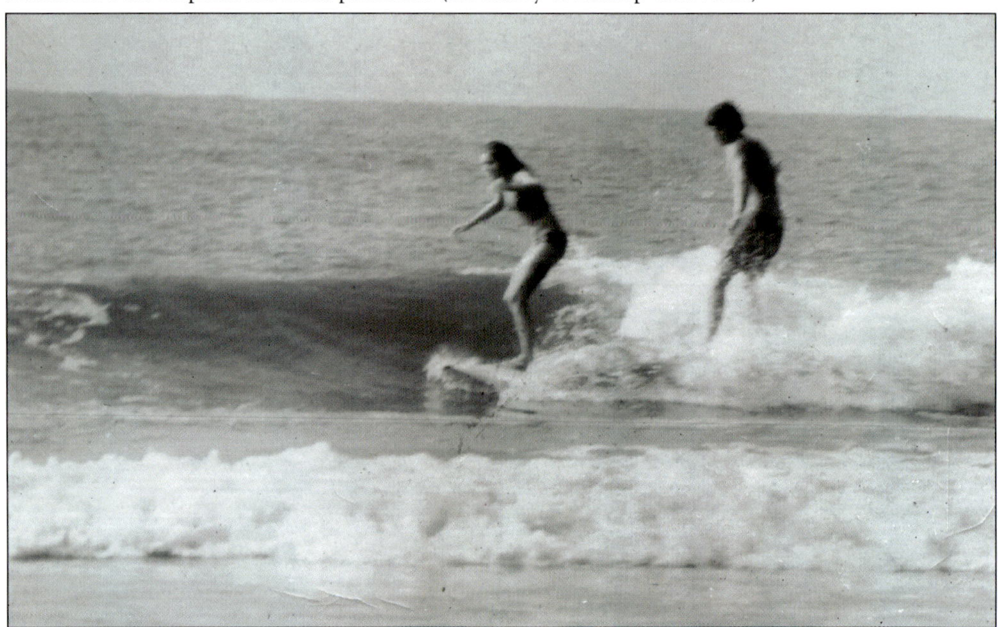

Nanci Polk's family had a beach house just up from Twelfth Street on Folly Beach. It was there that she learned to surf, borrowing her brother Greg's surfboard. She's shown here crowding out Jackie Peters right to keep position on the wave. (Courtesy of Polk-Weckhorst archives.)

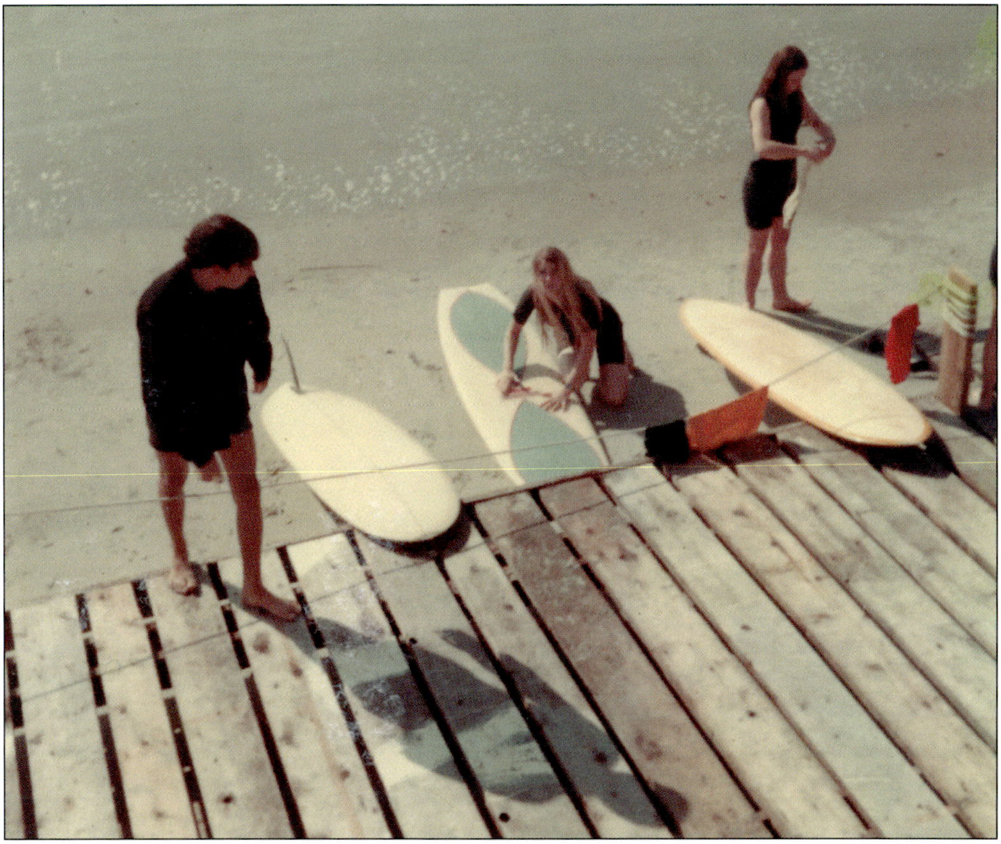

Nanci Polk began surfing local contests like the one above at the pier in Charleston in the mid-1960s. She is seen waxing her board, preparing for her heat. Moving up quickly through the ranks of the Eastern Surfing Association from novice to the more experienced divisions, she was soon winning contest after contest. At right, Nanci (front right) poses with some of her usual competition on a contest road trip. She remembers that in many contests all female surfers, regardless of age or ability, were put in the same heat to fill the slots, a far different scene from today when entire contests are held just for female surfers. (Both, courtesy of the Polk-Weckhorst archives.)

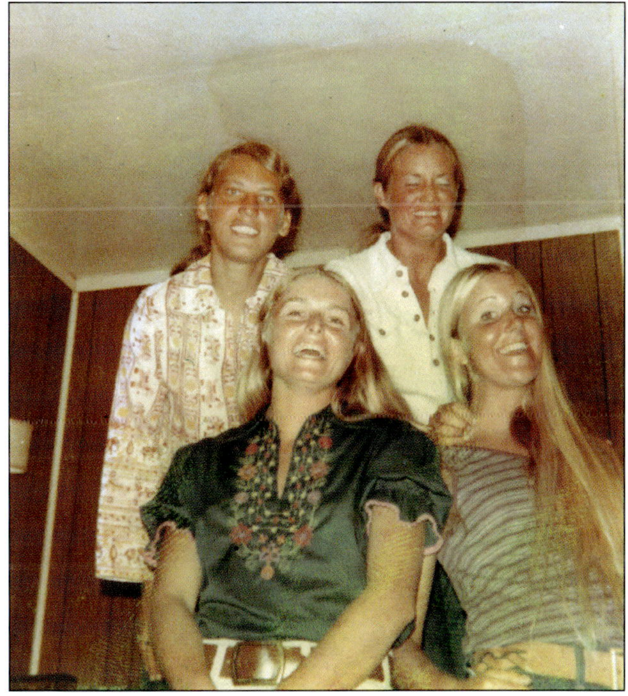

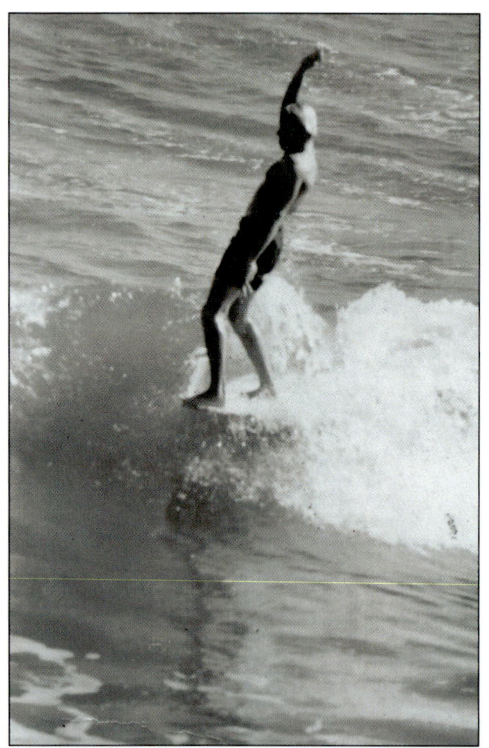

Jerre Weckhorst hangs five in this iconic pose made famous in the 1960s on the West Coast. He was part of the military influx into South Carolina during the Vietnam War era, bringing a love of waves with him to Folly Beach from South Florida. (Courtesy of the Polk-Weckhorst archives.)

Nanci Polk and Jerre Weckhorst both competed for and were chosen to represent the East Coast in the US Surfing Championship at Huntington Beach, California, in 1972. It is a unique event. While they were there, Nanci also competed for a slot on the US team for the World Surfing contest. They stayed with a military family, so they were able to surf the "forbidden" waves at Camp Pendleton. Here, Nanci shows off her award-winning style. (Courtesy of the Polk-Weckhorst archives.)

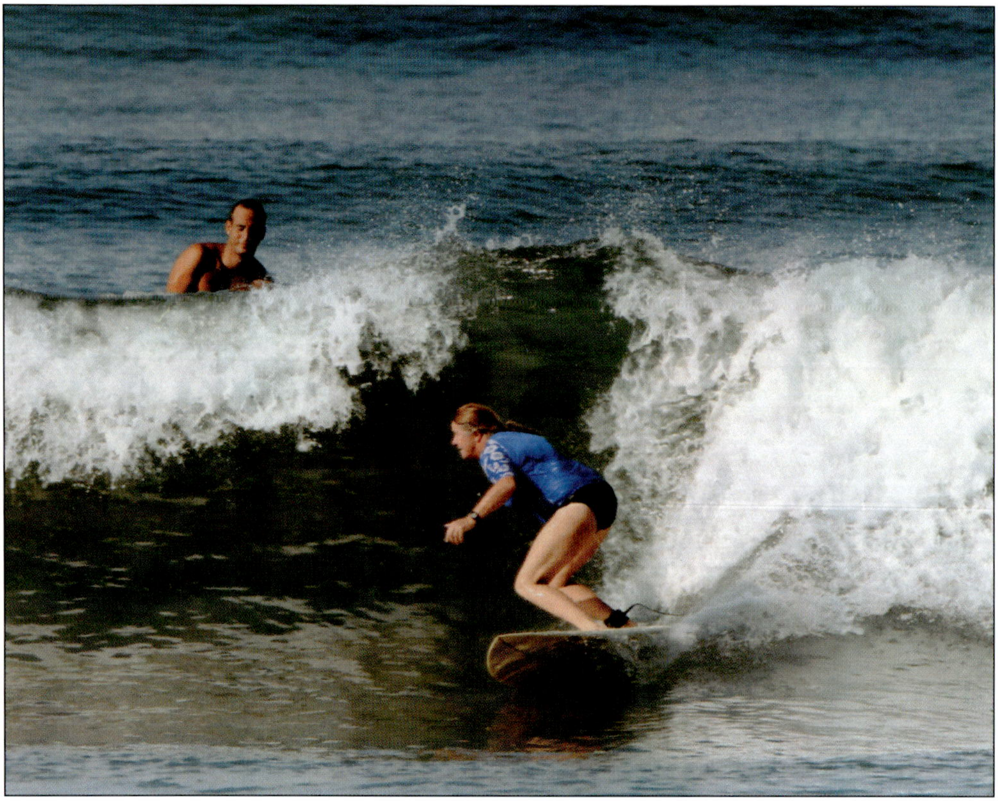

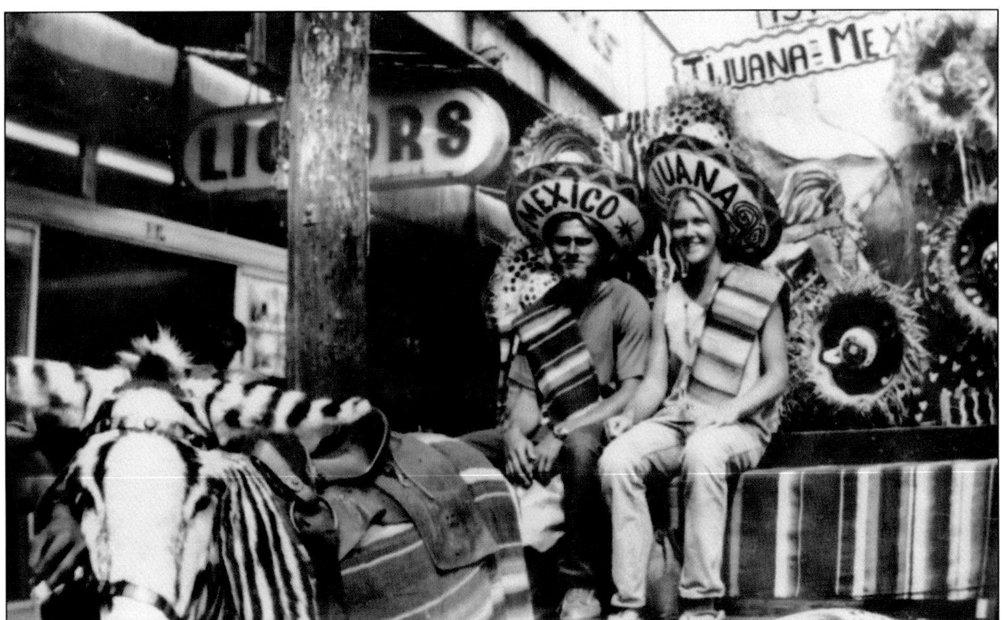

This great shot of Nanci and Jerre on a side trip to Tijuana, Mexico, in 1972 was taken during a break in competition. Later that year, the two moved to Hilton Head Island. In 1982, they opened Nan-Seas, fielding the island's first surf team. (Courtesy of the Polk-Weckhorst archives.)

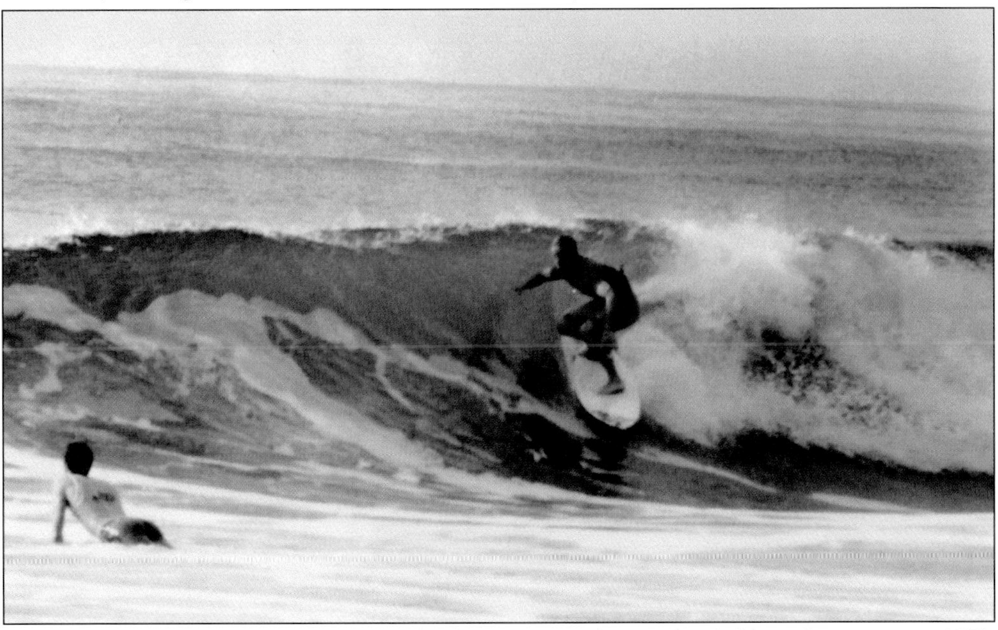

Hamp and Sis Sewell had operated Kindred Spirits, a surf camp for children, beginning in 1971. Nan-Seas stepped in to fill the void when they closed by catering to surfers and windsurfers. The business also housed their canvas shop until 2000, when Nanci and Jerre passed the torch to John Tolly and Sunny Daze Surf Shop. Concentrating on the canvas business, they still found plenty of time to catch any swell that came though. Jerre is seen scoring a sweet wave of his own. This surfing power couple defined the sport on the island for decades. (Courtesy of the Polk-Weckhorst archives.)

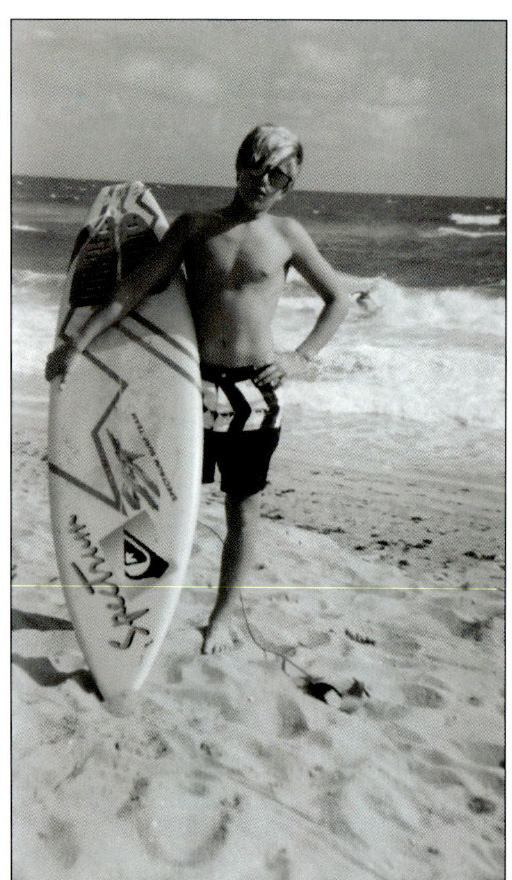

Byron Sewell was one of the top competitors on the Nan-Seas team in the 1980s, as one can see from these early photographs. He moved on to bigger waves in Central America, finally working as a private surf, dive, and fishing mentor on a private yacht. The crew explored 40,000 miles over the next three and a half years, from Costa Rica to Papua, New Guinea. While the locals dream of traveling off the island, Byron has returned to Hilton Head, guiding light-tackle and fly fishermen. His favorite thing nowadays is teaching kids to fish and surf and spreading aloha through the Lowcountry. (Both, courtesy of the Polk-Weckhorst archives.)

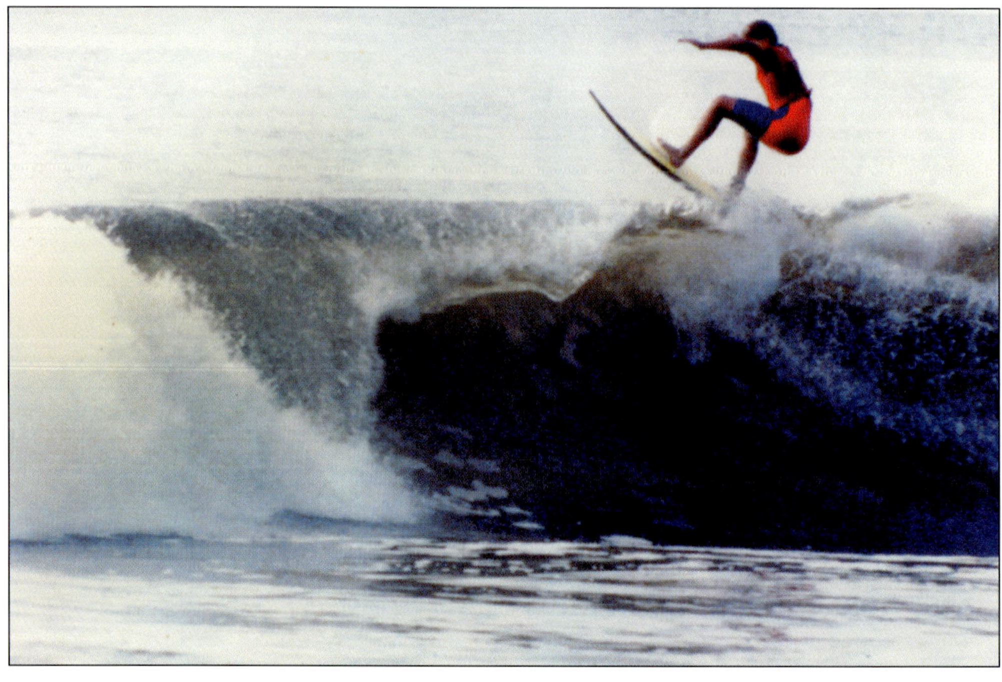

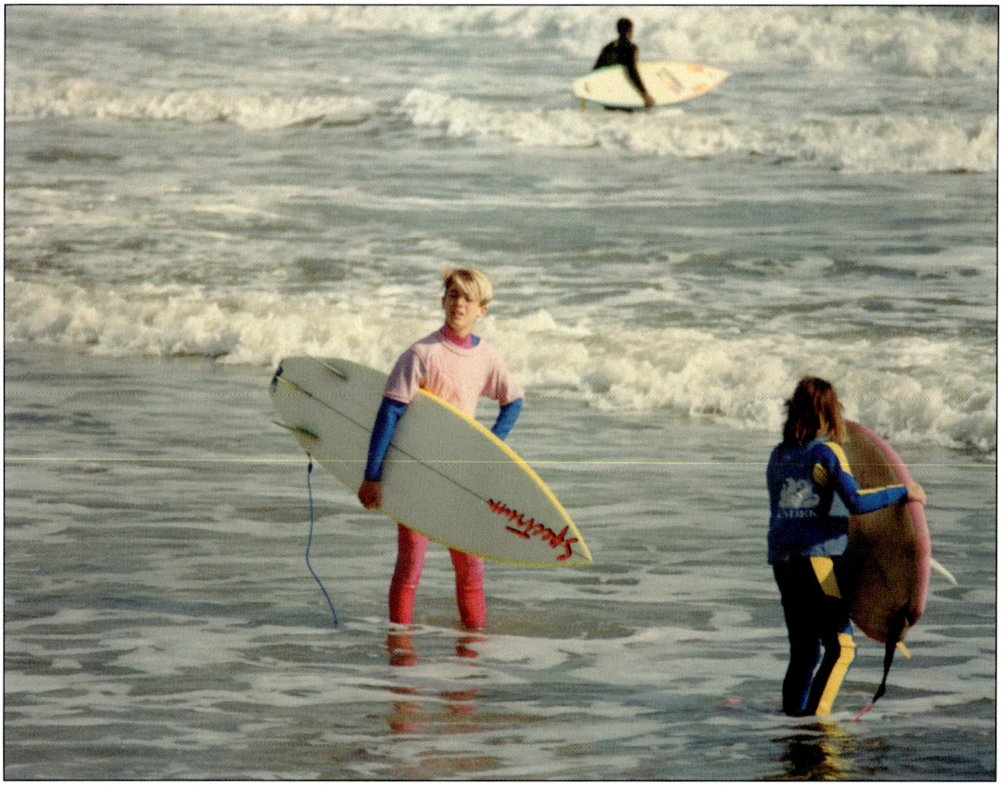

Gavin Daley stands impatiently posing for this shot while Chastity Goins plunges ahead into the waves. Gavin was also a top competitor on the Nan-Seas team but now travels the country as a top-tier tattoo artist. An excellent multitalented musician, people may find him sitting in with his family's band, the Lowcountry Boil. A reggae artist, the dreads and tattoos are instantly recognizable. (Courtesy of the Polk-Weckhorst archives.)

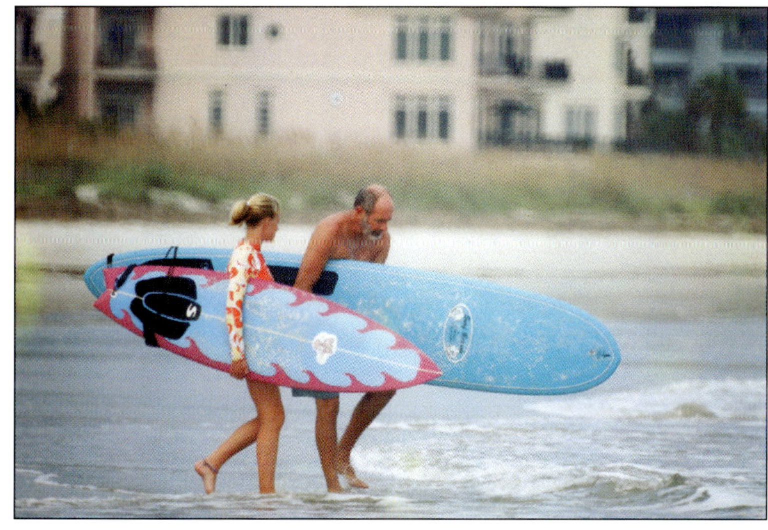

Rick Lawson spends a little quality water time with daughter Caitlin on her visit home. A veteran of the Eastern Surfing Association competition circuit, Caitlin now finds her home break in Puerto Rico. (Courtesy of Rick Lawson.)

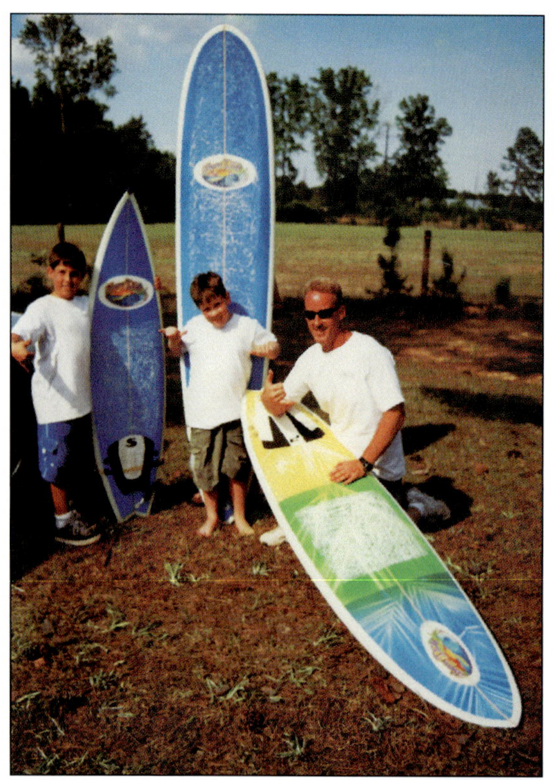

The Quintal family lived in Hilton Head, and when Justin was 11 years old, they began surfing in the Eastern Surfing Association contests held in Charleston. In this photograph, people may recognize Justin (left), Dane, and their father, Mike. In his first year, Justin was top ranked in his age group in short board and second in longboard. Mike, who considers himself more of a soul surfer, told the *Island Packet* that he was amazed at his son's talent. Dane, then eight, started competing as well. (Courtesy of John Tolly.)

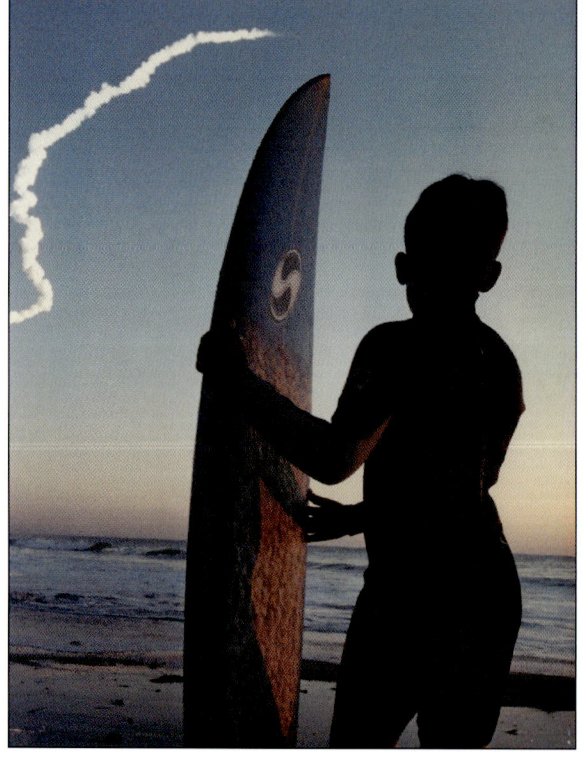

Moving to Florida, Justin's career skyrocketed. He surfs longboards and competes all over the world. In August 2015, he won his third consecutive Van's Joel Tudor Duct Tape Invitational, the US Open's specialty longboard event. Dane moved into skateboarding. Mike is still soul surfing, and Kim is a professional surf mom. (Courtesy of the Polk-Weckhorst archives.)

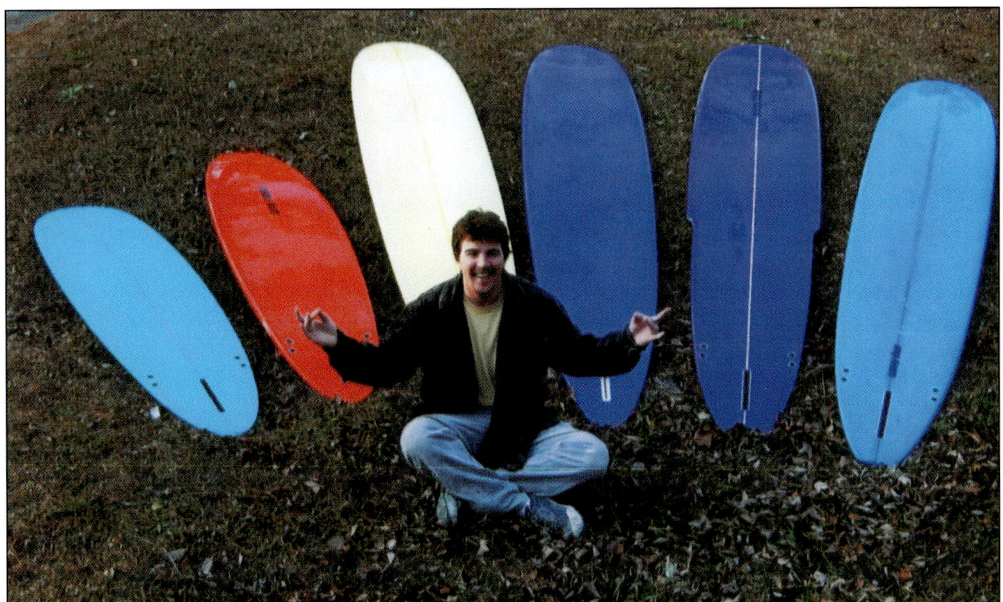

John Tolly poses with his quiver of boards. Surfers must have a board that will handle each of the different conditions that Mother Nature can throw at them—at least that is their story. After all, one would not ride a pig in storm surf. Having one's own shaping bay helps immensely, as boards can be made to suit any surfing style. (Courtesy of John Tolly.)

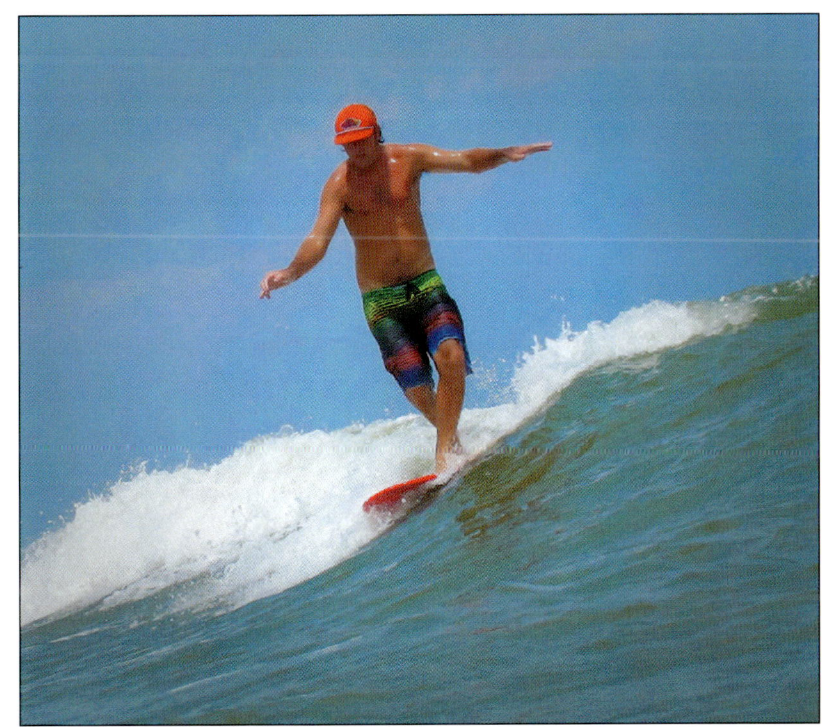

Here is "Mr. Sunny Daze" himself, John Tolly, showing a graceful cross step to the nose on a picture-perfect beach day. There are days when one has to slip out of the shaping room to catch a few, and Tolly is captured doing just that. (Courtesy of Jesse Cadman.)

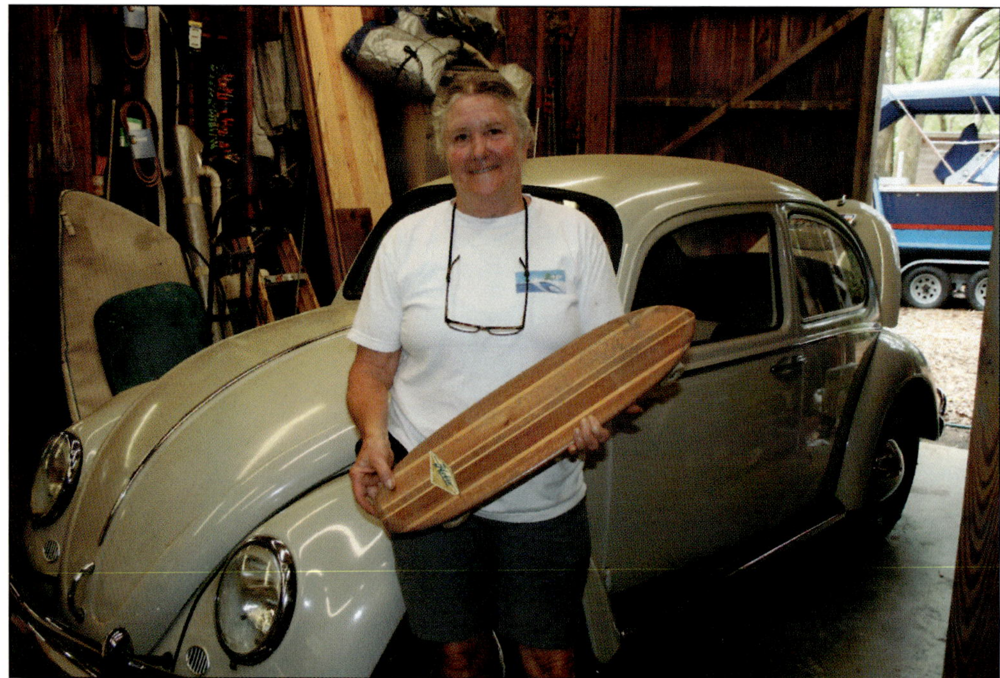

Above, Nanci Polk-Weckhorst holds the Hobie skateboard that she rode in her West Ashley neighborhood, beginning around 1967. She used it to practice her carving surfing turns. She still keeps it in the original canvas bag. Below, hanging in a place of honor, is the cypress board that was actually Nanci's grandmother's ironing board from the beach house on Folly Beach. Her dad used to swipe it and push her and her brother into the waves on Twelfth Street back when Nanci was a child. (Both, authors' collection.)

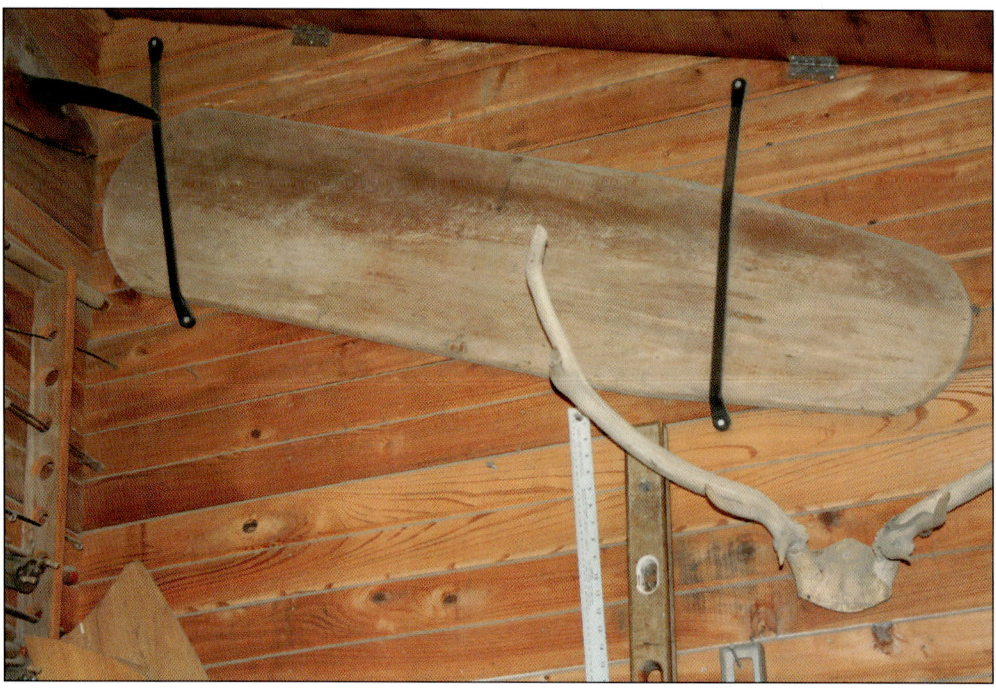

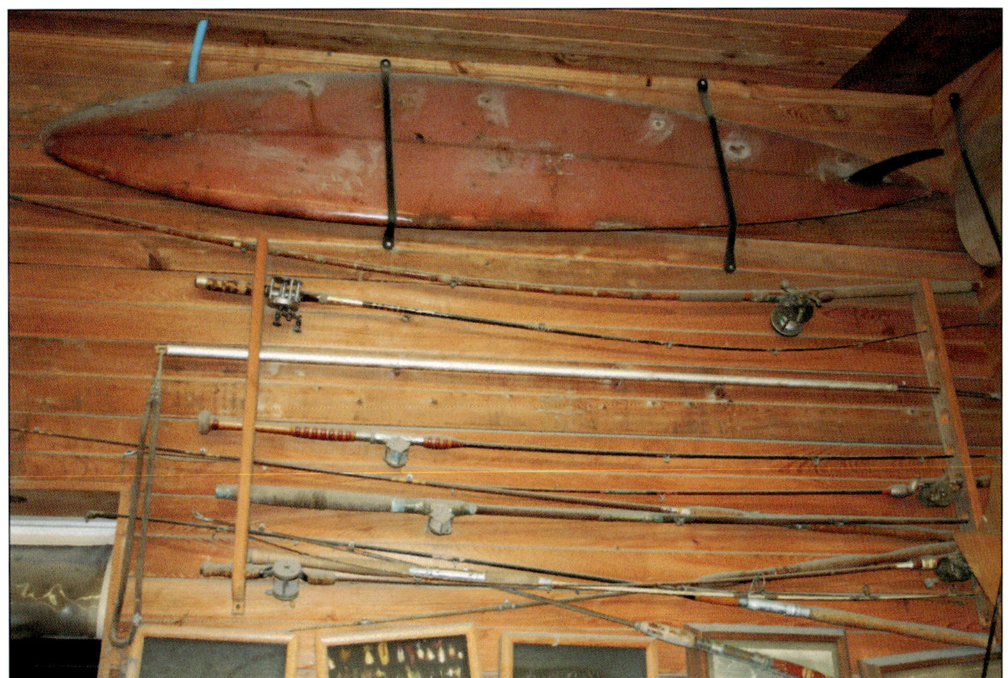

There is nothing like an old garage to bring back memories. This surfboard was the sign at the Revolution No. 9 Surf Shop located on Folly Road in Charleston in 1969. The shop, owned by Foster Folsom, sold Keinholz and Angell brand surfboards. (Authors' collection.)

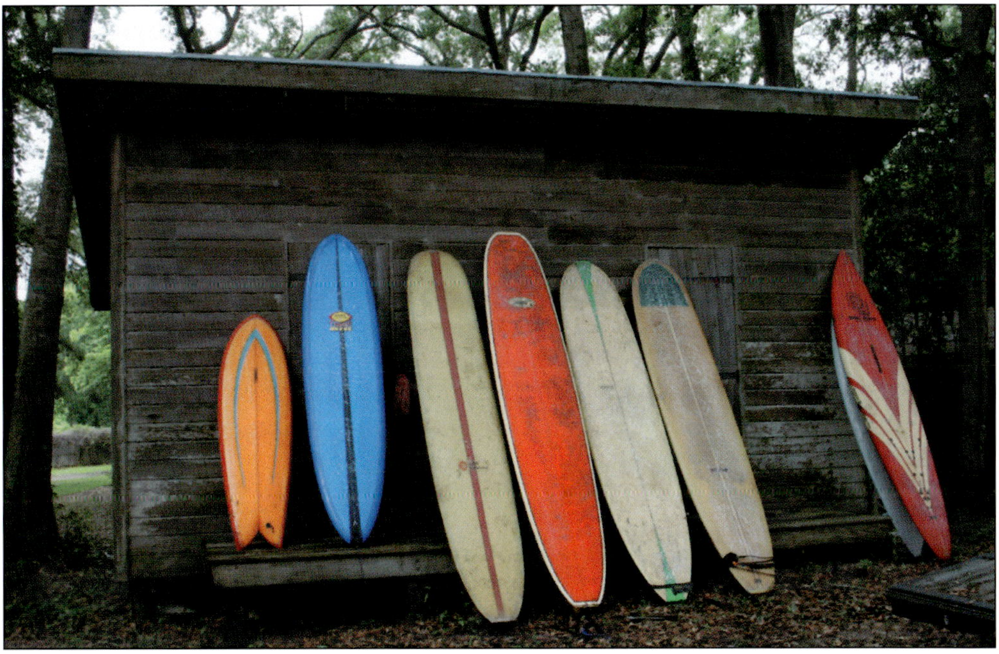

Collectors never know when a big score is hiding just out of sight. Clearing out garages and attics can yield a hidden treasure trove of antique surfboards. This shed in the back of a Hilton Head Island house yields a G&S, a Bing, a Con Ugly, a square-nosed Hansen, a G&S Hot Curl, a Dewey Weber Performer, and two early windsurfers. (Authors' collection.)

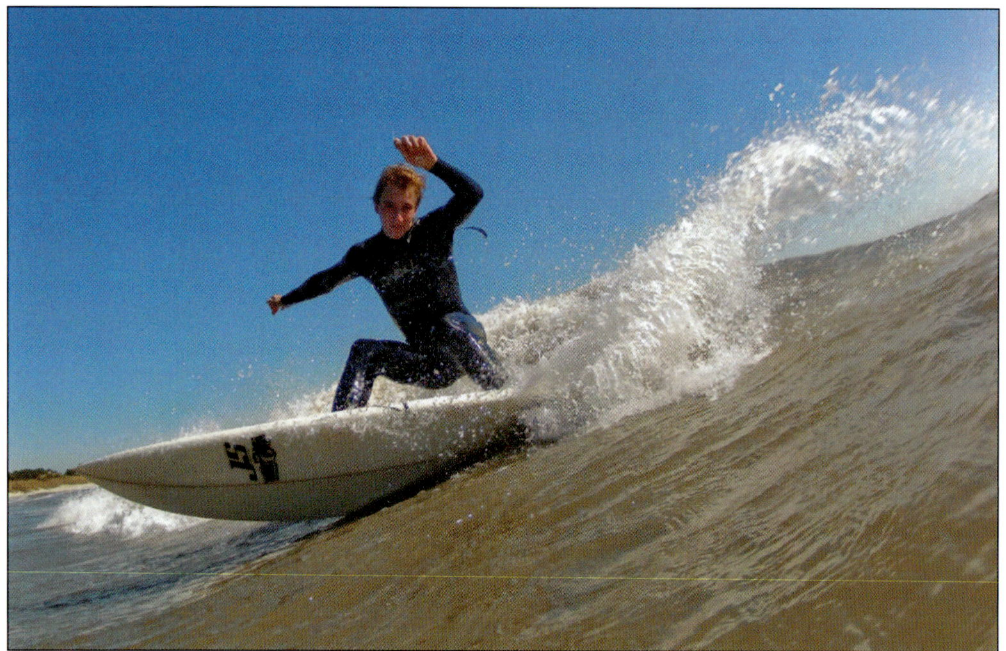

Hilton Head local James Urbin burns through a turn at Burke's Beach. James, along with his younger brother Will, are part of the younger pack shredding in the water these days. Hilton Head Island's surfing community keeps growing—but it is still tightly knit. Mike Quintal described it best, saying it is almost a tribal thing. (Courtesy of Jesse Cadman.)

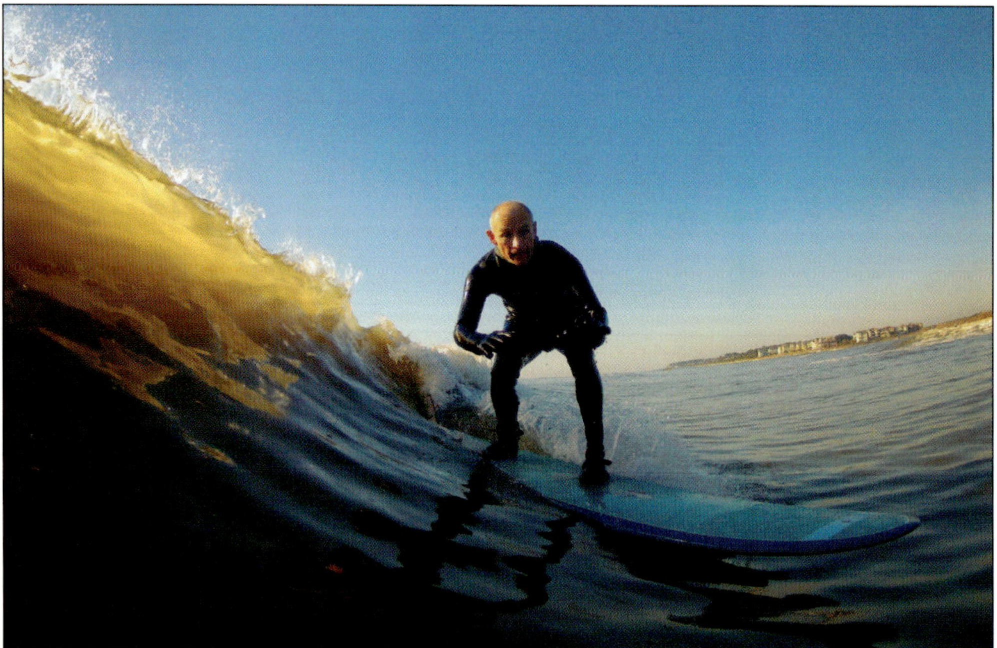

The Burke's Beach boys lightheartedly started calling a Rhode Island native the "chairman of the board" when they noticed he brings his trusty beach chair along with his board (rain or shine) whenever he goes to the beach. It is corny, but Michael "Chairman" Feinman does not seem to mind. (Courtesy of Jesse Cadman.)

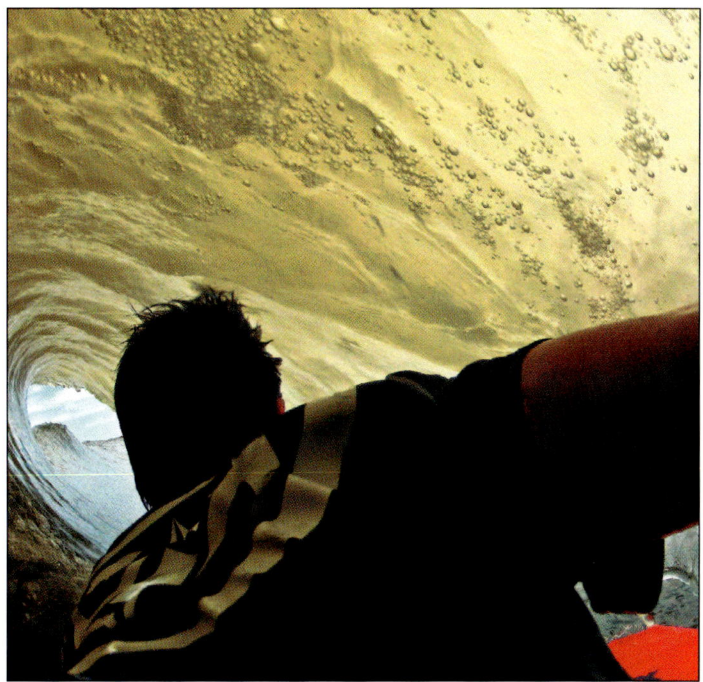

Jesse Cadman, a former professional bodyboarder, escapes the summer heat at Bradley Beach and pulls in for some much needed shade. If one does not catch him bodyboarding, stand-up paddleboarding, surfing, skimboarding, or shooting water photography, people can find him teaching his three-year-old, Jesse Dakota, the ways of waterman. (Courtesy of Jesse Cadman.)

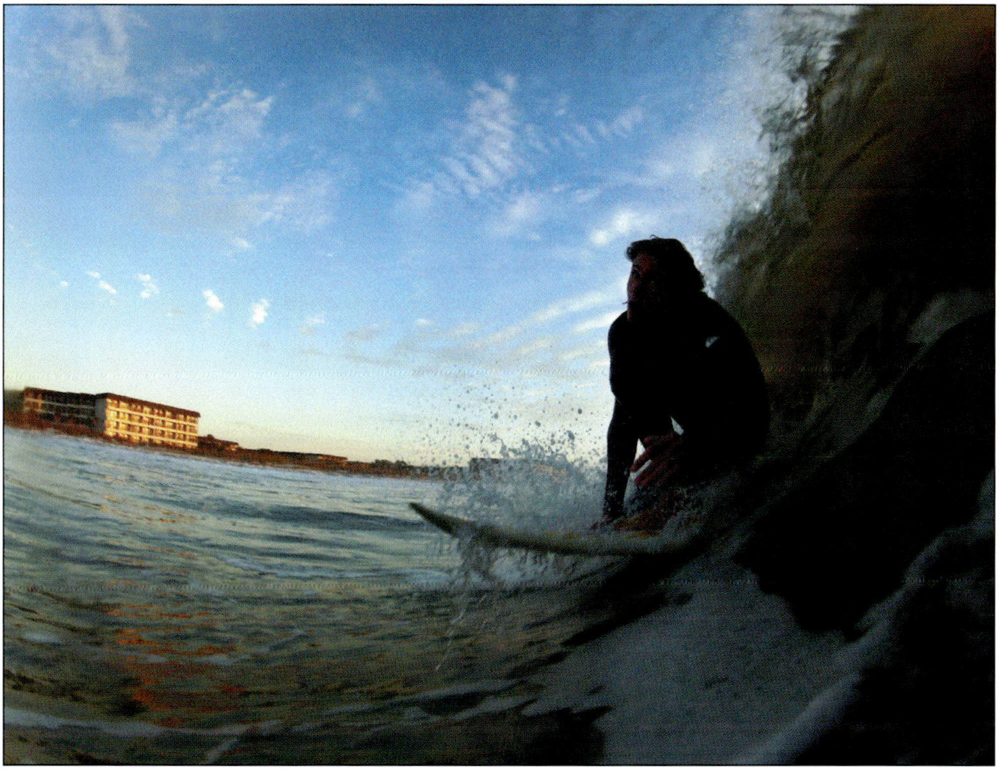

Hilton Head's Jordan Lemmon is talented both on and off the water. One of Hilton Head's top skateboarders, he is as comfortable slotted in the pocket as he is sailing high above the coping, as evidenced by this wave at Bradley Beach on Hilton Head Island. (Courtesy of Jesse Cadman.)

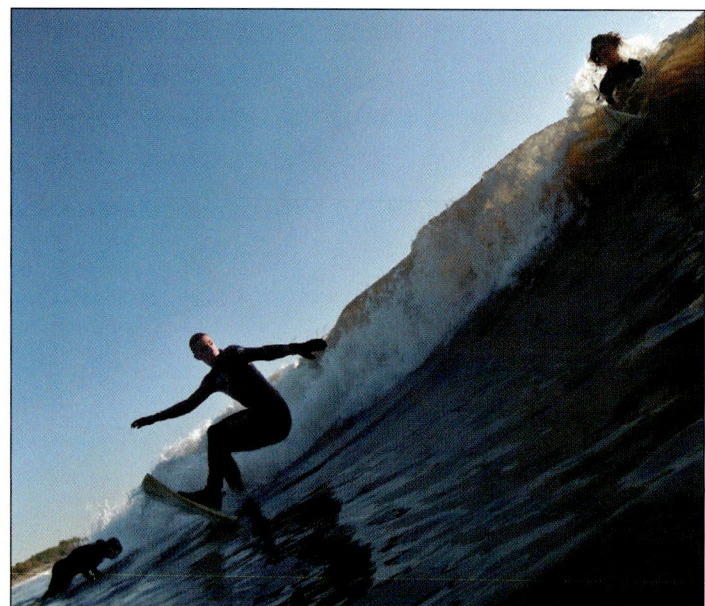

Michael Brewer recalls surfing at age 11. Since then, he has been proud to call the island his home break. The friends he grew up with there continue to be his most treasured relationships. Even with the pressure of balancing job and education, the ocean still grounds him. Mike says he can still clear his mind with one good wave. (Courtesy of Jesse Cadman.)

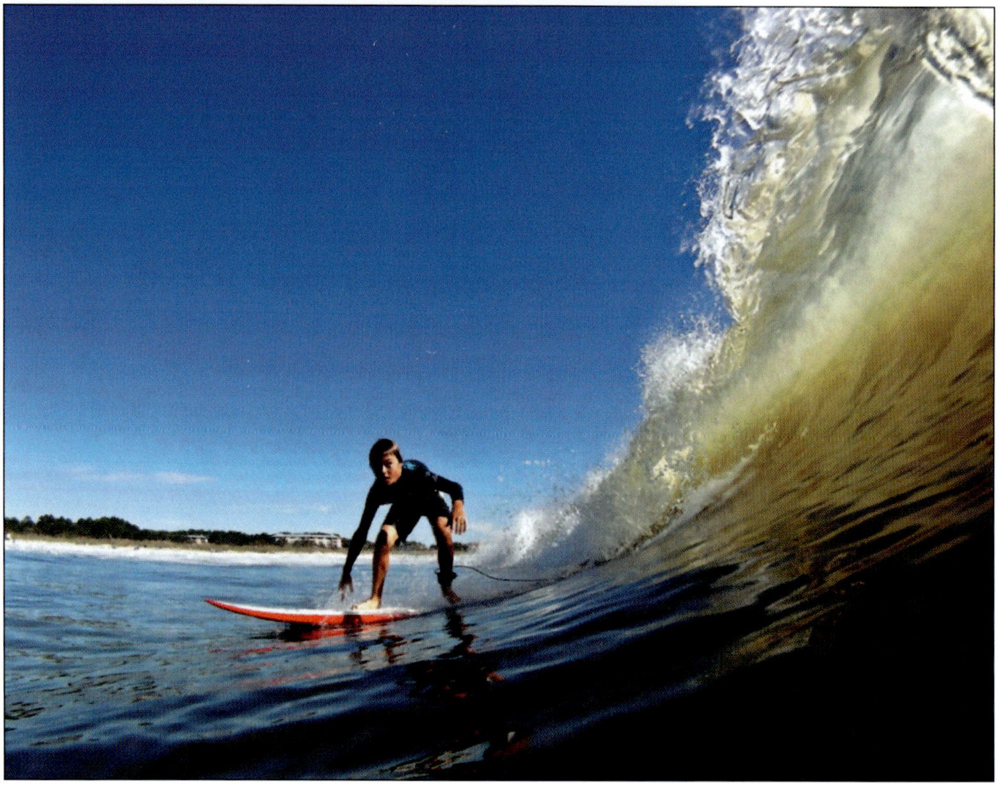

James Bartholomew rode his uncle's classic six-foot single fin when he was 10 years old, and that is all it took. He bought his first board the next day and has not looked back. Now he has done enough traveling to appreciate the variety of waves in different conditions. When on Hilton Head, he surfs Burke's Beach with an eye to the outer bars and nearby islands, which can produce good waves. (Courtesy of Jesse Cadman.)

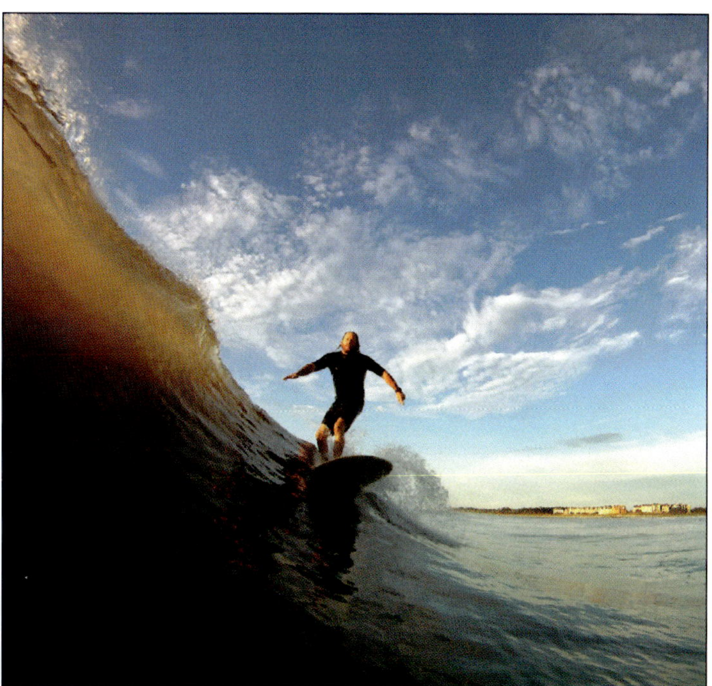

Billy Hughes gets his love of Indian motorcycles from his dad and his love of surfing from his mom, a former 1964 Greg Noll team rider. He was up on bikes at four years of age and surfing at 15 in Myrtle Beach in 1985. When people see him in his 1957 Chevy Bel Air with a 1967 Dewey Weber on top or riding his 1948 Indian, do not think he is a pretender—he comes by it honestly. (Courtesy of Jesse Cadman.)

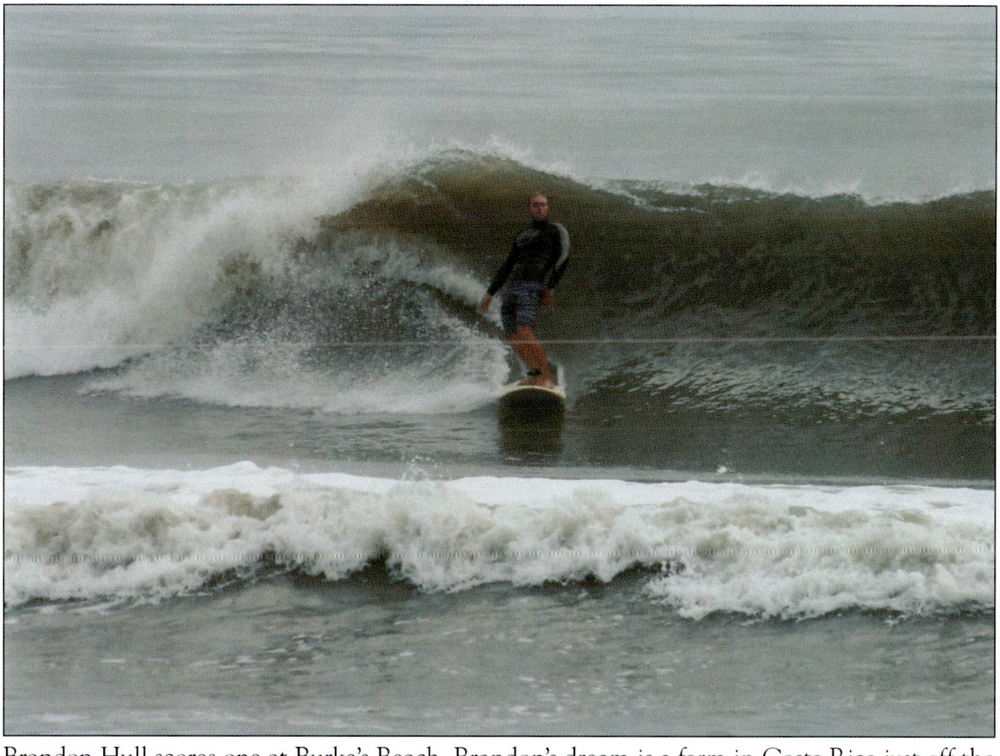

Brandon Hull scores one at Burke's Beach. Brandon's dream is a farm in Costa Rica just off the beach and all the waves he could want. In the meantime, he will have to be content with classic longboarding and a quick walk to the nose. (Courtesy of Jesse Cadman.)

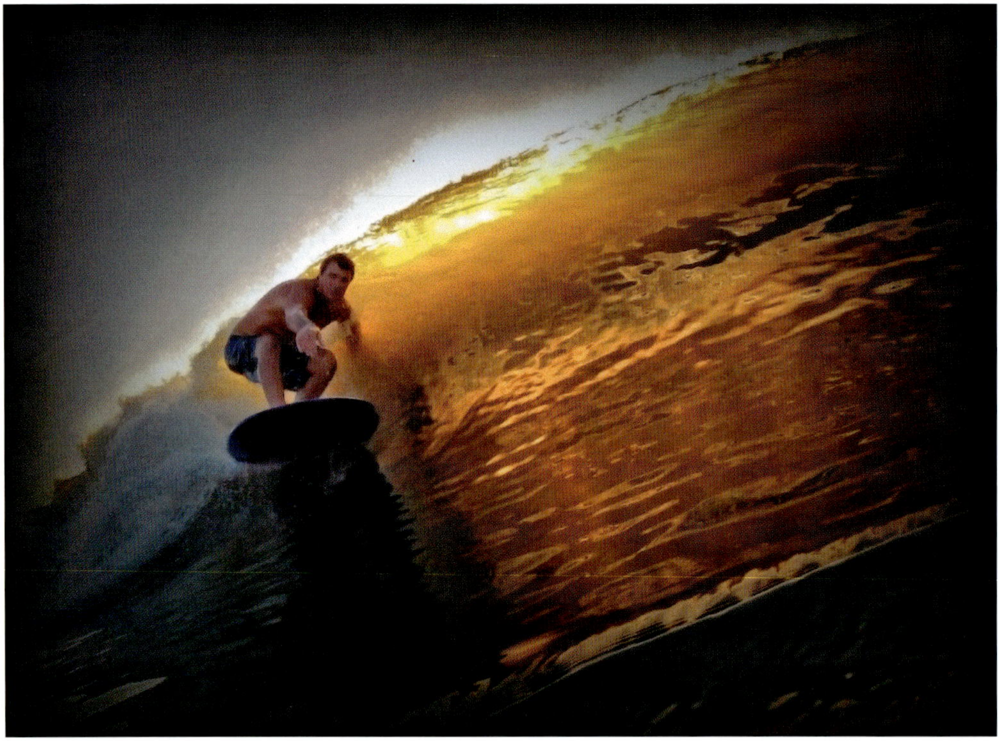

Above, John Tolly gets buried on this wave. John operated the Sunny Daze Surf Shop on Hilton Head from 2000 to 2009. He now makes custom boards from a shaping bay on the island. Below, when Patrick Farley Mills is not putting in long hours at the Sunny Daze Factory helping John, people can catch him at Burke's Beach. Pat is an avid fisherman and knows the local waters like the back of his hand. (Both, courtesy of Jesse Cadman.)

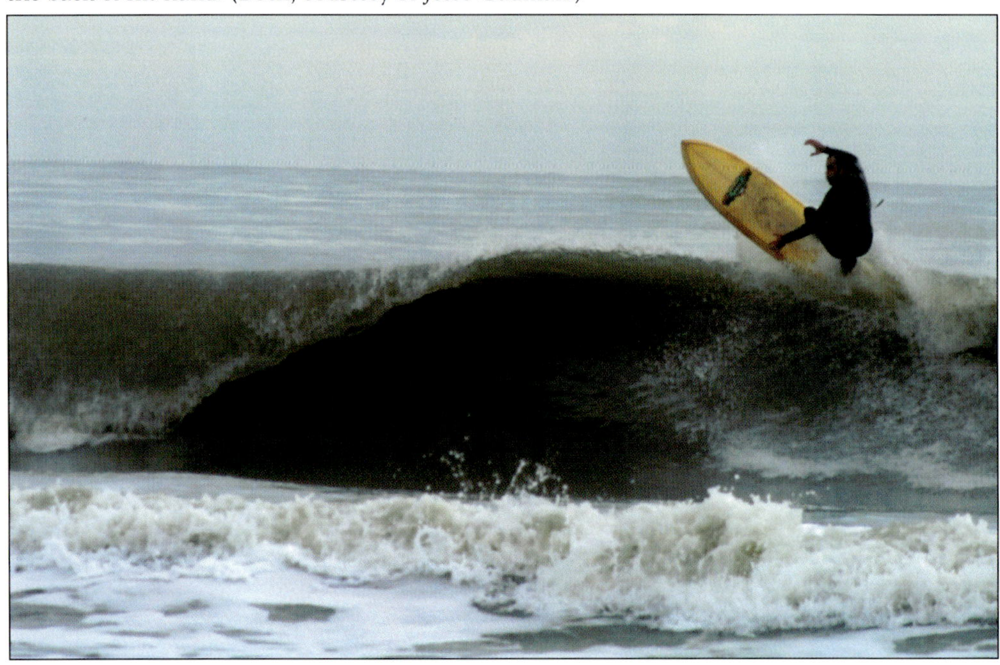

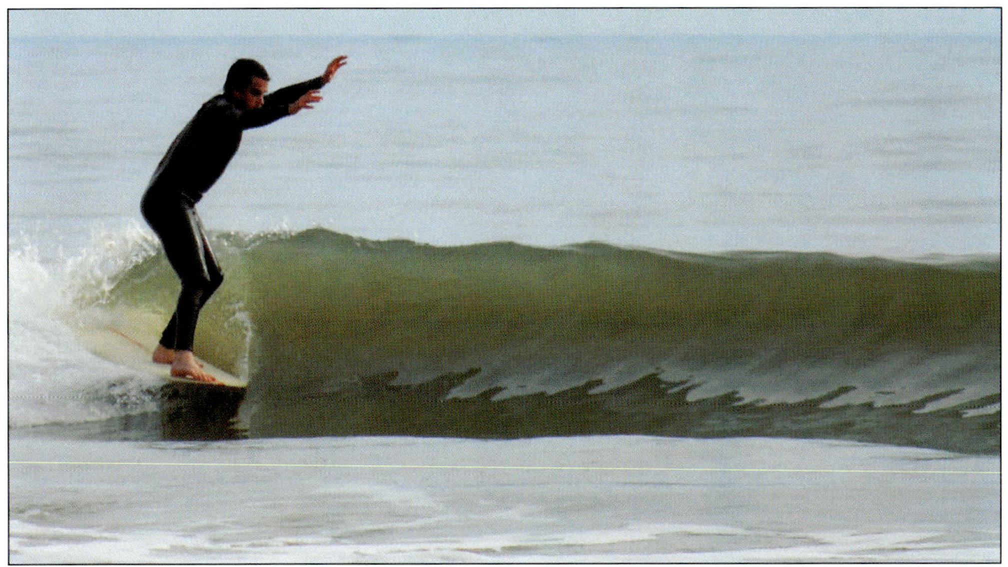

Jesse Cadman is perched on the nose, experiencing the glide in the clear waters at Burke's Beach on Hilton Head Island. Jesse is a talented in-water photographer, using a GoPro, so it is not often that a photograph of him surfaces. (Courtesy of Glen Barroncini.)

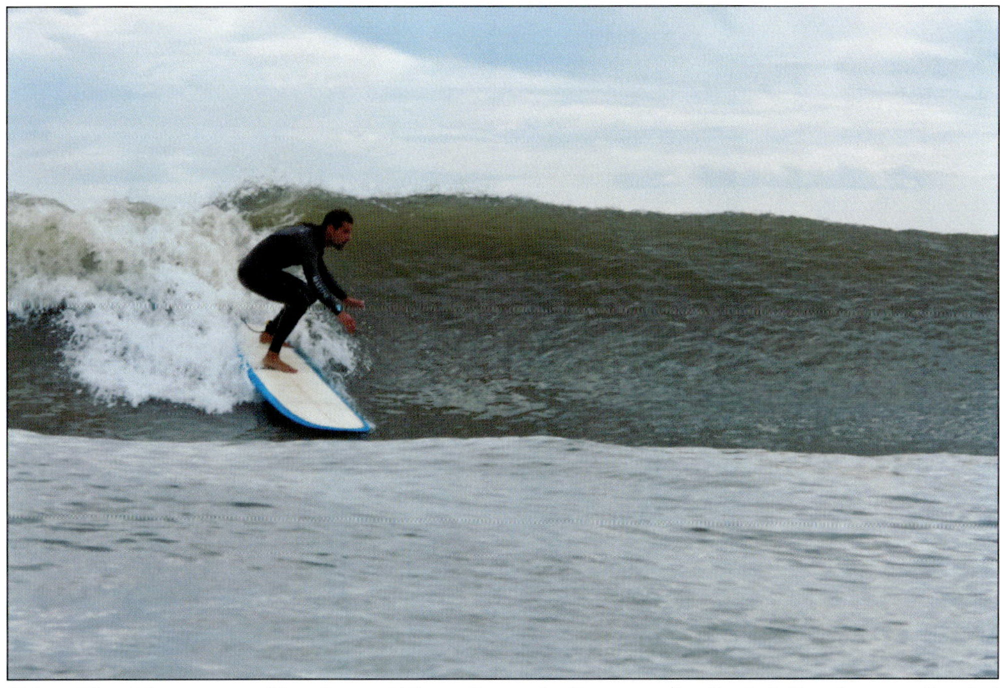

Hilton Head fire captain Tim Santini blazes down the line on a fun Burke's Beach wave. Santini honed his skills in Wilmington, North Carolina. He showed up in the lineup here 10 years ago fresh from a college sabbatical in Australia, where he acquired his all-time favorite board, a six-foot-three Skipps. (Courtesy of Jesse Cadman.)

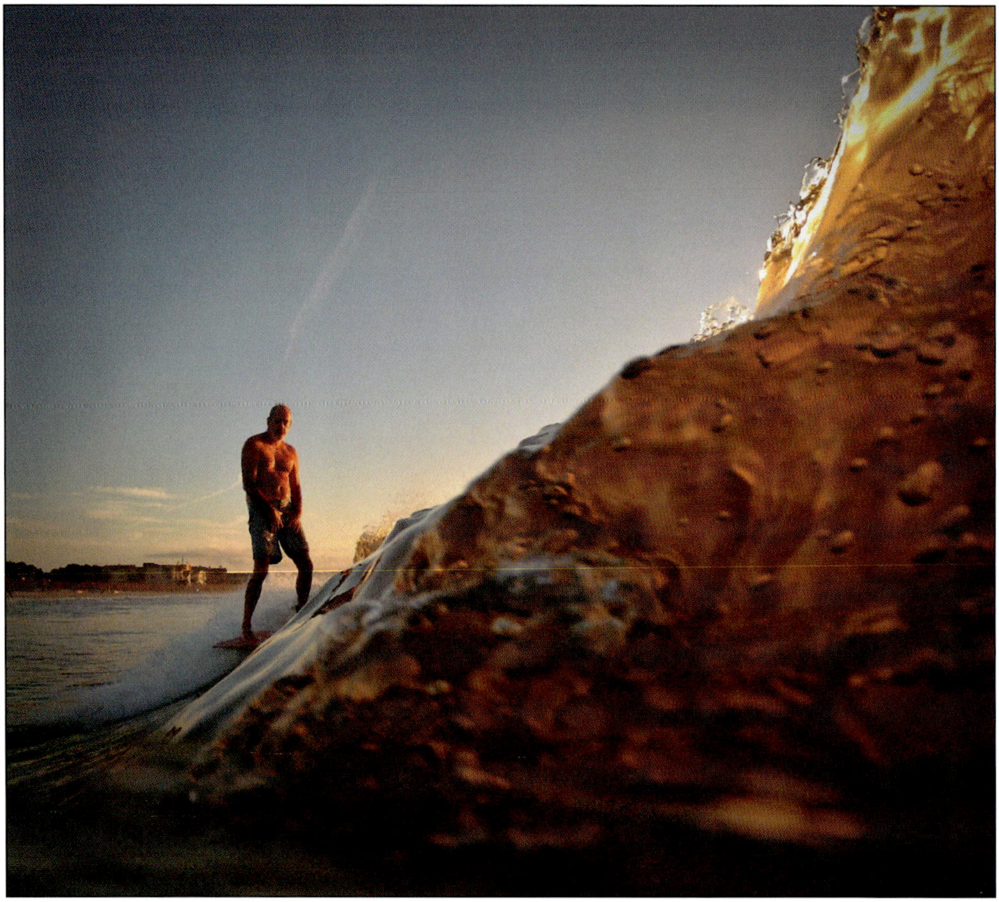

Above, Rick Lawson is a true inspiration to Hilton Head's younger surfers. Whether tinkering on his classic cars or ripping up and down the beach dodging tourists (and angry lifeguards) on his land sailor, Rick is considered one of Hilton Head's true legends. Below, local funnyman Will Hagins laces an early-morning peak at Burke's Beach. Will and his older brother Trey grew up surfing these same Hilton Head local waters. (Both, courtesy of Jesse Cadman.)

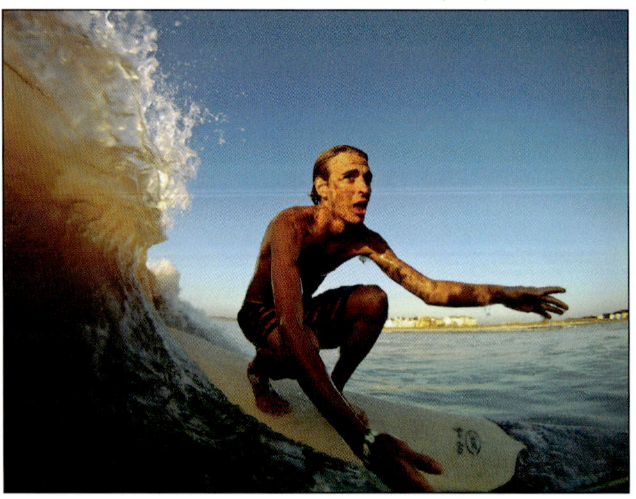

Four

Spin-Offs

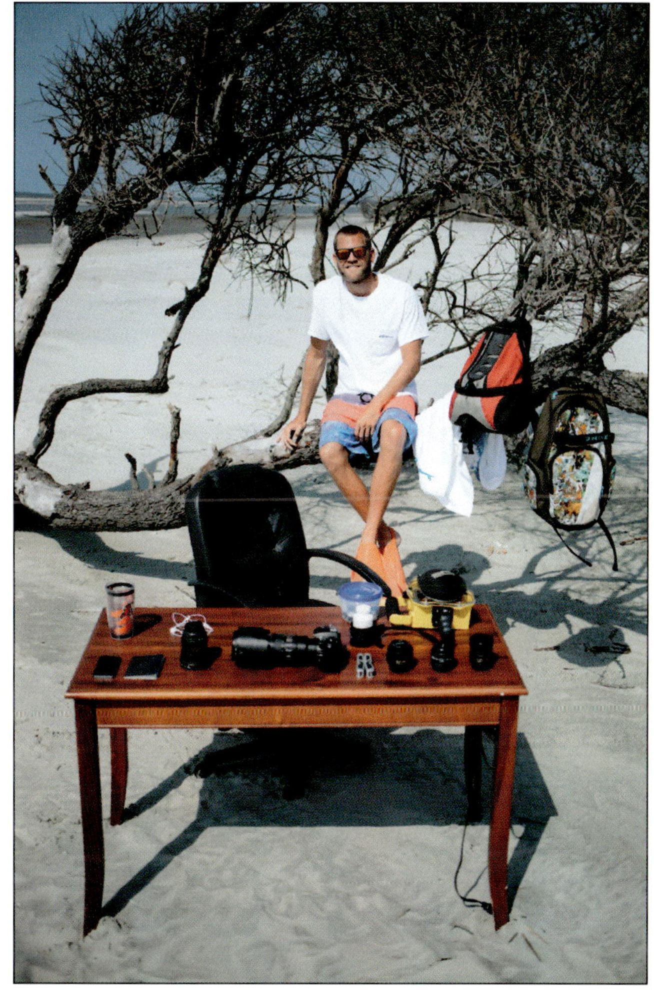

It is rare that one can make a living doing something what he or she loves. Every now and then, surfers can take their passion for waves, add a unique talent, and spin off a career. The sport of surfing has its spin-offs too. Skateboarding grew in popularity in the 1960s, and a good, hard ocean breeze encouraged kite and windsurfing. Prone paddling has become an elite event around the world, and stand-ups fight for their place in the sport. Justin Morris, a blogger at *Follyhood* and in-water surfing photographer, recently posed for a magazine shoot on Folly Beach. (Courtesy of Nickie Cutrona.)

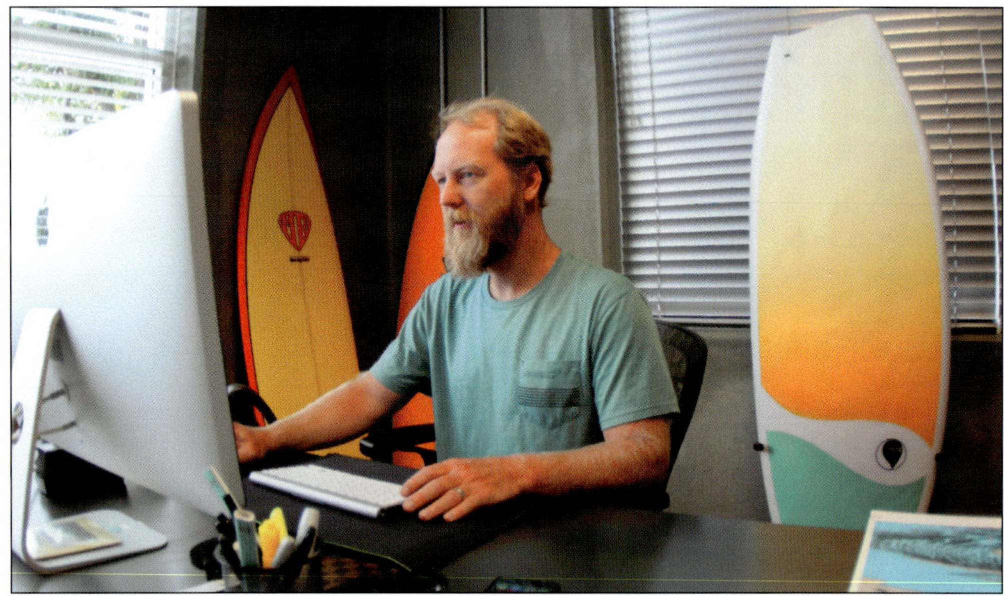

Rob McCarty began surfing at the Dunes Club in Myrtle Beach in the early 1980s. Airbrushing designs for Kelly Richard's Perfection Surfboards led him to pursue a degree in graphic design. Getting in on the ground floor with his sponsor, Rip Curl, Rob quickly advanced to lead designer. After a jump to Billabong, he and a handful of talented executives formed their company, Vissla. (Courtesy of Yoge Yoshida.)

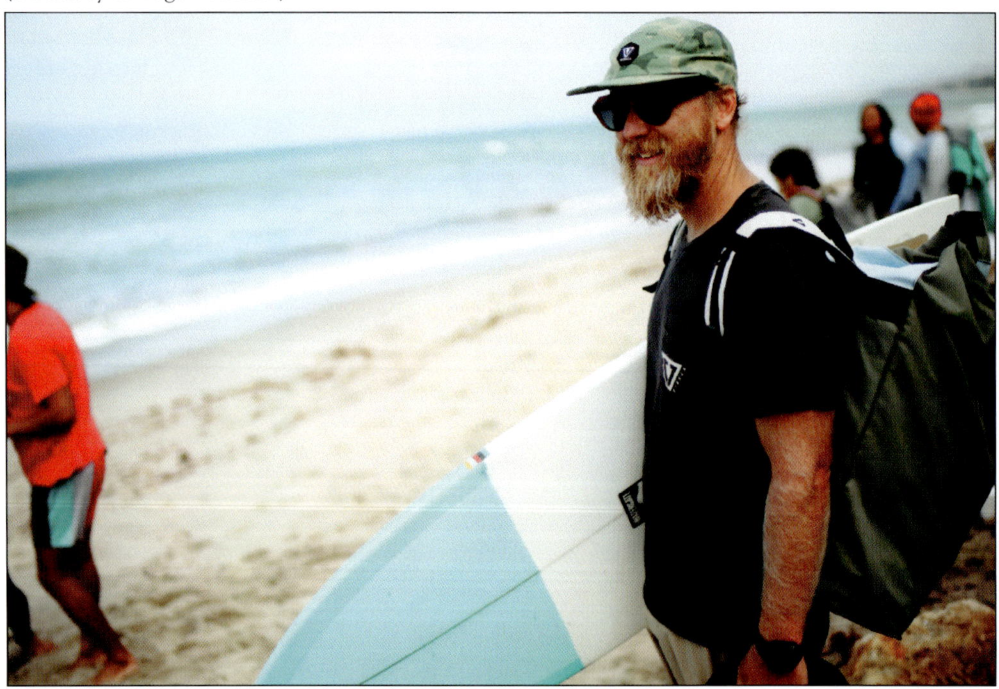

Members of Vissla began with a blank piece of paper and a dream of creating a modern surf brand. Six months later, Rob, vice president of design, delivered the first full line of wet suits and apparel. Coming full circle, Kelly Richard's Village Surf Shop received the East Coast's inaugural shipment, and Cam Richards was named their first surf ambassador. (Courtesy of Yoge Yoshida.)

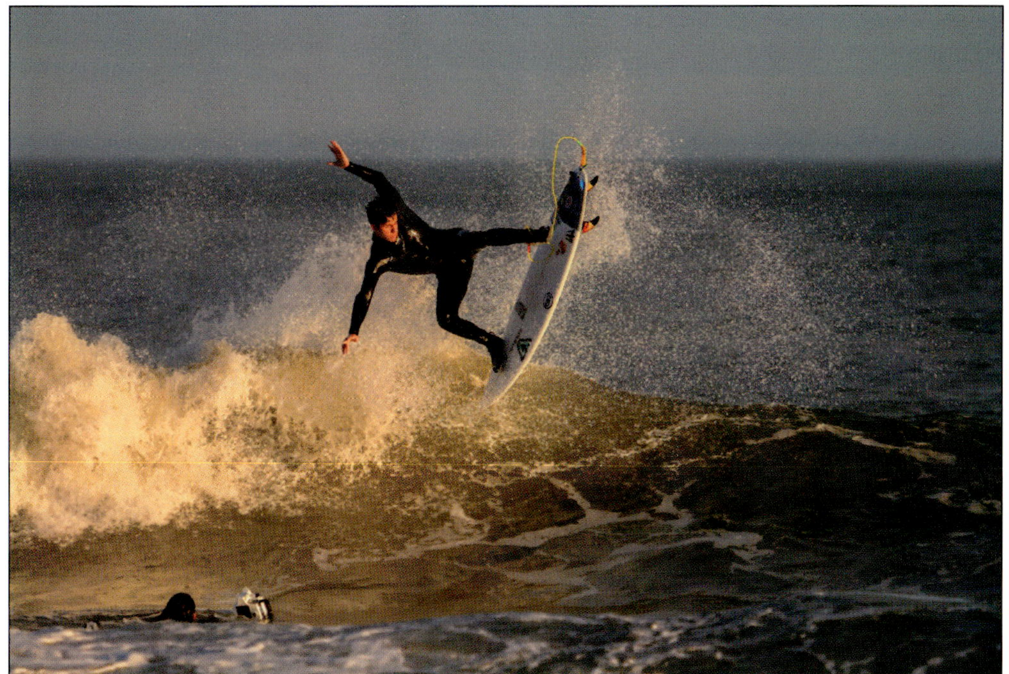

Cam Richards is living every young surfer's dream. The phenomenally talented surfer represents Vissla. He best describes his life as traveling the world, learning about different cultures, eating amazing food, seeing all the beautiful places, and surfing to his heart's content. That is enough to keep him busy and happy. (Courtesy of Kent Ficklin.)

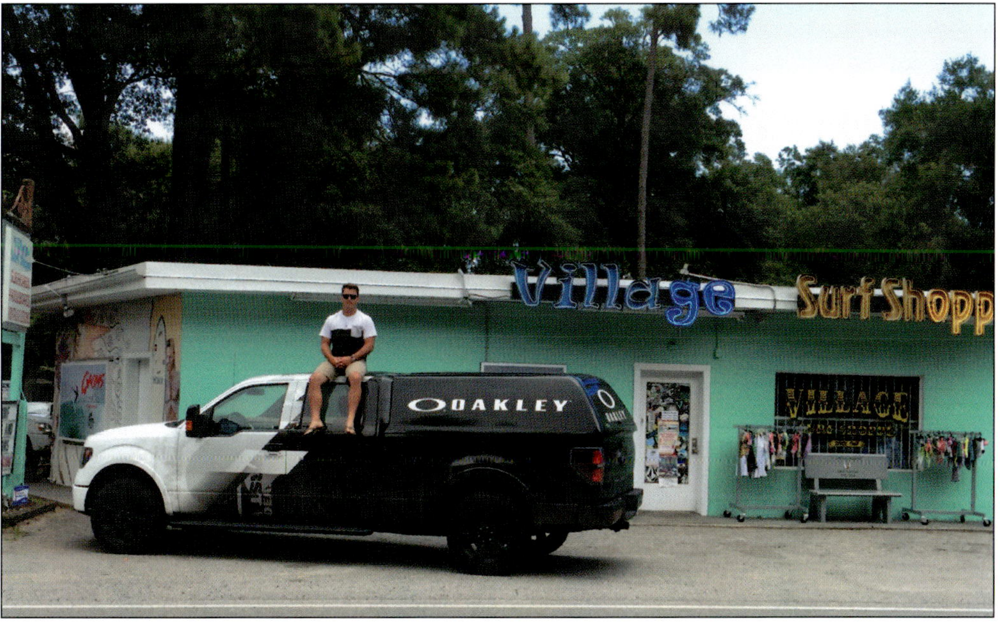

Cole Richards has taken his talents in an entirely different direction from brother Cam. He combined his surfing skills and love of fishing and golf into an exciting niche. He spends his time roaming from fishing to golf, tennis, and surfing tournaments representing Oakley sunglasses as the company's event coordinator. (Courtesy of Cole Richards.)

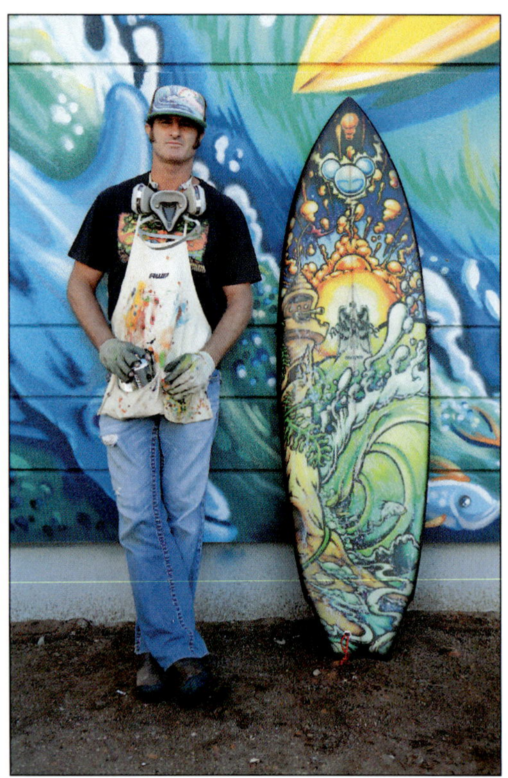

Surfing saved Drew Brophy's life and gave him a very special opportunity. He began painting surfboards in his nontraditional style at Kelly Richards's shop. Moving to the North Shore, he went from painting 10 surfboards a week to 10 per day. When he relocated to California in 1996, he hooked up with Matt Biolus, founder of Lost surfboards. They decided that Matt would shape and Drew would handle the art. The response was overwhelming. They have traveled the world surfing and creating. (Courtesy of Larry Beard.)

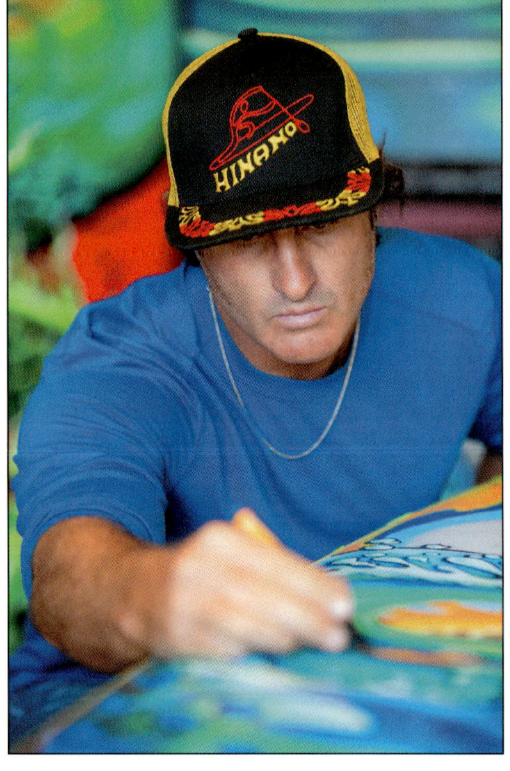

Now working within the heart of the surfing industry, Drew handles commissions from all over the world. He has always believed that surfers are so unique and colorful that their boards should reflect their personalities. His distinctive style does just that. (Courtesy of Larry Beard.)

Beau Flemister has always had a way with words. With his dad and fellow surfer, Kyle, he has been traveling the world, looking for waves his entire life. Based in Hawaii, he spent his high school days surfing The Washout at Folly Beach. Look for *Surfing* magazine's editor-at-large and his exotic dispatches from his around-the-world adventures with wife Rachel. (Courtesy of Mike Smolove.)

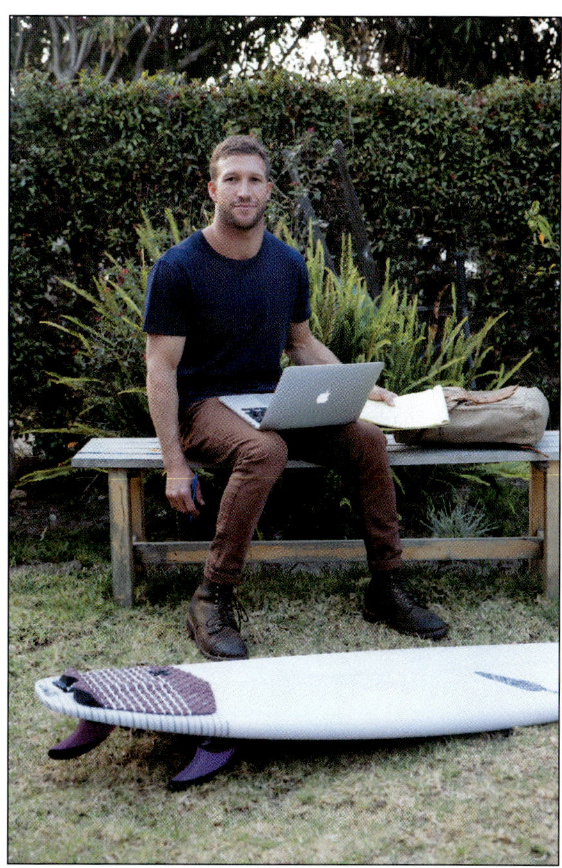

Chris Dixon, a Surfside Beach native, has parlayed his outdoor skills and writing talent to become a successful author, blogger, and freelance writer for outlets like the *New York Times*. His first full-length book, *Ghost Wave*, is centered on the phenomenon of the Cortes Bank and its elusive monster wave. Based out of Charleston, he has adopted Folly Beach as his home break. (Authors' collection.)

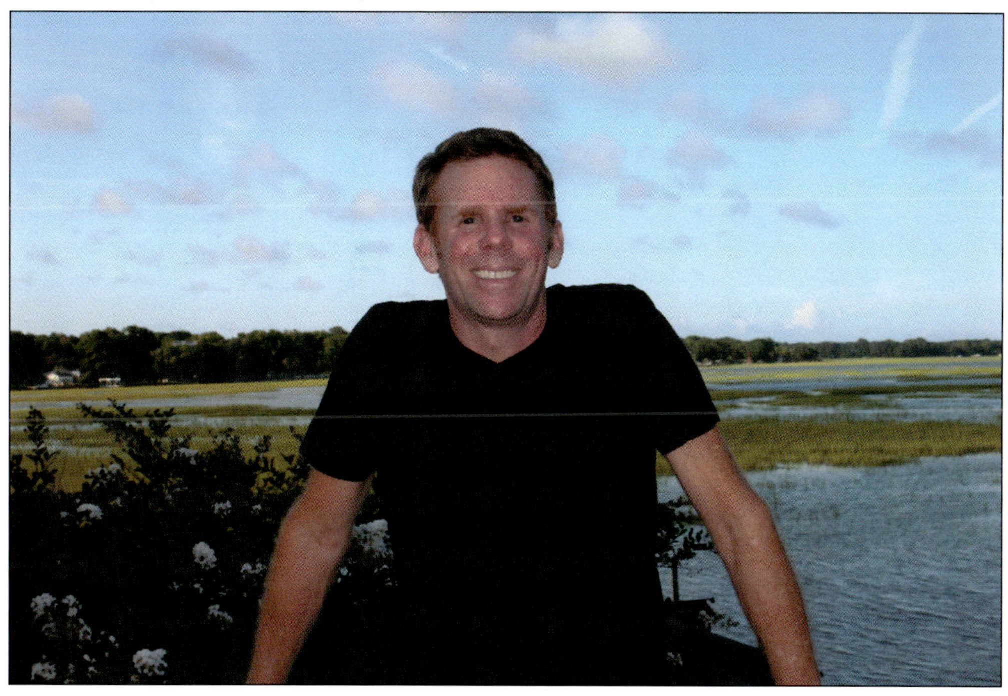

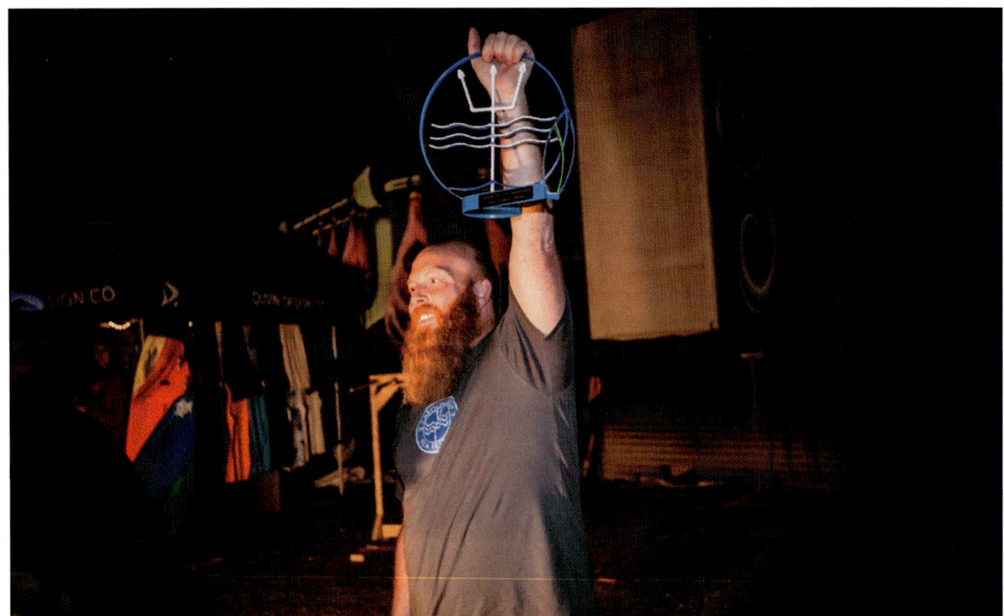

Chad Davis (pictured) was working as a runner for Madonna when he turned a chance encounter in Malibu into a company that sources music for surf movies. Bringing Triple 9 Music back to Charleston, he teamed up with fellow College of Charleston alumni Chuck Gainey (in the image below) to create the Carolina Surf Film Festival. The response was overwhelming. (Courtesy of J.B. McCabe.)

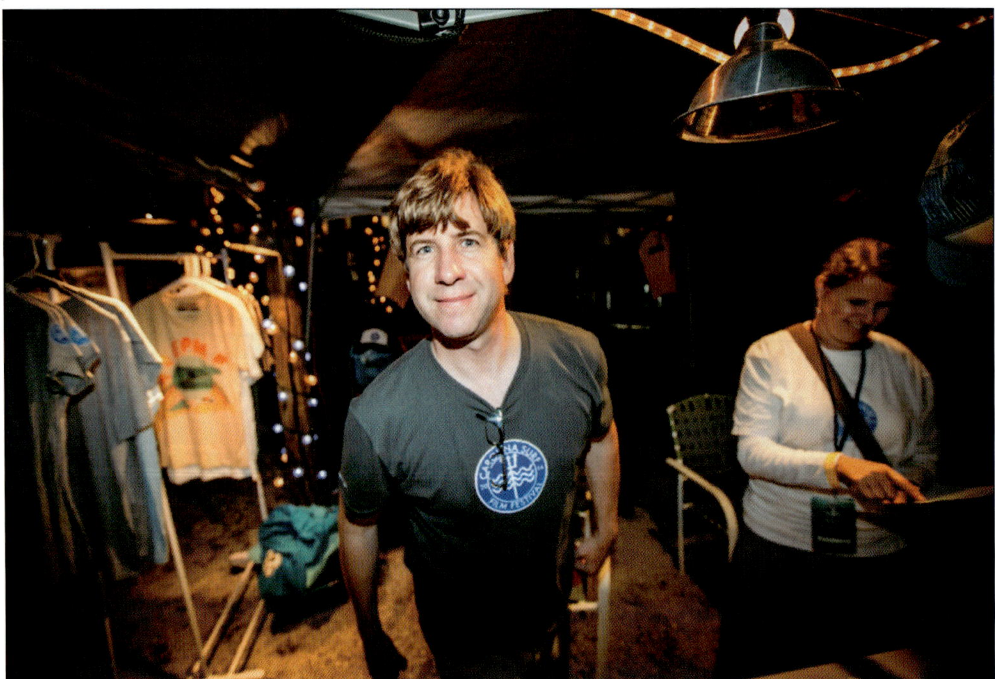

The group debuted a branded T-shirt, wax, and hat line in 2014, hoping to expand into a full Carolina Surf Brand clothing line. They are also eyeing other venues around the Carolinas to include in their surf film festival lineup. (Courtesy of J.B.McCabe.)

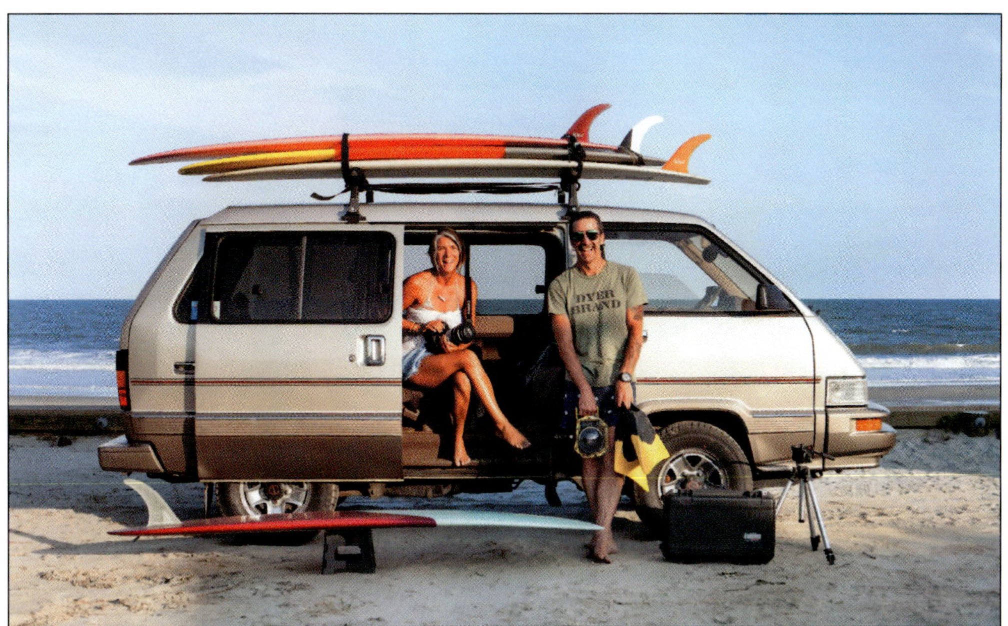

This creative duo has found the perfect place to match their love of surfing and their photographic skills. Combining Patrick Willey's guerilla-style video productions, Tanya Boggs's prowess with a still camera, and their eye for the unique, they created *Two Feet and Classy*, their first surfing movie. It celebrates the "love the one you are with" philosophy of home breaks. (Courtesy of Tanya Boggs Photography.)

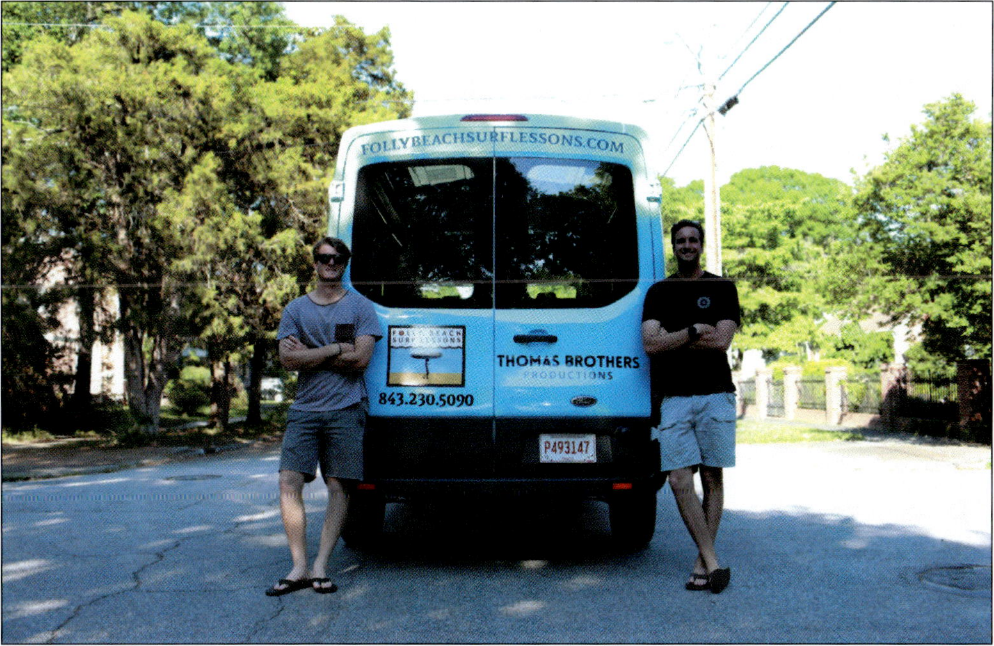

Surfing The Washout at Folly Beach led Bryant Thomas (left) to shoot, edit, and produce his first local surf film, *Waves in Our Pocket*, with brothers Ellison (right) and Robert in 2010. He followed it with *A Look to the Tropics* two years later. The freelancer now focuses his lens on professional surfing around the globe and commercial video productions. (Courtesy of Thomas Brothers.)

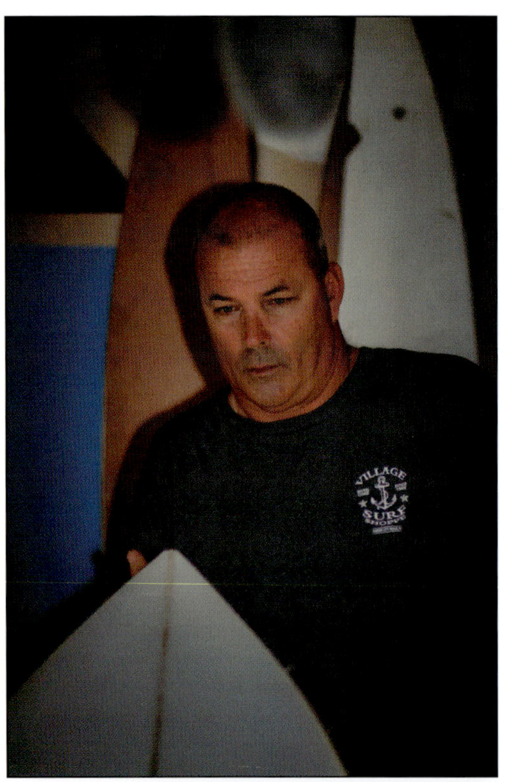

Kelly Richards grabbed a surfboard that was way too small for him and decided to learn the sport. After fighting it for six months, Kelly finally went into Village Surf Shop, was advised to buy a Bing that "fit," and never looked back. Since he was hanging around the shop, owner Eric Eason asked if Kelly would do some ding repair. By 1980, he was shaping his own line of boards, producing as many as 2,500 boards in a year under his Perfection label. (Courtesy of Kent Ficklin.)

Kelly purchased Village Surf Shop in 1988 and has continued the shop's practice of mentoring younger surfers to realize their potential, not only in the sport but in life. He has nurtured the careers of many youngsters in the sport, including sons Cam and Cole. (Courtesy of Kent Ficklin.)

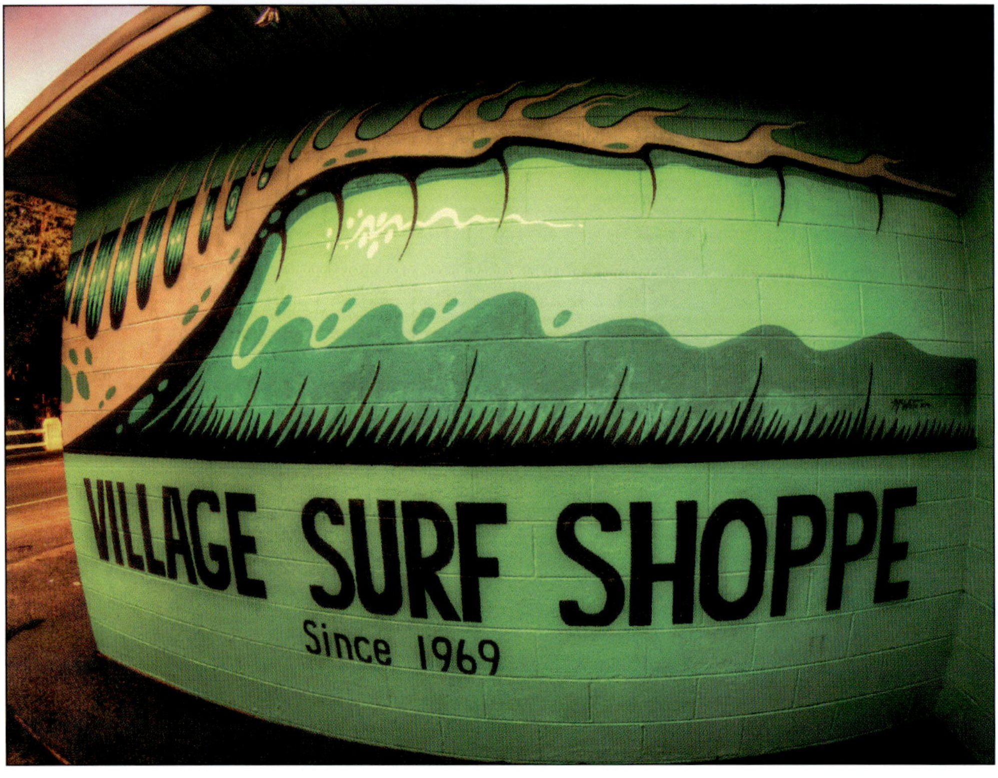

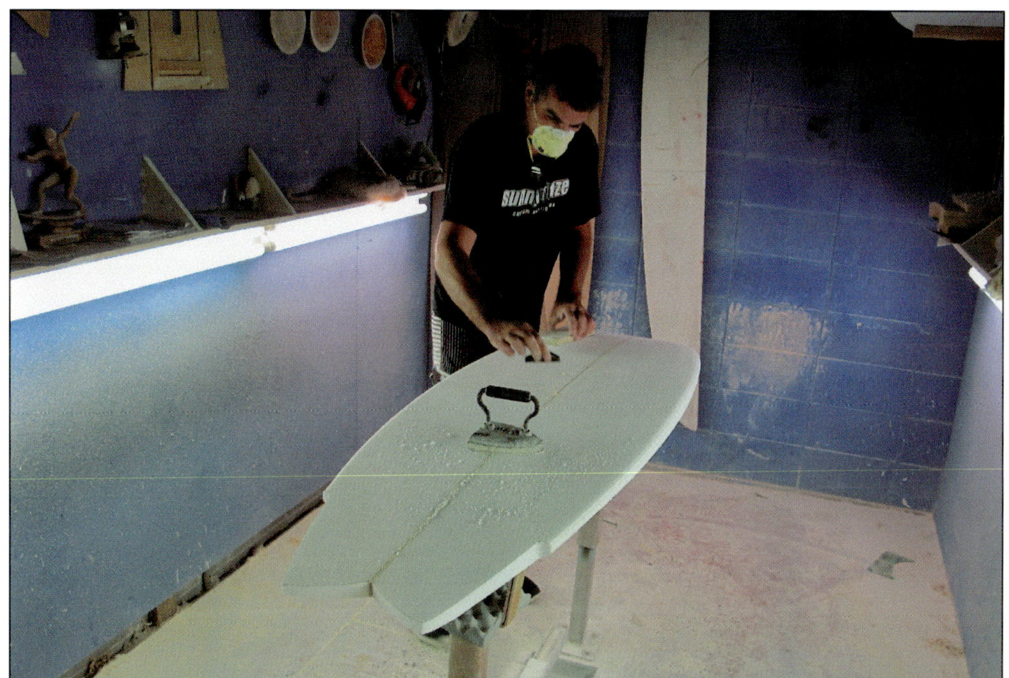

John Tolly grew up vacationing on Hilton Head and finally surrendered to the island's allure, moving there full-time in 1994. He opened Sunny Daze Surf Shop and fully immersed himself in the business of the sport. Branching out into shaping surfboards under the Sunny Daze brand was a natural progression for him. (Courtesy of Jesse Cadman.)

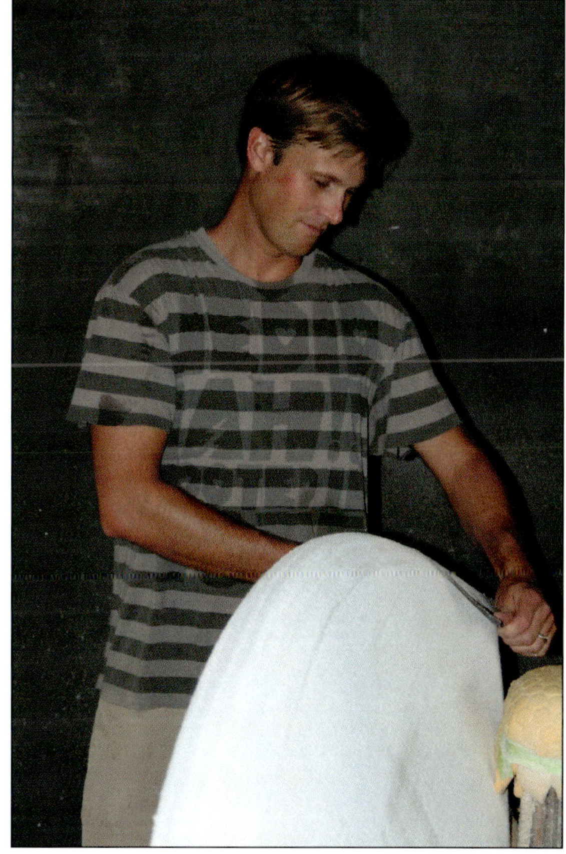

Richard Prause climbed onto his first surfboard on the beaches of Maui before he could walk and has photographs to prove it—that is life in a surfing family. Coming home to Charleston, he enhanced the stoke of surfing by building his own boards. This garage hobby became Grasshopper Surfboards. As he says, the magic of riding a wave is amazing, but riding it on a board he created is the ultimate feeling. (Authors' collection.)

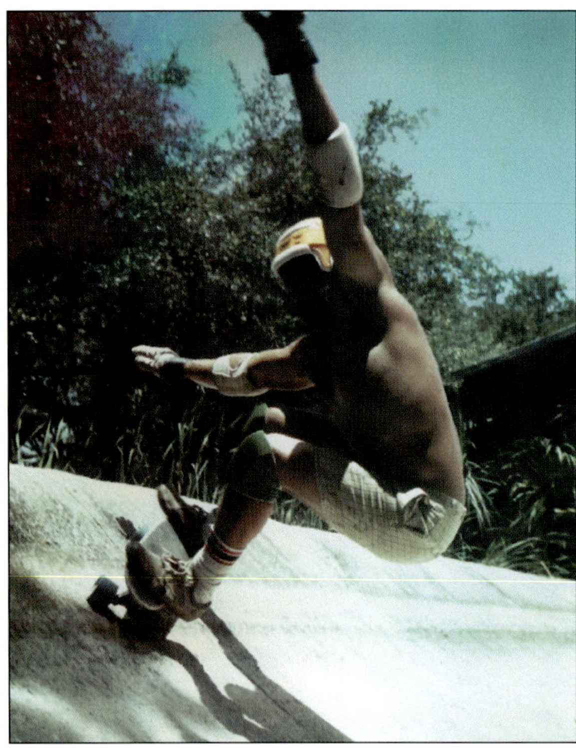

What is there to do when there is no surf? Find an empty swimming pool and grab a skateboard like Jerre Weckhorst is seen doing in the 1970s. Draining a bait pond at Hilton Head Harbor Marina gave him a free practice spot. It had the perfect shape, but he had to be careful not to lose his skateboard into the next pond, where an alligator had relocated. (Courtesy of the Polk-Weckhorst archives.)

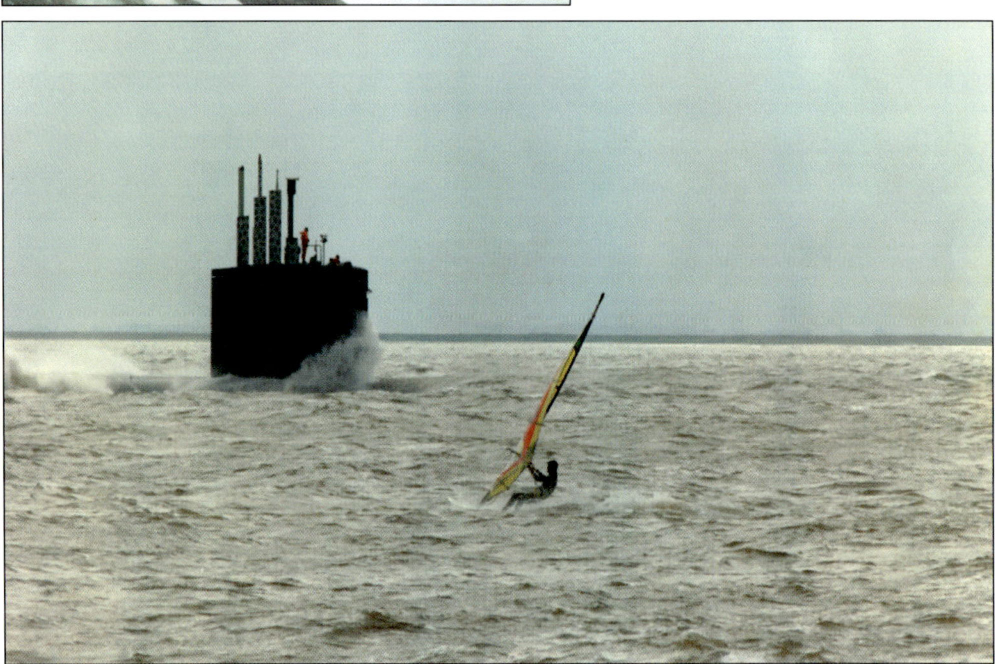

One never knows what is lurking under the water's surface. Glenn Tanner would launch at Fort Moultrie when a good hard nor'easter was blowing straight down the harbor and fly on his windsurfer. Some days, the obstacles were more formidable than others. He found out the hard way when a submarine appeared behind him in Charleston Harbor in the 1980s. (Courtesy of Glenn Tanner.)

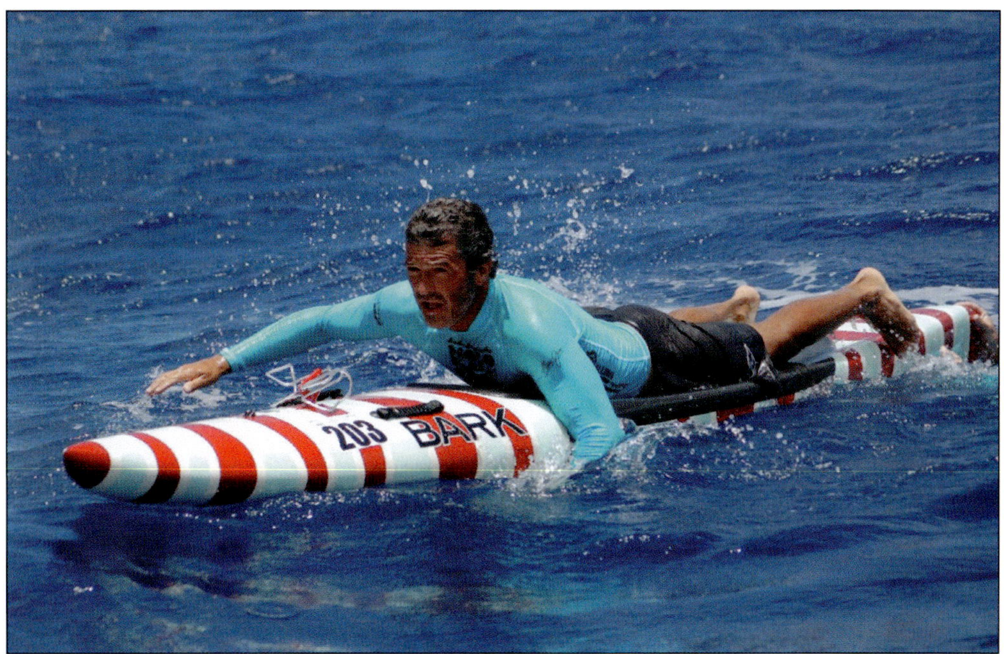

Expert prone-paddle racers like Don Alderman practice in local waters to prepare for elite events like Hawaii's M2O, the Molokai to Oahu race spanning 32 miles of open ocean. As of 2015, Alderman is a veteran of two solo finishes and one team finish. Technology has also impacted this traditional Hawaiian sport. The fiberglass boards may have become lighter and stronger, but the challenge remains the same. (Courtesy of Don Alderman.)

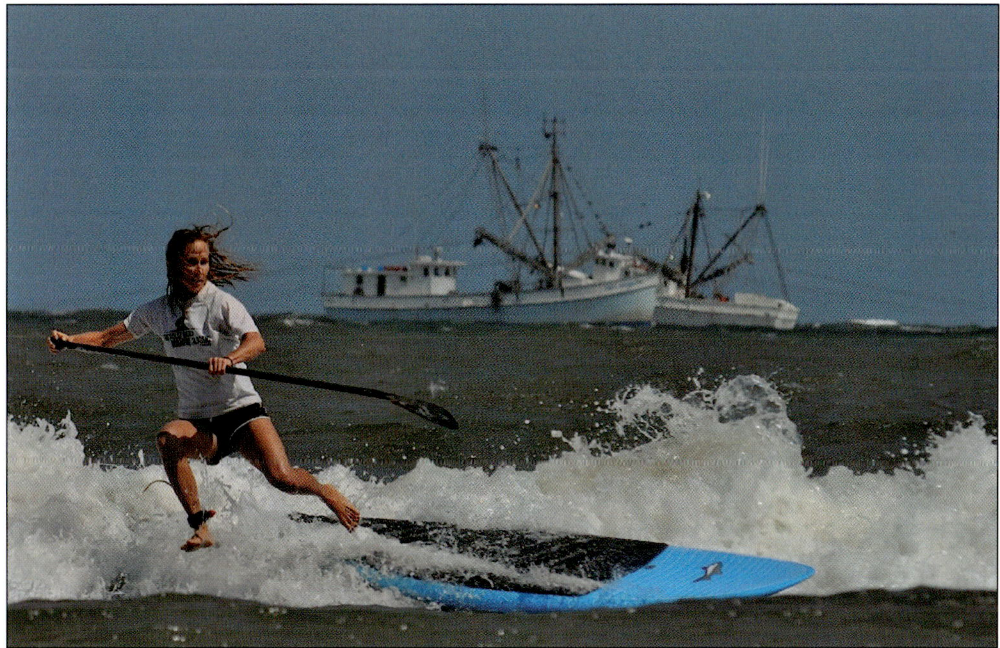

Jenny Alderman charges a wave on a stand-up paddleboard (SUP) at The Washout on Folly Beach. Seen in creeks, ocean, and rivers and commonly occupied by yoga classes and nature tours, SUPs are a common sight throughout the Lowcountry. (Courtesy of David Quick.)

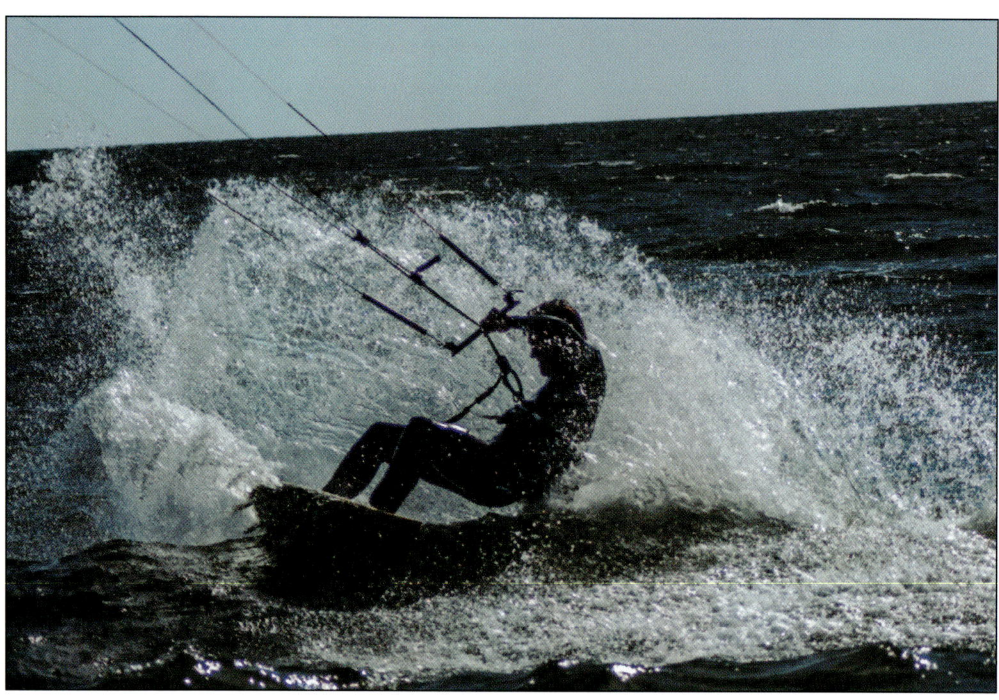

Tanner Schuck (above) takes advantage of a windy day to practice his kite surfing. Kiters are concentrating their sport on Sullivan's Island beaches. The colorful sails that dot the skies as they fly across the surface of the ocean are truly a sight to see. Reminiscent of photographs at hot-air balloon festivals, when the wind comes up these kiters rise above the dunes. (Above, courtesy of OceanFitness; below, Lindsey Lee Graham.)

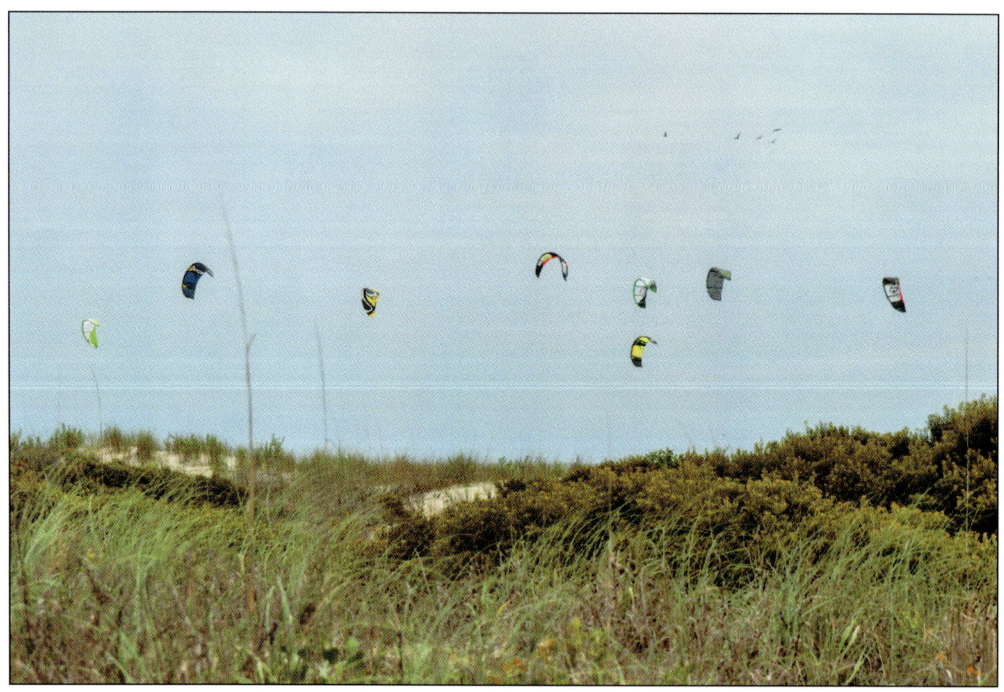

Of course, there are always innovators in every sport. Here an unidentified skater takes advantage of the renewable energy of the wind as he scoots down the Sullivan's Island beach on a skateboard. (Courtesy of Lindsey Lee Graham.)

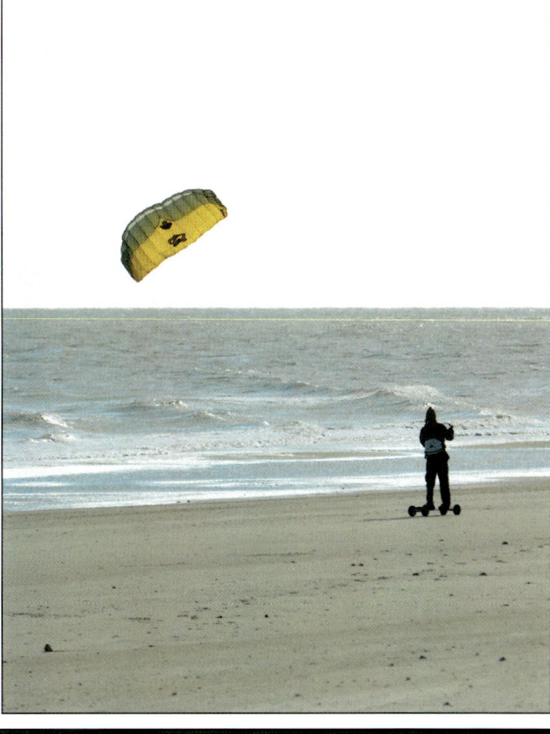

Paul Mulkey Jr. sets the standard for the wakeboarding set. This sport, the hybrid of snowboarding, water-skiing, and surfing, has the added attraction of stationary jumps, allowing the wakeboarder to gain air and execute maneuvers. This Trophy Lakes event on Johns Island in 2015 proves the popularity of the sport. (Courtesy of Paul Mulkey Sr.)

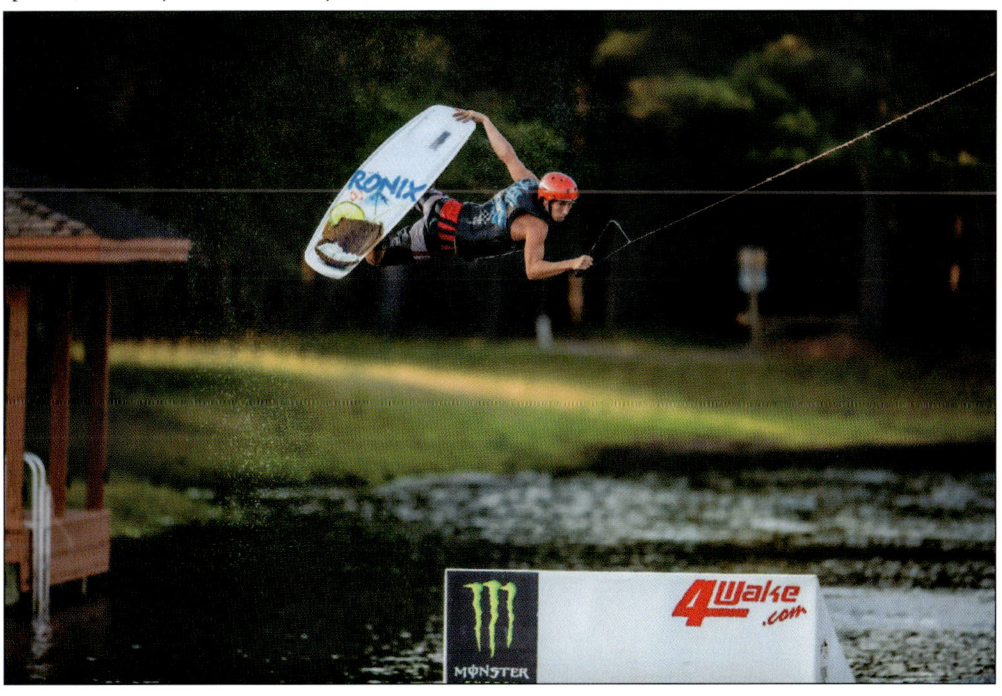

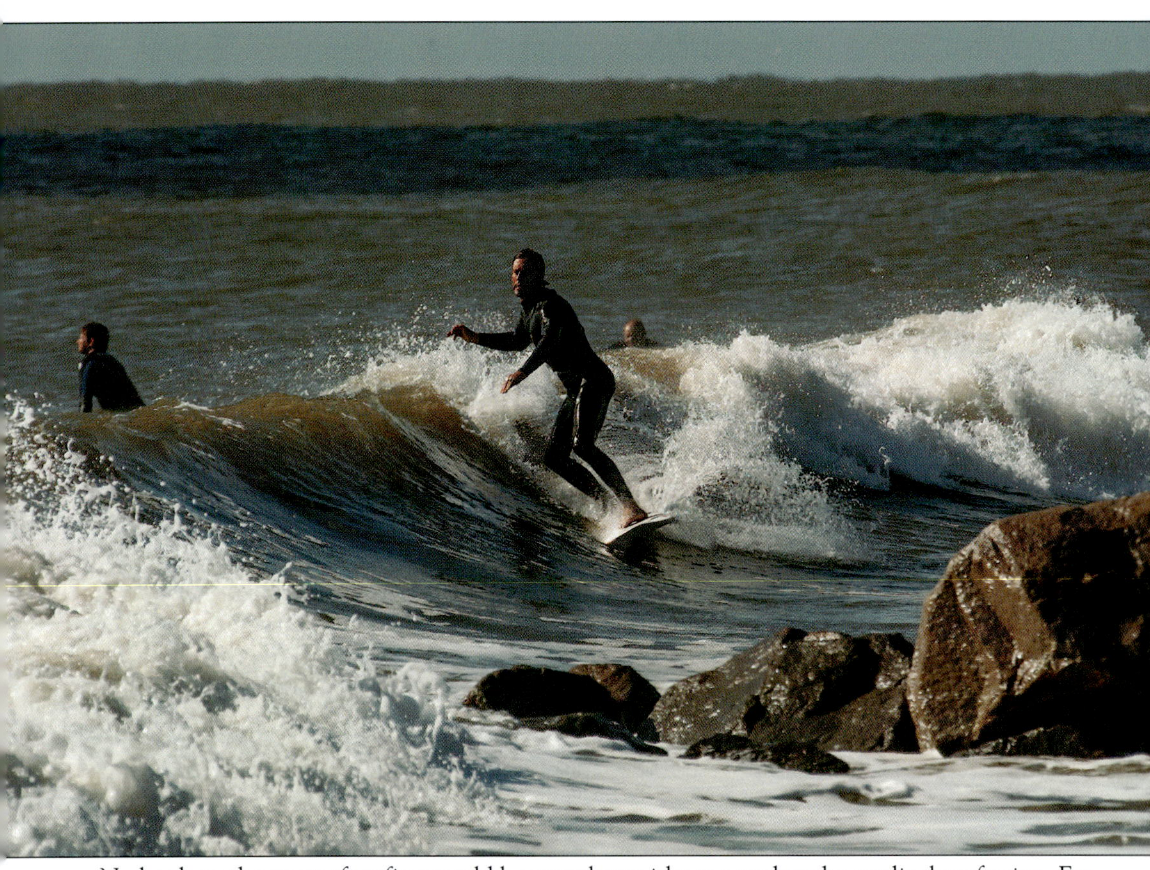

No book on the sport of surfing would be complete without a nod to the medical profession. For years, they have stitched and casted their way through the surfing population. One look at this unidentified surfer shows which way any ride can go. (He made it through just fine.) (Courtesy of Lew Harford.)

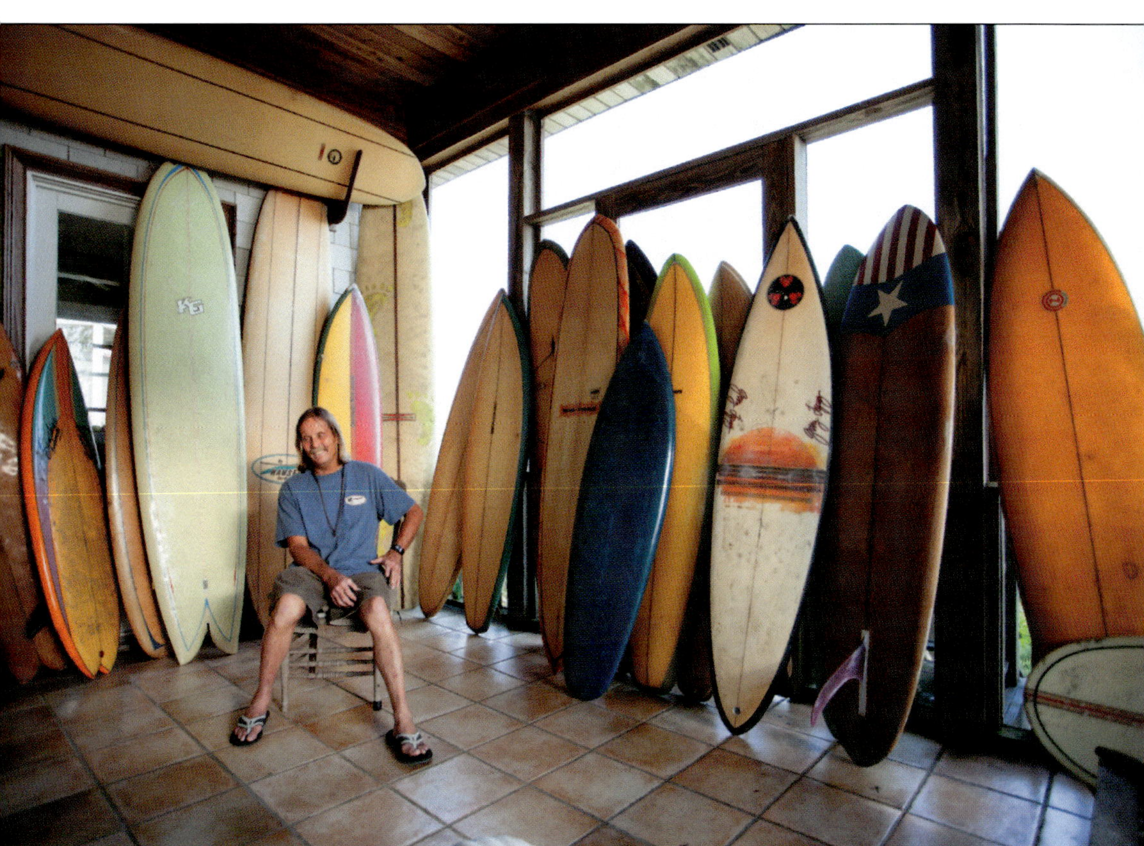

One true statement of surfing life is that one can never have too many surfboards. There are always new shapes or new fin setups to try. Charlie Newell in Myrtle Beach admits that he began collecting only red surfboards so his wife could not tell when he got another one. He now has one of the largest red surfboard collections in town. Foster Folsom (pictured) laughs at his obsession as he sits in front of part of his collection on his porch near Folly Beach. (Courtesy of Tanya Boggs Photography.)

Consistent with our mission to preserve history on a local level, this book was printed in South Carolina on American-made paper and manufactured entirely in the United States. Products carrying the accredited Forest Stewardship Council (FSC) label are printed on 100 percent FSC-certified paper.

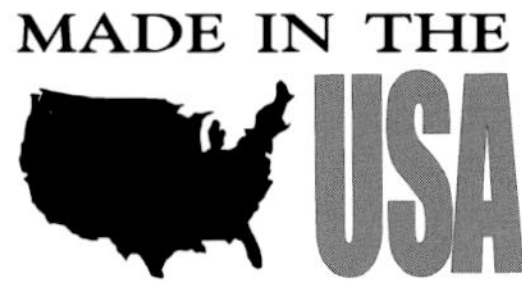